THE LAND OF PROMISE

Edited by

PHILIP JOHNSTON &
PETER WALKER

THE LAND OF PROMISE

BIBLICAL, THEOLOGICAL AND CONTEMPORARY PERSPECTIVES

APOLLOS

INTERVARSITY PRESS
DOWNERS GROVE, ILLINOIS 60515

APOLLOS (an imprint of Inter-Varsity Press),
38 De Montfort Street, Leicester LE1 7GP, England
World Wide Web: www.ivpbooks.com
Email: ivp@uccf.org.uk

INTERVARSITY PRESS
PO Box 1400, Downers Grove, Illinois 60515, USA
World Wide Web: www.ivpress.com
Email: mail@ivpress.com

First published 2000

British Library Cataloguing in Publication Data
A catalogue record for this book is available from the British Library.

UK ISBN 0–85111–469–5

Library of Congress Cataloging in Publication Data
This data has been requested.

US ISBN 0–8308–2659–9

Set in 11/13 Adobe Garamond
Typeset in Great Britain by The Midlands Book Typesetting Company, Loughborough
Printed in Great Britain by Creative Print and Design (Wales), Ebbw Vale

Contents

The contributors

Desmond Alexander is currently Director of Christian Training for the Presbyterian Church in Ireland, and was Lecturer in Semitic Studies at the Queen's University of Belfast from 1980 to 1999. His main field of research is the Pentateuch, about which he has written extensively in academic journals and books. Desmond also has a special interest in the relationship between the Old and New Testaments, and is co-editor of the *New Dictionary of Biblical Theology* (IVP, 2000).

Carl Armerding was for many years Professor of Old Testament and Principal at Regent College, Vancouver. In 1968–9 he held a post-doctoral fellowship in archaeology in Jerusalem. He is currently Director of the Schloss Mittersill Study Centre, Austria, and Senior Academic Adviser to the Oxford Centre for Mission Studies. In both capacities he works extensively with theological education in the emerging democracies of eastern Europe. Carl has published commentaries, a volume on Old Testament criticism and work on ancient Israel's charismatic leadership.

Naim Ateek is Director of the Sabeel Ecumenical Liberation Theology Center, Lecturer at the Tantur Ecumenical Institute, Jerusalem, and a well-known speaker locally and internationally. Previously he was parish minister of the Palestinian congregation at St George's Cathedral, Jerusalem. Naim has written *Justice and Only Justice: A Palestinian Theology of Liberation* (Orbis, 1989) and co-edited several other publications.

Colin Chapman is presently Lecturer in Islamic Studies at the Near East School of Theology in Beirut, and a former Principal of

Crowther Hall, Birmingham. He worked previously for thirteen years in Egypt and Lebanon with CMS, and wrote *Whose Promised Land?* (Lion, 1983) while resident in Beirut. His first degree was in biblical Greek and Hebrew, and his interest in the issues concerning the land began during that time.

Philip Johnston teaches Old Testament at Wycliffe Hall, Oxford. He has published studies of Israelite afterlife beliefs, and is a review editor for *Themelios*. Philip has lived and worked in the divided societies of Belgium and Northern Ireland, and has an interest in Israel past and present, a commitment to reconciliation and an editor's eye for detail.

Baruch Maoz is the founding pastor of Grace and Truth Christian Congregation in Rishon LeTsion, Israel, field leader for Christian Witness to Israel and a former national co-ordinator for the Lausanne Consultation on Jewish Evangelism (LCJE). He founded and directs HaGefen Publishing, and has edited several journals including *Mishkan*. Baruch is the author of several books in Hebrew, and a contributor to *Church Practice* (Carey) and *Jerusalem Past and Present* (Tyndale, 1992). He is presently engaged in writing an assessment of the Messianic Movement.

Palmer Robertson teaches at Knox Theological Seminary in Fort Lauderdale, Florida, USA, and at the African Bible College in Lilongwe, Malawi, Africa. His special interest is in the relation of the old-covenant Scriptures to the new. His publications include a study of *The Christ of the Covenants* (Baker, 1980), commentaries on some of the minor prophets, and an introduction to the theological significance of the land of the Bible. Palmer has been a regular participant in the Cyprus–Bethlehem Consultations on the Land.

Deryck Sheriffs teaches Old Testament and acts as course leader for the MA in Aspects of Biblical Interpretation at London Bible College, where practical training and research have an interdenominational and international ethos. His own research and publication interests lie in bridging the gap between the ancient Near East and today, as developed in his *The Friendship of the Lord: An Old Testament Spirituality* (Paternoster, 1996). Deryck's background and on-going teaching experience in South Africa have sensitized him to the issues of land, justice, racial identity and biblical interpretation.

Stephen Sizer is a vicar in Virginia Water, Surrey, England, and an area tutor for Westminster College, Oxford. He has undertaken postgraduate research into the ethical management of Holy Land pilgrimages and their impact on the indigenous church. He is currently pursuing further doctoral research on the history, politics and theology of Christian Zionism. Stephen has written extensively on the ethics of pilgrimages, dispensationalism and Zionism (accessible from www.virginiawater.co.uk/christchurch), and is the author of *Panorama of the Holy Land* (Eagle, 1998).

Gordon Thomas has been Lecturer in Biblical Studies and Dean of Students at Nazarene Theological College, Manchester, since 1988. He studied at York and Leeds Universities, at Nazarene Theological College and at London Bible College. For six years he taught English and Religious Education in mission schools in Swaziland, interspersed with four years of high-school teaching in inner Manchester. Gordon is currently Secretary of the Tyndale Fellowship Biblical Theology Study Group.

Peter Walker teaches New Testament at Wycliffe Hall, Oxford. He has published research on attitudes to Jerusalem in the fourth century AD (1990), in Christian theology (ed., 1992) and in the New Testament itself (1996). Peter is a frequent visitor to Israel, as a researcher, lecturer and accredited tour guide. He has been a regular participant in the Cyprus–Bethlehem Consultations on the Land, and is co-editor of its recently published papers, *The Bible and the Land: An Encounter* (Musalaha, 2000).

Paul Williamson teaches Old Testament at the Irish Baptist College, an accredited college of the Queen's University of Belfast. Before this Paul was pastor of the Baptist church in Omagh. The importance of territorial claims in Irish society has contributed to Paul's personal interest in the biblical theology of land. This has been intensified by his doctoral research, leading him to probe its enduring theological significance.

Foreword

God promised Abraham both a land and a seed. But that was some 4,000 years ago. How are we to interpret this double promise today?

The question becomes all the more perplexing as we watch political developments in the Middle East. It is now more than half a century ago that the State of Israel was established. Then in 1967 Jerusalem came under Jewish rule as a result of the Six Day War. Since then the so-called 'peace process' has ambled on, and I am writing in the aftermath of the failed Camp David talks promoted by President Clinton.

Evangelical Christians are of course committed to the supreme authority of Scripture. But equally biblical Christians, equally anxious to submit to its authority, reach different conclusions about Israel and the land of promise. This is why I felt it right in *Evangelical Truth* (1999) to include the interpretation of Old Testament prophecy among the so-called 'matters indifferent', which should not be allowed to rob us of our unity in the essentials of the gospel.

This does not mean, however, that we acquiesce in our disagreements. It is right rather to seek a greater measure of consensus. So I was glad in 1986 to host a discussion in London, which gave rise to a group called 'Evangelicals for Middle Eastern Understanding'. It is a movement which has since then gathered more momentum in the US than in the UK.

Let me declare my own position in this debate. Preaching in All Souls, Langham Place, in 1983 I said this:

> What about the promised land? Is the setting up of the State of Israel a fulfilment of prophecy? It is a reasonable view to hold, and many do hold it, and we regard them with respect and love. Others, among whom I number myself, do not hold that view. There is the risk of ignoring the justice of the Palestinians' cause; there are also biblical arguments.
>
> For example, the Old Testament promises about the land are nowhere repeated in the New Testament, except possibly in Luke 21:24. The prophecy of Romans 11 is a prophecy that many Jews will turn to Christ, but the land is not mentioned, nor is Israel mentioned as a political entity. So we need to be very cautious in simply jumping back to the Old Testament promises and ignoring how they are handled in the New.
>
> Instead, according to the apostles, the Old Testament promises are fulfilled in Christ and in the international community of Christ. A return to Jewish nationalism would seem incompatible with this New Testament perspective of the international community of Jesus.

These statements clearly need much more detailed argument; and opposing views need to be weighed. It is therefore a particular pleasure to welcome the essays in this volume. They come from a variety of evangelical scholars – Old Testament and New Testament specialists, British and American, a Jewish Christian and a Palestinian Christian. It is always good to see biblical Christians wrestling with the text of Scripture, and debating in a charitable and constructive spirit with those who share their high regard for Scripture but interpret it differently.

This book is the result. It is scholarly and readable, careful and Christ-centred, faithful to the ancient Scriptures and sensitive to current issues. I warmly commend these essays. Doubtless they are not the last word on the subject. Indeed I hope they will provoke further reflection and writing. Yet here is an excellent place to begin.

John Stott

Introduction

Land matters! It matters to all of us to have a place we call home, a group of people to whom we belong, a country we can call our own. Many of us living in settled western democracies have not experienced disputes about land at first hand, though recent conflicts in Northern Ireland and southern Europe remind us of their explosive power and often tragic consequences. For Israelis and Palestinians in Israel/Palestine, land certainly matters, as much as ever. Even the name of the land is contentious! It is their home, their people, their country – but they are two distinct and often hostile peoples.

In this millennium year, many senior religious and political leaders are visiting Israel and its neighbours. In early January all the patriarchs of the eastern churches were present together in Jerusalem to celebrate the Orthodox New Year, a remarkable gathering for an exceptional event. The President of Russia also attended. In March the Pope travelled to Israel to visit the land of Jesus, while the President of the United States visited the region to try to push forward the tortuous peace process. At the same time many ordinary Christians visit the 'Holy Land' on their own holiday pilgrimage. For all these visitors, too, the land matters, though in different ways.

Christians visit this particular land mostly because it was the land of Jesus. They know that the land was promised and given to the Jewish people in the Hebrew Scriptures, and they acknowledge the authority of these texts as part of the Christian Bible. But they also realize that they are part of the old covenant, which in various ways is qualified by the new covenant of Jesus Christ. And the new-covenant documents with their new, international perspective are virtually silent about the old promised land. So many Christians are uncertain how to integrate these different perspectives.

Most Christians are aware of recent Jewish history, at least in broad outline: the rise of Zionism and the early pioneer movement, the appalling horror of the Holocaust, the founding of the State of Israel in 1948, the various Arab–Israeli wars, and the current peace process. They are also aware of the uprooting and enforced exile of many Palestinians, the despairing terrorism, the *intifada*, and the emergence of a Palestinian Authority. Many accept instinctively that both Jews and Palestinians have a right to a homeland, but do not know how to reconcile these conflicting aspirations on the ground, or how to integrate their instincts of human justice with their biblical beliefs.

This book will help Christians to think through the meaning of both Old and New Testament teaching on the land. Its primary focus is the Bible and Christian theology, since these are foundational. We need to read closely and think carefully about what our authoritative texts say and mean. We need to ponder how to interpret the Old Testament, both in its own context of God's ongoing dealings with his people, and in the light of the radical newness of the gospel. And we need to interpret the New Testament in the context of first-century Jewish expectations and aspirations. We then need to build this unfolding biblical theology into an integrated Christian theology. Only when we have done this can we develop a distinctly Christian perspective on the current situation in Israel, to understand it, pray about it and contribute positively to it.

The volume also has a practical concern. Christians already do contribute to middle-eastern developments, whether aware of it or not. Western governments have often been influenced by different Christian theologies, whether of specific officials in power or of large and influential interest groups. Christians contribute economically by travel and pilgrimage. And Christians contribute in personal contact with Jews and Muslims who identify closely with one group or the other. So what we think matters enormously. It affects profoundly what we say and do.

This book has its origin in a study group of the Tyndale Fellowship, an association of evangelicals who study and teach theology in Britain. The Biblical Theology Study Group brings together some twenty or thirty members in an annual conference for spiritual and intellectual fellowship. In recent years the group has had a renewed desire for its study to be of wider service to the church, as well as of value to members. So with enthusiasm and energy the current secretary, Gordon Thomas, organized the 1999 conference on 'The Land', with a view to publishing the papers. The conference was collaborative in the best sense, in that each draft paper stimulated discussion and cross-fertilization of ideas, with fruitful insights offered by other members studying the same theme. While each author retains his particular perspective, they all showed a commendable openness to constructive dialogue both during the conference and later with the editors.

Despite the best efforts of several people, we were unable to have distinctly Jewish and Palestinian voices at the conference. But we still wanted their contribution to be part of the book, so we invited capable representatives to submit articles. We are very grateful to Baruch Maoz and Naim Ateek for preparing material in the midst of busy schedules, and to Baruch in particular for responding at very short notice when another contributor withdrew. Their chapters clearly and crisply remind us all of the issues at stake.

As the personal sketches show (above, pp. 7–9), all the contributors have reflected at length on biblical interpretation, land and nationhood. Several collaborated some years ago in a similar study of an equally contentious issue: *Jerusalem Past and Present in the Purposes of God* (ed. P. W. L. Walker, Tyndale, 1992, 1994), and many have already written on various aspects of the whole subject in publications too numerous to list. This present volume builds on the earlier one and widens the scope of study as we seek to understand the divine purpose.

Land matters, especially a land of promise. But is the ancient promise still valid? If so, on what basis? And if not, why not? This book may not resolve all the relevant issues. But it does present and discuss the key biblical, theological and contemporary issues, and should help us all to understand better the land of promise in the purposes of God.

Philip Johnston
Peter Walker

1. THE LAND IN ISRAEL'S STORY

1A
Promise and fulfilment: the territorial inheritance[1]

Paul R. Williamson

Introduction

If land is indeed one of the central themes of biblical faith (Brueggemann 1978: 3), it is nowhere more obvious than in Genesis–Kings. No other topic better highlights the fact that, in their final form at least, the Pentateuch and the Former Prophets belong together, and are intended to be read as a unified narrative. Whatever stages and developments the process of compilation went through, it is quite clear from their respective emphasis on the land that these are two parts of the same story. In that story the promise of land and its fulfilment undoubtedly plays a major role. It is a central tenet of the promise to the patriarchs, never far from sight throughout the ancestral history. It is the planned destination for those rescued from Egyptian bondage, to which they eventually make

[1] I am grateful to the Tyndale Fellowship Biblical Theology Study Group, and especially to Desmond Alexander, Raymond Banks and Philip Johnston, for suggested improvements on this paper.

their way. It is the territory conquered under Joshua and parcelled out among the Israelite tribes. It is centre stage for the military campaigns in the days of the judges, and the centre of the empire carved out by David and consolidated under Solomon. It is the focus of political intrigue during the divided monarchy, and expulsion from it is the tragic note on which the story is brought to its conclusion. In the promise–fulfilment schema of Genesis–Kings land is thus a major component (see Martens 1994: 104).

An examination of the scholarly literature reveals that there is at least a broad consensus in relation to the elementary aspects of the territorial promise. Despite clear differences of opinion over the fine details, most scholars readily accept that (a) the territorial promise relates primarily to a comparatively small geographical area whose borders are explicitly delimited; (b) the principal inheritors of this territorial promise are the Israelites, Abraham's descendants through Jacob; (c) the territorial promise is presented in Genesis–Kings as having been fulfilled (at least, to some extent) in Israel's history.

While these conclusions are certainly valid, they may nevertheless be somewhat misleading. They are so (a) if it is assumed that the promise of land is exhausted by the geographical parameters set out in a number of Old Testament texts; (b) if the patriarchs' physical descendants (i.e. the Israelites) are identified as the sole beneficiaries or inheritors of the promised land; and (c) if Israel's partial occupation of Canaan in the Old Testament period is seen as the comprehensive fulfilment of the territorial promise made to Abraham.[2]

Although primarily relating to Israel's settlement in the land of Canaan, the territorial promise also encompasses a much larger area, incorporates a lot more people and still awaits its ultimate fulfilment. The basis for this inference is as follows: first, the precise role of the promised land within the larger promissory agenda developed in Genesis–Kings; secondly, the complex nature of the territorial inheritance within Genesis–Kings; and thirdly, the degree of fulfilment of the promise of land in Genesis–Kings.

[2] For a discussion of the geographical differences between the boundaries of the patriarchal promise, Canaanite territory and the land of Israel, see Kallai 1997.

The role of 'land' within the programmatic agenda of Genesis 12:1–3

While land is certainly not an inconsequential theme in Genesis 1 – 11,[3] it takes on particular significance in the second part of Genesis and beyond. As an integral part of the divine blessing announced in the programmatic agenda of Genesis 12:1–3,[4] land becomes an important focal point for the outworking of the divine promises made to Abraham. Although the Abraham narrative contains at least three core divine promissory threads (i.e. phenomenal posterity, national territory and global prosperity),[5] the programmatic agenda is essentially twofold: it involves blessing on a national scale and, subsequently, blessing on an international scale.[6] While each of these two prospects in God's programmatic agenda is picked up and elaborated in the rest of the Abraham cycle, two chapters are especially significant: 15 and 17. In the former, the prospect of nationhood (encompassing the promised blessings of 'seed' and 'land') is solemnly guaranteed by a covenant between God and Abraham.[7] Then, in Genesis 17, the prospect of international blessing comes to the fore, with the announcement that Abraham will become 'father of many nations' (i.e. in the sense of becoming their spiritual benefactor) and the anticipation of a further covenant that will solemnly guarantee this dimension of the divine agenda. The linchpin connecting these two programmatic elements (national and international blessing) is Abraham's 'royal seed' – from the great nation descended from Abraham will come a royal individual who will mediate blessing to all the

[3] As suggested by Brueggemann (1978: 15), and more recently illustrated by McKeown (1997). See too Alexander's essay in the present volume, pp. 35–50.

[4] Although the territorial dimension is not mentioned explicitly as part of the divine promise in Gen. 12:1–3, it is clearly implicit in v. 1 and, significantly, becomes explicit as soon as Abraham has migrated to Canaan (v. 7).

[5] See Williamson 2000a for a discussion of these and their theological significance.

[6] This twin agenda has been proposed by Alexander (1994) and recently defended by Williamson (2000b).

[7] Because of the ritual involved in its establishment this covenant is sometimes described as the 'covenant between the pieces', and distinguished from the 'covenant of circumcision' introduced in Gen. 17. For a detailed examination of the relationship between these two covenants, see Williamson 2000b.

nations of the earth.[8] Thus understood, Genesis 15 and 17 describe two different but related covenants which develop the twin programmatic threads of Genesis 12:1–3.[9]

Such a reading of the Abraham narrative is further supported by the final recorded interaction between God and Abraham (Gen. 22:1–18), in which the covenant anticipated back in Genesis 17 is actually established. Once again, the climactic emphasis here (Gen. 22:16–18; cf. 18:19) is on the blessing of the nations through an individual 'seed' of Abraham.[10] Given this emphasis, and the significance of this pericope within the literary structure of the Abraham narrative,[11] it seems reasonable to infer that the climax of God's programmatic agenda is not the establishment of a nation, but rather the blessing of the nations.

The promise of land must be understood within this broader context of God's programmatic agenda, an agenda that culminates in the blessing of all the nations of the world through Abraham's seed (cf. Gal. 3:6ff.; Rev. 7:9). Since the latter aspect of the divine plan is patently non-territorial (in the sense that it is not restricted to any one geographical location), the national dimension of the territorial promise should probably be understood as a transitional stage in the outworking of God's ultimate plan. It is certainly difficult to envisage the necessity of a strictly localized fulfilment of the territorial promise *after* the climactic element in the programmatic agenda has begun to materialize. Surely Abraham's multitudinous and international descendants require a much larger, indeed a global, inheritance.

In view of this, however, the precise nature of the promise of land within Genesis–Kings needs to be examined more carefully. Does it refer merely to the transitional stage in the outworking of salvation history, or does it also incorporate a much greater

[8] The 'kings' who will come from Abraham (v. 6) are clearly identified with the promised seed (cf. Gen. 17:16; 35:11), thus establishing a strong link between them. Cf. also Ps. 72:17, in which the role formerly associated with Abraham is transferred to an ideal Davidic king.

[9] For a detailed defence of the above interpretation, see Williamson 2000b, esp. ch. 6.

[10] See Alexander 1997 and Williamson 2000b, ch. 7, 4c.

[11] The climactic significance of Gen. 22 in the Abraham narrative is suggested not only by the chiastic pattern detected by a number of recent scholars, but also by the computer-assisted literary analysis of Bergen (1990: 313–326).

inheritance – one encompassing the *'ereṣ* (earth/land) in its global sense?[12]

The nature of the territorial promise in Genesis–Kings

Given the function of the territorial promise within the larger programmatic agenda of Genesis 12:1–3, it is clear that, in its primary sense at least, the promised land must be understood in terms of earthly real estate, viz. the national territory promised to Israel. However, some scholars – mainly on the basis of texts in the latter part of the Old Testament and in the New Testament – understand the territorial promise more comprehensively, in a way that transcends geographic and political limitations altogether.[13] Although others (e.g. Kaiser 1981: 302) consider these two interpretations of the territorial promise to be mutually exclusive, a case can be made from the Genesis–Kings material for understanding the territorial promise in both ways: regionally, as the territory occupied by the Israelites for the greater part of their national existence in biblical times, and globally, as the eternal abode of all Abraham's spiritual 'seed', whether Jew or Gentile.

National or international?

Basic to any such discussion is the question of whether the territorial promise relates exclusively to Abraham's national descendants (i.e. the 'great nation' of Gen. 12:2) or whether it also encompasses the patriarch's international descendants (the 'many nations' of Gen. 17:4–6). The latter is certainly given some credence by the inclusion of the territorial dimension of the promise in Genesis 17:8 (cf. 35:11) and, albeit indirectly, by the apparent allusion to territorial conquest in Genesis 22:17b.

[12] Recently Sailhamer (1996) has made the novel suggestion that the *'ereṣ* (earth/land) of Gen. 1 – 11 should be understood as the *'ereṣ* of subsequent chapters (i.e. the term is generally used in its restricted, territorial sense *throughout* the book of Genesis). While this seems untenable (even Sailhamer is forced to admit the global meaning in Gen. 1:1; 18:25), it could be argued that the use of the same term subtly suggests that the promised land of the patriarchal stories is a microcosm of the 'earth' in the primeval prologue.

[13] E.g. Hoekema 1979: ch. 20; Dray 1984; LaRondelle 1983: ch. 9; McComiskey 1985: 199–209; Crenshaw & Gunn 1985: ch. 17; Holwerda 1995: ch. 4.

While these texts agree that it is Abraham's 'seed' (NIV 'descendants') who will inherit the promised land, this 'seed' cannot simply be equated with the nation of Israel or identified exclusively with Abraham's biological descendants. Rather, in Genesis 17 Abraham's 'seed' must also encompass the 'multitude of nations' to which Abraham will become 'father' (i.e. benefactor), whereas in Genesis 22:17b the 'seed' relates to an individual descendant who will mediate blessing (presumably incorporating his territorial conquest) to all the nations of the earth. Both passages therefore imply that the ultimate inheritors of the patriarchal promises (including the territorial dimension) are not a national entity but an international community. Thus understood, it is difficult to see how the territorial promise could be exhausted by any political borders, whether Israelite or otherwise.

Regional or global?

Clearly pertinent to the above discussion is the question of whether the promised land was ever restricted absolutely to any one geographical locale, or whether, from the beginning, it could also have a much broader connotation – one that would eventually encompass the whole earth. While there can be no doubt that the territorial promise is given localized parameters in Genesis–Kings, a close examination of the relevant promissory texts may actually support a wider interpretation of the promised land. Specific geographical boundary markers are highlighted in a number of texts: Genesis 15:18; Exodus 23:31; Numbers 34:1–12; Deuteronomy 11:24; 34:1–4; Joshua 1:2–4. Significantly, the actual borders in these texts are rather imprecise. Moreover, the extent of the promised land is certainly not identical in each (e.g. the boundaries reflected in Deut. 11:24 are much broader than those of Num. 34).[14] While this has generally been interpreted as evidence of different layers of redaction,[15] the fact that no steps were taken to impose uniformity suggests an element of flexibility difficult to harmonize with rigidly

[14] See the discussion in Weinfeld 1993: ch. 3. Even Townsend (1985: 324–328), who attempts to resolve the disparity by differentiating between 'general' and 'specific' land descriptions, is forced to acknowledge that his solution is not 'entirely satisfactory'.

[15] E.g. von Waldow 1974: 498; Weinfeld 1993: ch. 3.

defined territorial borders. It could reasonably be inferred from this that the map of the promised land was never seen as permanently fixed, but was subject to at least some degree of expansion and redefinition.

Such a conclusion is further suggested by other texts, in which the territorial inheritance is described more generally: (a) in terms of its pre-Israelite occupants; namely '(the land of) Canaan/the Canaanite(s)' etc. (Gen. 12:5; 15:19–21; 17:8c; Exod. 3:8, 17; 6:4b; 13:5a, 11a; 23:23, 28; 33:2; 34:11; Lev. 14:33; 18:3; [20:24]; Num. 13:1; 33:51–53; Deut. [1:20]; 2:24); (b) in terms of the geographical location of the beneficiaries: 'this land/the land that you see/the land on which you are lying/the land ... where they lived as aliens' (Gen. 12:1, 7; 13:14–15 [cf. v. 17]; 15:7 [cf. v. 16]; 17:8b; 24:7; 28:13, 15; 48:4; Exod. 6:4c); (c) in terms of the ancestral promise (Gen. 35:12; 48:21; 50:24; Exod. 6:8; 13:5b, 11b; 32:13; 33:1; Num. 14:[16], 23, 30; Deut. 1:8, 21; 6:10, 18, 23; 7:13; 8:1, 18; 9:5; 10:11; 11:9, 21; 19:8; 26:3; 27:3; 28:11; 30:20; 31:7, 20–23; 34:4).

Clearly, none of these descriptions ties down the geographical parameters sufficiently to reconstruct a map of the promised land. The first category – in which the land is described in terms of its pre-Israelite inhabitants – comes closest to supplying us with a thumbnail sketch, but again the various texts reflect a noticeable degree of fluidity.[16] While it is reasonable to conclude that the promised land, strictly speaking, was the territory formerly occupied by the Canaanites, Amorites, Hittites, Perizzites, Hivites and Jebusites, the inclusion of additional groups in such lists, to give what are probably symbolic totals of seven and ten, may suggest that the ideal envisaged is less susceptible to rigid delineation than many have imagined. This would also account for the rather vague description of the promised land in terms of present location or the ancestral promise. The territorial promise, in its most comprehensive sense, was not limited by geographical borders, therefore such

[16] It has long been recognized that the various lists of pre-Israelite inhabitants of the promised land are far from uniform. Whereas a list of ten nations is found in Gen. 15:19–21, most of the lists in the Pentateuch and the Former Prophets contain only six nations (listed in slightly different order): Exod. 3:8, 17; 23:23; 33:2; 34:11; Deut. 20:17; Josh. 9:1; 11:3; 12:8; Judg. 3:5 (cf. Neh. 9:8). In three passages the inclusion of the Girgashites makes a total of seven (Deut. 7:1; Josh. 3:10; 24:11). In two texts, Exod. 13:5 and 1 Kgs. 9:20 (cf. 2 Chr. 8:7), only five nations are listed, while only three are mentioned in Exod. 23:28.

borders were not mapped out with the rigidity and consistency which otherwise we might expect.

Of particular significance in this latter respect are texts in which further expansion of the territorial promise is at least implicit (e.g. Gen. 26:3–4; Exod. 34:24; Num. 24:17–18; Deut. 19:8–9). These texts seem to suggest that the promised land could extend beyond strict geographical parameters indicated elsewhere. Admittedly, this expansion is restricted in the first instance to the full regional extent of the patriarchal boundaries. However, the unique plural ('lands') in Genesis 26:3–4 should undoubtedly be read in conjunction with the oath to which it alludes (Gen. 22:17–18), making it synonymous with Abraham's seed possessing/inheriting the gate of his enemies. This supports the above interpretation of Genesis 22:17b and provides a firm exegetical basis for Paul's assertion that Abraham would inherit 'the world' (Rom. 4:13; see McComiskey 1985: 53). Thus understood, Canaan was simply the preliminary stage in the ultimate unfolding of God's programmatic agenda – an agenda which not only involves all peoples of the earth but also encompasses all regions of the earth.[17]

Therefore, while the promised land was primarily a specific, regional territory, there is ample reason to infer that it was also something more. The fact that the promised land was of more than political significance has often been overlooked, especially by those who still anticipate some sort of future, national fulfilment of the territorial promise. When the global significance of the promised land is taken on board, a future fulfilment in a narrow, regional sense appears largely redundant, and indeed somewhat anticlimactic.

Unconditional or provisional?

A further important question is whether or not the territory could have been forfeited permanently through Israel's disobedience. While some texts in the Pentateuch appear to pledge the land to Abraham and his descendants unconditionally,[18] in other passages

[17] The latter is a corollary of the former: as the promise of offspring expands in scope, so too must the promise of land. And this is precisely how both promises unfold in Scripture; see McComiskey 1985: 48–51.

[18] E.g. Gen. 12:7; 13:15, 17; 15:7, 18–21; 28:13, 15; 35:12; Exod. 3:8, 17; 6:8.

possession of the land is qualified with certain provisos,[19] thus raising the vexed question: is the territorial promise unconditional or provisional in nature? The biblical text plainly suggests that both are somehow true.

Those looking at the texts through a diachronic lens see the explanation of such a paradox in editorial layers underlying the final form of the text.[20] All such theories, however, ultimately come up against the insuperable problem of why redactors would wish to combine two antithetic traditions, or to qualify the tradition of an unconditional promise on such a selective basis themselves. In any case, if the final redactor was somehow able to harmonize the unconditional and provisional passages, this must also be possible for those who wish to understand the text in its final form. Significantly, even those today who affirm the permanent, unconditional nature of the territorial promise have little difficulty in reconciling this premise with the passages that qualify the promise in some way.[21]

So then, how can the territorial promise be both unconditional and provisional? In what sense is it the former and in what sense is it the latter? An examination of the relevant texts reveals that, while the territorial promise was irrevocable, it was provisional with respect to actual experience of the inheritance. As Kaiser (1978: 90–91) explains: 'The conditionality was not attached to the promise but only to the participants who would benefit from these abiding promises ... participation in the blessings depended on the individual's spiritual condition.'[22] This can be illustrated by the example of the wilderness generation. While enjoyment of the promised land was denied to those who lacked faith and were disobedient, the behaviour of that one generation did not result in the nullification of the promise. Rather, 'the promise continued

[19] Cf. Exod. 20:12; 23:23–33; 34:24; Lev. 18:3, 24–27; Deut. 4:1–5, 40; 5:33; 6:18; 8:1; 11:8ff.; 16:20; 18:9–14; 19:8–9; 21:23; 24:4; 25:15; 30:16; 32:47.

[20] E.g. von Rad 1943; Weinfeld 1993: ch. 8; Habel 1995: esp. ch. 8. For a concise critique of different diachronic and synchronic approaches to this issue, see Millar 1998: 57–60.

[21] See e.g. Townsend 1985: 322–324; Kaiser 1998: 210–213.

[22] Elsewhere (1973: 145), Kaiser draws more fully a helpful analogy with the Davidic covenant, observing that 'the "if" in the Davidic covenant (Ps 132:12; 89:29–32; 2 Sam 7:14b–15; 1 Kings 2:4; 8:25; 9:4–5) can only refer in those contexts to *individual* and *personal* invalidation of the benefits of the covenant, but they can never affect the certainty of God's eternal oath'. Cf. 2 Sam. 7:13, 16; Ps. 89:27, 28, 35, 36; 2 Sam. 23:5; Is. 55:3.

even though possession of the land was deferred' (Holwerda 1995: 89).[23]

The unconditional nature of the territorial promise is highlighted especially in Genesis 15, where God solemnly guarantees his promise to make Abraham into a great nation. Here the obligation is markedly one-sided. God alone (represented by the theophany) passes between the divided animals, emphasizing that 'He alone had something to promise' (Dillmann 1897: 2:65). The promise of nationhood (i.e. seed and land) was guaranteed absolutely at this stage by God himself. Significantly, however, nothing is said in the present context to suggest that Abraham's descendants will *retain* possession of the specified territorial inheritance in an unqualified manner. Indeed, the possibility of expulsion is at least implicit in the reason given for the delay in the fulfilment of the territorial promise (v. 16).

Even in the passages that appear to qualify the territorial promise, the future possession of the promised land by Abraham's seed is not in any doubt. Indeed, it is generally assumed (cf. Deut. 11:8–12). What is under review in these texts is the question of who will enter into the inheritance and/or how long they will remain there. It is clear from these passages that, to obtain a share in the inheritance, more is required than mere biological descent from the patriarchs. Experience and continued enjoyment of the territorial inheritance demanded loyalty to the God of the patriarchs. Nevertheless, while the actual inheritance of the promised land is qualified in this way, the promise itself is unconditional; its fulfilment is guaranteed by God himself, and therefore it is difficult to see how it could be forfeited permanently through the disobedience of any one generation of Abraham's descendants. Apparently the latter possibility (i.e. permanent expulsion) is not actually envisaged in Genesis–Kings (cf. Lev. 26:40–45; Deut. 30:1–5), nor does such a prospect square with the hope expressed in Israel's prophetic literature.[24]

[23] The lesson was surely not lost on the original readers of Genesis–Kings, who were in all probability still in exile in Babylon.

[24] Significantly, it is on the basis of Yahweh's faithfulness to his covenant promises that the Old Testament prophets base their confidence in a future restoration of the promised land; cf. Jer. 30–33; Ezek. 36–37.

Temporal or eternal?

This, however, gives rise to another fundamental question regarding the nature of the territorial promise. Is it possible to locate its ultimate consummation in the past (i.e. within Israel's history), or does its biblical expression imply or even demand a more permanent realization in the future? In other words, should we view the territorial promise as just a temporal phase or also as an eternal dimension of the programmatic agenda?

There is at least some indication within Genesis–Kings that the territorial dimension of the promise, while in one sense a temporary phase in the outworking of the programmatic agenda, speaks metaphorically of something greater. To start with, there is the juxtaposition of Genesis 1 – 11 and Genesis 12, suggesting that, among other things, 'the land promise in 12:7 is a reversal of the pattern of expulsion that dominates Genesis 3 – 11' (Estes 1990: 409). This, and the thinly veiled allusion to God's primeval imperative to humankind (cf. Gen. 1:28; 9:1) in God's promise to make Abraham extremely numerous (Gen. 17:2, 6), strongly suggests that the divine answer to humanity's plight is not ultimately limited by physical or temporal restraints. Consequently, the territorial dimension of the divine promise may well speak of something more secure than national borders. Thus understood, there may be some exegetical basis for the New Testament claim that Abraham was anticipating something rather more permanent than a relatively small parcel of earthly real estate (cf. Heb. 11:8–16). As Estes (1990: 412) observes, 'the juxtaposition of the call of Abram with the building of a city in Genesis 11:1–9 provides a plausible biblical matrix for the assertion in Hebrews'.[25]

Furthermore, on several occasions within the ancestral story the territorial promise is actually said to be 'everlasting' (Gen. 13:15; 17:8; 48:4; cf. Exod. 32:13; Josh. 14:9). Here caution must be exercised, for one could easily read too much into the Hebrew term *'ôlām*.[26] Nevertheless, the contextual usage certainly permits us to

[25] Also Alexander in the present volume (pp. 35–50).

[26] For *'ôlām* Barr (1969: 73–74) suggests a semantic range between 'remotest time' and 'perpetuity', noting that 'the question of the extent of time involved by relating an object to *'ôlām* is ... relative to what the object is'.

understand the territorial promise in the fullest sense; viz. as long as the *'ereṣ* itself lasts. Therefore, although the Hebrew term is not necessarily as infinite as it sounds in English, the parallels that some have drawn with similar promises concerning the Rechabites and the levitical priesthood are inexact.[27] Moreover, Genesis 17 suggests that the territorial promise will at least be as 'everlasting' as the covenant itself, a covenant which relates primarily to the blessing of the nations through Abraham's royal seed and, by implication, is truly everlasting.

Admittedly, this gives rise to a major crux: how can the territorial promise, explicitly described in Genesis 17 as 'the whole land of Canaan', be understood as 'everlasting' in any real sense? There are, it would appear, only two ways to resolve this. Either the promise of specific national territory is indeed everlasting, in which case Abraham's 'seed' will possess the land of Canaan for ever,[28] or else the land in question here incorporates a meaning that extends beyond the geographical parameters of national territory. The precise identity of the Abrahamic 'seed' to whom this promise actually belongs is clearly crucial. If, as the immediate context seems to suggest (see above), Abraham's 'seed' here incorporates not one nation only (i.e. Israel), but rather 'many nations' (i.e. his spiritual posterity), it is difficult to interpret 'the whole land of Canaan' in a strictly localized manner. Rather, as Keil pointed out over a century ago:

> If the whole land of Canaan was promised to this posterity, which was to increase into a multitude of nations (ver. 8) [*sic*], it is perfectly evident ... that the sum and substance of the promise was not exhausted by the gift of the land, whose boundaries are described in chap. xv. 18–21, as a possession to the nation of Israel, but that the extension of the idea of the lineal posterity ... to the spiritual posterity ... requires the expansion of the idea and extent of the earthly Canaan to the

[27] E.g. Wright 1994: 5–6. Unlike the temple, in which the Rechabites and the levitical priesthood were to serve God perpetually, the promised land still exists today.

[28] Significantly, even some dispensationalists are reluctant to carry the territorial promise into the eternal state, although this is surely the logical corollary of their insistence that the land of Canaan (in its strict, geographical sense) has been promised to Israel (the 'great nation' promised to Abraham) for ever.

> full extent of the spiritual Canaan, whose boundaries reach as widely as the multitude of nations having Abraham as father (Keil & Delitzsch 1976–7: 1:226).[29]

A further indication that the territorial promise relates to something of an enduring nature is the associated concept of rest. This aspect is not explicitly connected with the promised land until the book of Deuteronomy (e.g. 3:20; 12:9–10; 25:19; cf. Josh. 1:13), but the concept itself does appear earlier (Gen. 49:15[?]; Exod. 33:14). Indeed, a strong case can be made for connecting this promised 'rest' with the divine rest spoken of in the Genesis creation narrative (cf. Exod. 20:11; Deut. 5:15; Heb. 3:7 – 4:11).[30] Understood in this light, securing possession or inheritance of the promised land typifies entering into God's eternal rest, of which the land of Canaan was merely a symbol. God intended humankind to share such a rest with him from the beginning (as reflected in the Edenic Paradise described in Gen. 2). The territorial promise thus anticipated the full restoration of the Edenic conditions that had been lost initially and jeopardized persistently through human disobedience.[31] It is reasonable to conclude, therefore, that anything less than a permanent restoration of the conditions that pertained in Eden stops short of a comprehensive fulfilment of the territorial promise.

From the above discussion of the nature of the territorial promise, the following conclusion may be drawn: while the promised land includes the territory occupied by Israel for the greater part of her history, it also encompasses something more. However, the latter is no less terrestrial than the former, in the same way that the paradisal conditions of Eden are no less earthly than those of the 'new earth' anticipated by the prophets. Thus as Martens (1994: 121) aptly concludes:

[29] While Keil has apparently failed to influence many recent commentators, his suggestion clearly provides further rationale for the apostle Paul's claim that Abraham received a promise that 'he would inherit the world' (Rom. 4:13).

[30] See Kaiser 1973: 145–149, Lincoln 1982: 209–210, and Alexander in the present volume (pp. 35–50).

[31] As Dumbrell (1984: 120) observes in relation to the Deuteronomic vision of Canaan's fertility (Deut. 26), 'one can hardly escape the impression that what is being depicted through such references is Eden recaptured, paradise recovered'. See too Alexander in the present volume (pp. 35–50).

> Land, then, is more than acreage or territory. It is a theological symbol, through which a series of messages are conveyed ... But if land is more than acreage or territory and symbolic of promise, gift, blessing and lifestyle, it is nevertheless still soil and territory. It has theological aspects, but it is not thereby an ethereal thing, nor should it be spiritualized.[32]

Such a conclusion is clearly borne out by the ways the territorial promise is actually fulfilled in the biblical corpus under review.

Fulfilments of the territorial promise in Genesis–Kings

In the Genesis–Kings corpus, the territorial promise is apparently depicted as having been fulfilled at least twice in Israel's history: during the days of Joshua and during the reign of Solomon (cf. Josh. 21:43–45; 1 Kgs. 4:20–21). However, the fact that the promise of land was fulfilled more than once leaves open the possibility of multiple fulfilments and also raises the question of its ultimate fulfilment. Was the fulfilment in the days of Joshua the first realization of the territorial promise, and was that of the Solomonic era the last?

In the patriarchal era

Several scholars have sought to locate partial fulfilments of the territorial promise within the ancestral history itself: in Abraham's purchase of a family tomb (Gen. 23), and in Jacob's purchase of a camp site (Gen. 33:18–20). However, Turner's comment (1990: 103) is apposite:

> If *buying* property could be construed as fulfilling the promise, one wonders why Abraham – laden down with this world's goods – had not made similar offers for desirable properties before. He had used his own initiative in trying to push the posterity promise along, but even Abraham realizes that land

[32] A distinction should be maintained between 'spiritualizing' the Old Testament promise of land (i.e. emptying it of all physical significance) and drawing out its full, global importance.

> bought – at any price – is not a *gift* from Yahweh ... His purchase of this small plot simply emphasizes the non-fulfilment of the promise.

It is doubtful, in any case, whether the patriarchs anticipated any such immediate fulfilments. One of the key texts (Gen. 15:13–16) envisages a considerable time-lapse before the territorial promise is actually fulfilled. In the same context God's reply to Abraham's query is significant: Abraham asks for reassurance that he personally will inherit the land, whereas Yahweh confirms that it will be given to Abraham's descendants (cf. vv. 8, 18). Elsewhere, possession of the promised land is expressly associated with Abraham's descendants, sometimes exclusively so,[33] a further indication that fulfilment of the territorial promise should not be sought within the ancestral history. While it may be objected that in several texts the patriarchs personally are said to be the inheritors of the territory,[34] their description as 'aliens' – even after their purchases of real estate (cf. Gen. 35:27; Exod. 6:4) – strongly suggests that they never actually enjoyed anything more than temporary-resident status (cf. Gen. 34:30; Acts 7:5; Heb. 11:13). Moreover, the conjunction linking the patriarch and his descendants in some of the texts mentioned above might in fact have an explanatory function, in which case the second clause simply qualifies the sense of the first.[35]

Therefore the way the relationship of the patriarchs to the land is described would appear to militate against seeing even partial fulfilments of the territorial promise in the patriarchal era. This is not to deny, however, that 'this purchased plot of land is equivalent to a symbolic down payment on Canaan as Israel's legal possession' (Habel 1995: 123).[36] Nor does it detract from the fact that the burial of the patriarchs and their families in the promised land was an act of faith in the eventual fulfilment of the promise. But to interpret Abraham's purchase of a burial site as anything more than

[33] Cf. Gen. 12:7; 22:17; 24:7.

[34] E.g. Gen. 13:15, 17; 15:7; 17:8; 26:3; 28:4, 13; 35:12.

[35] I.e. the conjunction may be a *vav explicativum*: 'I will give to you, *that is*, to your descendants ...' For more on this, see Williamson 2000a.

[36] Both Brueggemann (1978) and Habel (1995) draw attention to the use of the term *ʾaḥuzzah* (possession) in Gen. 23:20; cf. 17:8.

a symbol of or an allusion to the later fulfilment of the promise seems to go further than the text permits.[37] For the actualizing of the territorial promise we must look elsewhere.

In the settlement period

Without doubt, the first fulfilment of the promise categorically underlined in Genesis–Kings is that which resulted from Joshua's military campaigns. While there is a certain ambivalence in the book of Joshua,[38] it is nevertheless clear that the promise of land was realized, albeit partially, in the settlement period.

The conquest is clearly presented as a significant stage in the promise–fulfilment schema of Genesis–Kings. It is the climax of the expectation that has been building up steadily in Numbers and Deuteronomy (Josh. 1:2–6). In some measure, under Joshua, Israel entered the rest forbidden to Moses and the generation that died outside Canaan (cf. Josh. 11:23; 21:44; 22:4; 23:1). To some extent God fulfilled the territorial promise made to the patriarchs (Josh. 21:43–45).

Nevertheless, while the territorial promise was fulfilled in the conquest of Canaan, it was only partially fulfilled, or rather, this was only the first stage of fulfilment (Josh. 13:1–2). Although the land had been allocated to the various tribes, Israelite control of the territory was still limited. As long as there were pockets of resistance, there could be no permanent state of rest, and the latter (see above) lay at the very heart of the promise. Moreover, as repeatedly emphasized in Deuteronomy, the continual enjoyment of such rest was dependent on covenant loyalty (cf. Deut. 4:25–28), without which Israel's experience of the 'good and spacious land' would be short-lived (cf. Josh. 23:12–13). Thus the fulfilment of the territorial promise in Joshua's day fell short, not only in relation to the

[37] Even Turner (1990: 103–104 n. 3) is prepared to admit that 'there is a very close connection – but not that of promise/fulfilment'.

[38] Although some texts strongly affirm that the entire land was taken (cf. 11:23; 21:43–45; 23:14), others indicate that the land was not yet fully possessed (cf. 13:1, 6–7; 15:53; 23:4–13). Since the latter picture is confirmed in Judges, it is the former passages that present the greater challenge to commentators. For a concise discussion of traditional and more recent attempts to reconcile the absolute nature of these texts with an incomplete conquest, see Hess 1996: 284–286.

geography, but also – and more significantly – in respect to the ideology of the promised land.

In the Davidic-Solomonic empire

The later fulfilment in the period of the United Monarchy was certainly more comprehensive in both respects. In this period the borders of Israel were extended to those mentioned in Genesis 15:18–21 (cf. 1 Kgs. 4:21).[39] Moreover, a degree of rest was attained beyond that experienced under the leadership of Joshua (cf. 2 Sam. 7:1; 1 Kgs. 4:24–25; 5:4). The latter is underlined in a number of ways,[40] not least of which is the fact that it is precisely in such a context of rest that David and later Solomon implement plans to erect a centralized sanctuary for worship (cf. Deut. 12:10).

However, even though the territorial promise met with a greater degree of fulfilment in the Davidic–Solomonic era, this still fell far short of the ideal encapsulated by the promised land. Like the earlier generation, the 'rest' experienced under David and his successor was short-lived. The economic prosperity envisaged in Deuteronomy (e.g. 15:4–6; 28:11–12) remained somewhat elusive. Soon the land was under threat once again, as history repeated itself with the cycle of covenant disloyalty and divine judgment. Although further allusions to the fulfilment of the territorial promise may be detected in the ensuing story, its climax in Israel's expulsion from the land illustrates that, in the final analysis, 'the enjoyment of the land was ... a token of an even greater fulfilment that Israel never experienced in any enduring way' (VanGemeren 1995: 175). Therefore, although the material in Genesis–Kings emphasizes how the territorial promise has been fulfilled in Israel's history, it nowhere suggests that this dimension of the divine plan has been fulfilled in its most comprehensive sense. Rather, as the exilic readers were undoubtedly meant to infer, just as God had fulfilled this promise in the past, so he would do in the future also.[41]

[39] *Pace* Townsend (1985: 330), who maintains that Philistia was not under Israelite control. The third geographical reference in 1 Kgs. 4:21 makes it clear that Solomon's control included Philistia; cf. the reference to Gaza, in the far south of Philistia, in v. 25.

[40] E.g. the establishment of the Davidic covenant in the context of the realization of the promise of a 'great nation' (cf. 2 Sam. 7:9–13, 23–24); an allusion to the promise of innumerable posterity in 1 Kgs. 4:20 (cf. Gen. 22:17).

Nevertheless, it was left to the prophets and others to fill out the picture of a grandiose fulfilment in the future.[42]

Conclusion

This examination of the territorial promise has demonstrated that, while the promise of land was certainly fulfilled to some extent in the period covered by Genesis–Kings, it was never fully realized. Rather, its fulfilment in the nation was but a preliminary stage and a symbol of its climactic fulfilment. It is not surprising, therefore, that other Old Testament writers should envisage a future and more permanent fulfilment of the territorial promise – one that would impact not just Israel, but all the nations of the earth.

Bibliography

Alexander, T. D. (1994), 'Abraham reconsidered theologically', in *He Swore an Oath: Biblical Themes from Genesis 12 – 50*, Carlisle: Paternoster: 7–28.

——— (1997), 'Further observations on the term "seed" in Genesis', *Tyndale Bulletin* 48.2: 363–367.

Barr, J. (1969), *Biblical Words for Time*, London: SCM.

Bergen, R. D. (1990), 'The role of Genesis 22:1–19 in the Abraham cycle: a computer-assisted textual interpretation', *Calvin Theological Review* 4: 313–326.

Brueggemann, W. (1978), *The Land: Place as Gift, Promise, and Challenge in Biblical Faith*, London: SPCK. US edn 1977.

Crenshaw, C. I., and G. E. Gunn (1985), *Dispensationalism Today, Yesterday, and Tomorrow*, Memphis: Footstool.

Dillmann, A. (1897), *Genesis Critically and Exegetically Explained*, 2 vols., Edinburgh: T. and T. Clark.

Dray, S. P. (1984), 'The land: a forgotten element in biblical hope', *Evangel* 2: 1:2–4.

[41] Unless one assumes that the message of the Deuteronomistic History is entirely negative, the emphasis on God fulfilling his promises (of judgment and blessing) in the past must surely contain some measure of encouragement and hope for those who had been exiled from the promised land. For more on the latter, see Fretheim 1983: 44ff.

[42] As Dray (1984: 3) correctly points out: 'the prophetic expectation, howsoever spiritual, remains stubbornly "this-worldly" even if it necessitates a dramatic event of cosmos renewal to accomplish it (see Isaiah 65:17; 66:22). The earth remains the final and enduring place of experienced salvation.'

Dumbrell, W. J. (1984), *Covenant and Creation: A Theology of the Old Testament Covenants*, Exeter: Paternoster.
Estes, D. J. (1990), 'Looking for Abraham's City', *Bibliotheca Sacra* 147: 399–413.
Fretheim, T. E. (1983), *Deuteronomic History*, Nashville: Abingdon.
Habel, N. C. (1995), *The Land is Mine: Six Biblical Land Ideologies*, Minneapolis: Fortress.
Hess, R. S. (1996), *Joshua*, Tyndale Old Testament Commentaries, Leicester: IVP.
Holwerda, D. E. (1995), *Jesus and Israel: One Covenant or Two?* Leicester: Apollos.
Hoekema, A. A. (1979), *The Bible and the Future*, Grand Rapids: Eerdmans.
Kaiser, W. C. (1973), 'The promise theme and the theology of rest', *Bibliotheca Sacra* 130: 135–150.
——— (1978), *Toward an Old Testament Theology*, Grand Rapids: Zondervan.
——— (1981), 'The promised land: a biblical-historical view', *Bibliotheca Sacra* 138: 302–311.
——— (1998), 'The land of Israel and the future return (Zechariah 10: 6–12)', in H. W. House (ed.), *Israel: The Land and the People: An Evangelical Affirmation of God's Promises*, Grand Rapids: Kregel: 209–227.
Kallai, Z. (1997), 'The patriarchal boundaries, Canaan and the land of Israel: patterns and application in biblical historiography', *Israel Exploration Journal* 47: 1–2, 69–82.
Keil, C. F., & F. Delitzsch (1976–7), *Biblical Commentary on the Old Testament*, 10 vols., Grand Rapids: Eerdmans.
LaRondelle, H. K. (1983), *The Israel of God in Prophecy: Principles of Prophetic Interpretation*, Berrien Springs: Andrews University Press.
Lincoln, A. T. (1982), 'Sabbath, rest, and eschatology in the New Testament', in D. A. Carson (ed.), *From Sabbath to Lord's Day: A Biblical, Historical and Theological Investigation*, Grand Rapids: Zondervan: 197–220.
McComiskey, T. E. (1985), *The Covenants of Promise: A Theology of the Old Testament Covenants*, Leicester: IVP.
McKeown, J. (1997), 'The theme of land in Genesis 1 – 11 and its significance for the Abraham narrative', *Irish Biblical Studies* 19: 51–64, 133–144.
Martens, E. A. (1994), *God's Design: A Focus on Old Testament Theology*, Leicester: Apollos.
Millar, J. G. (1998), *Now Choose Life: Theology and Ethics in Deuteronomy*, Leicester: Apollos.
Rad, G. von (1933), 'There remains still a rest for the people of God: an

investigation of a biblical conception', in *The Problem of the Hexateuch and Other Essays*, London: Oliver and Boyd, 1966: 94–102.
——— (1943), 'The promised land and Yahweh's land in the Hexateuch', in *The Problem of the Hexateuch and Other Essays*, London: Oliver and Boyd, 1966: 79–93.
Sailhamer, J. H. (1996), *Genesis Unbound: A Provocative New Look at the Creation Story*, Sisters, OR: Multnomah.
Townsend, J. L. (1985), 'Fulfilment of the land promise in the Old Testament', *Bibliotheca Sacra* 142: 320–334.
Turner, L. A. (1990), *Announcements of Plot in Genesis*, Journal for the Study of the Old Testament Supplement Series 96, Sheffield: JSOT Press.
VanGemeren, W. A. (1995), *The Progress of Redemption: From Creation to the New Jerusalem*, Carlisle: Paternoster.
Waldow, H. E. von (1974), 'Israel and her land: some theological considerations', in H. N. Bream, R. D. Heim & C. A. Moore (eds.), *A Light Unto My Path: Old Testament Studies in Honor of Jacob M. Myers*, Philadelphia: Temple University Press: 493–508.
Weinfeld, M. (1993), *The Promise of the Land: The Inheritance of the Land of Canaan by the Israelites*, Oxford: University of California Press.
Williamson, P. R. (2000a), 'Abraham, Israel and the church', *Evangelical Quarterly* 72: 99–118.
——— (2000b), *Abraham, Israel and the Nations: The Patriarchal Promise and its Covenantal Development in Genesis*, Journal for the Study of the Old Testament Supplement Series 315, Sheffield: JSOT Press.
Wright, C. J. H. (1983), *Living as the People of God: The Relevance of Old Testament Ethics*, Leicester: IVP.
——— (1990), *God's People in God's Land: Family, Land, and Property in the Old Testament*, Exeter: Paternoster.
——— (1994), 'A Christian approach to Old Testament prophecy concerning Israel', in P. W. L. Walker (ed.), *Jerusalem Past and Present in the Purposes of God*, Carlisle: Paternoster: 1–19.

1B

Beyond borders: the wider dimensions of land

T. Desmond Alexander

Introduction

The final quarter of the twentieth century witnessed a growing interest in the subject of land in theological writings on the Bible.[1] This was undoubtedly encouraged by the recognition that the concept of land permeates the biblical writings, especially the Old Testament, to a much greater extent than had previously been observed.[2]

An important reason for the prominence of land is clearly the metanarrative, recorded in the books of Genesis to Kings, which focuses on how the ancient Israelites came to possess the territory known today as Israel/Palestine. As we have already observed (in the preceding chapter), the account in Genesis–Kings is bound

[1] E.g. Brueggemann 1977, Wright 1990, Weinfeld 1993, Habel 1995.

[2] As Martens observes (1994: 103), 'land' (Hebrew *'ereṣ*) 'is the fourth most frequent noun or substantive in the Old Testament: it occurs 2,504 times' (2,505 times according to BibleWorks 4.0). Cf. Janzen 1992: 143.

together by a literary plot which moves from promise to fulfilment, or perhaps more accurately, partial fulfilment, since not all the divine promises made in Genesis are fulfilled by the end of 2 Kings.[3]

While the promise of land and its fulfilment are undoubtedly very important in Genesis–Kings, they are intimately bound to a number of other theological ideas. These are noteworthy because they enable us to comprehend better the significance of land within a broader biblical theology framework.

As the book of Genesis stands, the divine promises given to Abraham in Genesis 12:1–3 are clearly intended to be read in the light of the events recorded in Genesis 1 – 11 (cf. McKeown 1977). The divine summons to Abraham to 'leave your country, your people and your father's household and go to the land I will show you' (Gen. 12:1) stands in marked contrast to prior developments within Genesis. Whereas Genesis 3 – 11 mentions banishment (3:23–24), restless wandering (4:12–16) and scattering (11:8–9), Abraham is directed by Yahweh to a specific land. While these former events are occasioned by divine disfavour, the relocation of Abraham is associated with the promise of divine blessing (12:2–3). Out of this comes the idea that developments associated with the promise of land to Abraham represent a reversal of all that has occurred as a result of Adam and Eve's rebellion against God in the Garden of Eden. In the remainder of this chapter we shall explore a number of interrelated themes which shed important light upon the promise of land to Abraham and its fulfilment.

The land as a place of rest

Rest is an important aspect of the promise of land. Land and rest are often mentioned together, both being described as gifts from God (e.g. Deut. 3:20; 12:9–10; 25:19; Josh. 1:13–15; 21:43–44; cf. Josh. 22:4). Deuteronomy, for example, speaks of the land as being 'the resting place and the inheritance the LORD your God is

[3] The promise of land plays a secondary role to the promise of the nations being blessed through a royal descendant of Abraham. See Alexander 1998b: 191–212.

giving you' (Deut. 12:9). In the context of the Pentateuch, the divine gift of rest stands in marked contrast to the experience of the Israelites in Egypt and the subsequent period of forty years spent as nomads in the wilderness. The promised land holds out the possibility of rest from oppression by enemies, hard labour and wandering (cf. Gen. 15:13–14). Rest, however, is not merely a fortunate by-product of being given the land. As Exodus 33:14 reveals, it is a distinctive, divine gift which may be considered in its own right.[4]

In the books of Deuteronomy–Kings rest is often associated with deliverance from enemies (e.g. Deut. 12:9–10; 25:19; Josh. 21:43–44; 23:1; cf. Josh. 11:23). While Deuteronomy anticipates rest from enemies, and the book of Joshua concludes with it having been achieved, this rest is only temporary. Judges describes how the enemies of Israel regain power, bringing to an end the rest that was achieved under Joshua. The period from Joshua's death to the start of the monarchy is marked by events which revolve around various judges who bring periods of peace from war lasting forty or eighty years (Judg. 3:11, 30; 5:31; 8:28; cf. Josh. 11:23; 14:15, which also speak of the land having rest from war).[5] Brief references to these intervals of peace, however, merely emphasize the overall absence of rest during this period. Later, with the establishment of David as king in Jerusalem, 2 Samuel 7:1 draws attention to the rest which God gave him 'from all his enemies around him'. The Chronicler also introduces the theme of rest into his account of David's reign. According to 1 Chronicles 22:9, David received the divine promise: 'But you will have a son who will be a man of peace and rest, and I will give him rest from all his enemies on every side. His name will be Solomon, and I will grant Israel peace and quiet during his reign.'[6] While this promise is not recorded in the books

[4] In Exod. 33:14 the Lord says to Moses, 'My Presence will go with you, and I will give you rest.'

[5] In these verses the verb used is *šāqaṭ*, 'to have peace', rather than *nûaḥ*, 'to rest/settle'. Here the use of *šāqaṭ* appears to be determined by the subject 'land' (*'ereṣ*). As 2 Chr. 14:5 and 20:30 illustrate, *šāqaṭ* tends to be used of places, whereas *nûaḥ* is normally used to refer to what God does for persons.

[6] The name Solomon (in Hebrew *šᵉlōmōh*) is closely related to *šālôm*, 'peace'. 1 Chr. 22:9 brings together the concepts *šeqeṭ*, 'peace', *nûaḥ*, 'rest' and *šālôm*, 'peace'.

of Kings, 1 Kings 8:56 states that Solomon gave praise to God for rest.[7]

Rest from oppression by enemies is only part, however, of a larger picture. As Leviticus 26 reveals, both positively and negatively, the promised land is also portrayed as being very fertile and producing abundant harvests. This fruitfulness is encapsulated in the frequently used expression, 'a land flowing with milk and honey' (Exod. 3:8, 17; 13:5; Lev. 20:24; Num. 14:8; 16:13–14; Deut. 6:3; 11:9; 26:9, 15; 27:3; Josh. 5:6; cf. Exod. 33:3; Num. 13:27; Deut. 31:20). A vivid image of the land's richness is found, even before the Israelites take possession of it, in the account of the twelve spies returning with a cluster of grapes that has to be carried on a pole or wooden frame between two of them (Num. 13:23). Later, Moses portrays the bounty of the land in glowing terms: 'For the LORD your God is bringing you into a good land – a land with streams and pools of water, with springs flowing in the valleys and hills; a land with wheat and barley, vines and fig-trees, pomegranates, olive oil and honey; a land where bread will not be scarce and you will lack nothing; a land where the rocks are iron and you can dig copper out of the hills' (Deut. 8:7–9; cf. 11:10–12). The fruitfulness of the land obviously reinforces the idea that it will be a place of rest. Within this bountiful domain human beings will enjoy God's blessing and favour.

It is impossible to consider the concept of rest without noting its association with the Sabbath. In spite of substantial differences in wording, the Exodus and Deuteronomy versions of the Decalogue both associate the Sabbath with rest. Yet, whereas Exodus 20:11 refers explicitly to the divine institution of the Sabbath on the seventh day of creation (cf. Gen. 2:1–3), Deuteronomy 5:15 highlights Yahweh's deliverance of the Israelites from Egypt. This suggests that the deliverance of the Israelites from bondage in Egypt and their subsequent settlement in the promised land were viewed

[7] Further references to rest and/or peace come in 2 Chr. 14:5–6; 15:15; 20:30 in connection with two of the kings of Judah, Asa and Jehoshaphat. While Yahweh is the source of peace and rest, special attention is drawn to the fact that this peace comes through a divinely appointed ruler. In the pre-monarchic period, peace was associated with judges; in the monarchic period, rest comes through righteous kings. Interestingly, Is. 11:10 anticipates a time when a future Davidic king will be surrounded by nations and 'his place of rest will be glorious.'

as in some manner paralleling God's rest following the completion of his creative activity.[8] In the light of this we should not lose sight of the prominence given to the Sabbath in the covenant made at Sinai between Yahweh and the Israelites. Not only is the Sabbath the sign of the covenant (Exod. 31:16–17), but sabbatical principles underlie various regulations and practices mentioned in the Book of the Covenant and elsewhere.[9]

Rest from oppression, wandering and toil requires the provision of suitable land. Such rest, when experienced fully, represents a return to the idyllic conditions which existed prior to the expulsion of Adam and Eve from the Garden of Eden. In part it involves the restoration of a harmonious relationship between the ground and human beings. Interestingly, this appears to be the rest for which Lamech hoped when he named Noah: 'He will comfort us in the labour and painful toil of our hands caused by the ground the LORD has cursed' (Gen. 5:29).[10]

While the gift of land to the Israelites is obviously viewed as a positive blessing from God, bringing rest to the people following their exploitation in Egypt, the narrative of Genesis–Kings reveals that this rest never became a permanent feature of their time in the land. On the contrary, at best they enjoyed it only for relatively short periods. Not surprisingly, therefore, the hope of permanent rest became an important component of Israel's future expectations.[11]

The land as sacred space

A significant, but often neglected, part of the Genesis–Kings narrative is the account of the building of the tabernacle. The importance

[8] Although Gen. 2:1–3 does not use the verb *nûaḥ*, preferring the verb *šābaṯ*, Exod. 20:11 employs *wayyānaḥ*, 'and he rested', clearly understanding this to correspond with the expression 'he rested (*šābaṯ*) from all his work' which comes twice in Gen. 2:2–3. The verbs *nûaḥ* and *šābaṯ* are also used together in Exod. 23:12 in relation to the keeping of the Sabbath.

[9] We see this, for example, in the release of slaves in the seventh year (Exod. 21:2–6; cf. Deut. 15:12–18); the land being left uncultivated in the seventh year (Exod. 23:10–11; cf. Lev. 25:1–7); no work being performed on the seventh day (Exod. 23:12); the returning of property in the year of jubilee (Lev. 25:8–55); the cancelling of debts in the seventh year (Deut. 15:1–11).

[10] In Hebrew the name Noah (*nōaḥ*) resembles closely the verb *nûaḥ*, 'to rest'; Gen. 5:29 also contains a word-play between Noah (*nōaḥ*) and the verb *nāḥam*, 'to comfort'. See Mathews 1996: 316–319.

[11] Cf. Kaiser 1973, Gowan 1986, Wright 1999.

of this project is underlined by the extensive space devoted to recording the giving of the instructions (Exod. 25–31) and their fulfilment (Exod. 35–40). At the heart of this enterprise is the construction of a tent which becomes Yahweh's dwelling-place in the midst of the Israelites. Not only does this contribute to setting the Israelites apart from other nations as holy (cf. Exod. 19:6), but the same holds true for the ground where the tabernacle is located; it becomes sacred space. By coming to dwell among the Israelites, Yahweh gives to the promised land a unique status.

As well as distinguishing the land of Canaan from all other lands, the construction of the tabernacle is clearly perceived as being a restoration, in part at least, of the conditions which originally existed in the Garden of Eden. Biblical scholars have noted various parallels between the tabernacle (as well as the later Jerusalem temple) and Eden, not all of which are equally compelling.[12]

- Eden and the later sanctuaries are entered from the east and guarded by cherubim (3:24; Exod. 25:18–22; 26:31; 1 Kgs. 6:23–29).
- The tabernacle menorah (or lampstand) probably symbolizes the tree of life (2:9; 3:22; cf. Exod. 25:31–35).
- The LORD God walked in Eden as he later did in the tabernacle (3:8; cf. Lev. 26:12; Deut. 23:15; 2 Sam 7:6–7).
- The man's work in Eden is described using terminology that is later associated with service in the tabernacle. The Hebrew verbs in God's command 'to work it [the garden] and take care of it' (2:15) are only used in combination elsewhere in the Pentateuch of the duties of the Levites in the sanctuary (cf. Num. 3:7–8; 8:26; 18:5–6).[13]
- Gold and onyx, which are mentioned in Genesis 2:11–12, are used extensively to decorate the later sanctuaries and priestly garments (e.g. Exod. 25:7, 11, 17, 31).[14] Gold in particular is associated with the divine presence.[15]

[12] Most of these parallels are set out more fully by Wenham (1986).

[13] The relevant Hebrew terms are *'ābad*, 'to serve', 'to till'; *šāmar*, 'to keep', 'to observe'.

[14] There are about one hundred references to gold and seven to onyx in the Exodus account of the building of the tabernacle.

[15] It should be noted, however, that Gen. 2:11–12 does not state that this gold and onyx were located within Eden.

- The river flowing from Eden (2:10) is reminiscent of Ezekiel 47:1–12 which envisages a river flowing from a future Jerusalem temple and bringing life to the Dead Sea.[16]

These parallels between Eden and the tabernacle lend support to the idea that the promised land was viewed as being, in part at least, a re-creation of Eden (cf. Gen. 13:10). Yet, although the Israelites have the opportunity to enjoy fellowship with God at the tabernacle (and later at the Jerusalem temple), direct access into God's immediate presence is restricted to the high priest, and then only once a year on the Day of Atonement (cf. Lev. 16). In the light of this it is hardly surprising that other biblical passages look forward to a much fuller and grander restoration of Eden.[17]

The decision of Yahweh to establish his dwelling among the Israelites has important implications as regards the land. To sustain Yahweh's presence the land must remain undefiled. This is echoed repeatedly in Deuteronomy, which speaks of the Israelites' need to purge the evil from among them (Deut. 13:5; 17:7, 12; 19:19; 21:21; 22:21–22, 24; 24:7).

While the construction of the temple in the reign of Solomon is a high point in the Genesis–Kings narrative, subsequent years witness a gradual decline, leading eventually to the destruction of the temple by the Babylonians. This, however, as the final chapters of Ezekiel testify, does not bring to an end the hope that God's presence will be located permanently in the midst of his people. But this eventuality requires the provision of a sacred location which cannot be defiled by human sin.

The land gives identity to the people of God

The promise of land to Abraham must also be considered in terms of nationhood. Indeed, when God summons Abraham to leave his own land in Genesis 12:1–3, the promise of land is subsumed

[16] Cf. Dumbrell 1985: 41. Interestingly, Dumbrell also notes various links between sanctuary (tabernacle), creation and rest/Sabbath.

[17] The final chapters of Revelation, for example, envisage the creation of a garden-city, without a temple, 'because the Lord God Almighty and the Lamb are its temple' (21:22), where human beings will have open and direct access to God.

under the concept of nationhood. Yahweh says to Abraham, 'I will make you into a great nation' (Gen. 12:2). This is developed more fully in Genesis 15, where particular attention is given to the two main elements of nationhood: descendants (vv. 1–6) and land (vv. 7–21). While interest in Genesis focuses largely on the numerical growth of Abraham's descendants, with this becoming particularly important in the early chapters of Exodus, the Israelites' deliverance from Egypt and their settlement in the promised land are obviously viewed as establishing them as a nation in their own right.

When Moses brings the Israelites to Mount Sinai, Yahweh introduces the covenant which he wishes to make with them by affirming that they are to be distinguished from all other nations by being his 'treasured possession' (Exod. 19:5). Moreover, they are to be a 'kingdom of priests and a holy nation' (Exod. 19:6; cf. Deut. 7:6; 14:2). Since nationhood is normally understood as being a community of people sharing a common government and living in a clearly defined geographical region, possession of land is essential for Israel to become a 'holy nation'.

Yet more than land is required in order for the Israelites to establish their unique identity as God's holy people among all the other nations of the earth. On the one hand, their holy status depends upon Yahweh being in their midst. Consequently, the building of the tabernacle is especially significant, for it is Yahweh's divine presence which sanctifies the people (cf. Lev. 20:8; 21:8, 15, 23; 22:9, 16, 32).

On the other hand, Israel's status as a 'holy nation' means that the people must adopt a distinctive lifestyle. The book of Leviticus, in particular, is dominated by regulations and instructions which are designed to enable the Israelites to live in Yahweh's presence. Not only do these highlight the requirements for holy living, but they also have the practical effect of distinguishing the Israelites from other nations. This is particularly so as regards the rules concerning clean and unclean foods.[18]

Land obviously plays an essential role in giving identity to the people of God as a 'holy nation'. This is recognized by Moses when he exhorts the Israelites to keep the decrees and laws of Yahweh.

[18] Cf. Soler 1979, Wenham 1981, Houston 1993.

> Observe them carefully, for this will show your wisdom and understanding to the nations, who will hear about all these decrees and say, 'Surely this great nation is a wise and understanding people.' What other nation is so great as to have their gods near them the way the LORD our God is near us whenever we pray to him? And what other nation is so great as to have such righteous decrees and laws as this body of laws I am setting before you today? (Deut. 4:6–8; cf. 26:19).

The divine election of Israel and the creation of a distinctive nation are clearly essential elements in God's redemptive plan for the world.[19]

While the nation of Israel is intended to play a central role in the outworking of God's purposes in the world, it is apparent that these cannot be fulfilled through Israel alone. Both at creation and following the flood, God gives instructions that human beings are to 'be fruitful and increase in number' and 'fill the earth' (Gen. 1:28; 9:1).[20] While the establishment of Israel as a nation may be viewed as being in keeping with this creation mandate, especially given their remarkable numerical growth, this can only be viewed as a partial fulfilment, for Israel's national borders are never expected to extend to the ends of the earth.[21] For God's creation plans to be completed, other nations apart from Israel must also be included. Israel, however, has a special role to play *vis-à-vis* these nations.

The land as the arena where faith and obedience are tested

Throughout Genesis–Kings, possession of land is often closely linked to human trust in Yahweh and obedience to him. Abraham is expected to respond in faith to the promises Yahweh gives him. Before he can take possession of the land he must obey the divine

[19] Cf. Alexander 1995a: 174–186.

[20] These parallels are part of a larger pattern in which the flood narrative is portrayed as being the re-creation of the earth; cf. Smith 1977.

[21] While the borders of the promised land are set out in various passages with relative precision, there is no indication that Israel as a nation was to possess the whole earth. Nevertheless, there is the expectation that one day the Israelites will have a uniquely righteous king whose authority will extend over all the earth (e.g. Pss. 2:8–12; 72:8–11).

call and leave the security of his homeland and family. Later, he must continue to believe Yahweh's promise in spite of the land of Canaan's being occupied already by others. This pattern is often repeated. The Israelites must exercise faith in Yahweh's power if they are to leave Egypt and take possession of Canaan. However, their subsequent lack of faith results in disaster; due to their unbelief they die in the wilderness. Through faith Joshua succeeds in taking possession of the promised land. In marked contrast, the faithlessness of succeeding generations of Israelites leads to reversals in their fortunes. This is especially evident during the period of the judges. While the reigns of David and Solomon see the fulfilment of God's covenantal promise of land to Abraham in Genesis 15, the disobedience of subsequent kings results in the loss of land, first for the northern kingdom of Israel and then for the southern kingdom of Judah.

For Abraham and his descendants the promise of land provides a means by which their faith may be tested. In this way land is used to determine the strength or otherwise of the Israelites' trust in God and their willingness to obey him. This remains true even after they have taken possession of the land, for their covenant relationship with Yahweh promises a good life within the land only if they are obedient. Disobedience will result in expulsion from the land.[22]

Land as a source of divine blessing or cursing

The opening chapters of Genesis highlight a special relationship between human beings and the earth. This is revealed positively in the description of Adam's creation from the dust of the ground, and reflected linguistically in the correspondence between the Hebrew terms *'ādām*, 'man' and *'ᵃdāmâ*, 'ground'. While these factors point to the existence of an initially harmonious relationship between human beings and the land, this is subsequently transformed when Yahweh pronounces judgment upon the human couple for eating

[22] Cf. Lev. 26:1–45; Deut. 27:15–26; 28:1–68. Here, as in Gen. 2–3, obedience and disobedience are associated with rest and restlessness respectively. Since human history may be viewed as being dominated by the rejection of God's sovereignty, it is hardly surprising that it is marked by individual and group migrations, often resulting in conflicts between nations. The absence of true peace and rest in our world is a constant reminder of humanity's ongoing alienation from God.

from the tree of the knowledge of good and evil. Because the ground is divinely cursed, human beings must struggle with nature in order to sustain themselves.

Whereas Adam and Eve's actions result in humanity's coming under God's curse, the call of Abraham holds out the hope of blessing for 'all the families of the ground' (Gen. 12:3, my translation).[23] Later, this blessing is expressed in terms of 'all nations on earth' (Gen. 18:18; 22:18). The fulfilment of this promise is guaranteed through the eternal covenant which Yahweh announces to Abraham in Genesis 17. The establishment of this covenant is linked to a special line of Abraham's descendants, and is traced in Genesis from Abraham to Isaac, from Isaac to Jacob and from Jacob to Joseph. When Jacob eventually blesses Joseph's younger son, Ephraim, the expectation is created that it will be through his descendants that the blessing of the nations will come (cf. Gen. 48:1–22; 49:22–26). However, the book of Genesis also anticipates that the blessing of the nations will be fulfilled through another of Jacob's sons, Judah. When the account of Joseph's being sold into slavery in Egypt is interrupted by Genesis 38, attention is focused on the unusual events surrounding the continuation of the line or 'seed' of Judah. The possibility of a royal line descending from Judah is also anticipated in Jacob's blessing in Genesis 49:8–12.[24] Later this expectation is confirmed when Yahweh rejects the line of Ephraim and appoints David son of Jesse to become king over Israel (cf. Ps. 78:67–72). While the divine promise of blessing for the nations of the earth remains to be fulfilled, it is now linked to the royal line of David and guaranteed by the covenant which Yahweh makes with David in 2 Samuel 7.[25] As Psalm 72 affirms, especially verse 17, all nations will be blessed through a future royal descendant of David.[26]

[23] This should not be interpreted as a promise of universal blessing in the sense that every human being will benefit. The final statement in Gen. 12:3 needs to be read in the light of that which immediately precedes it: those who bless Abraham will be divinely blessed; those who curse Abraham will be disdained by God.

[24] For a fuller discussion of this passage, see Alexander 1995b: 32–37.

[25] Although the term 'covenant' is not used in 2 Sam. 7, the events of this chapter are understood elsewhere as constituting the making of a covenant (cf. Pss. 89:3–4, 26–37; 132:11–12).

[26] According to the writers of the New Testament, these expectations find their fulfilment in Jesus Christ. Cf. Alexander 1998a: 121–168.

The promise to bless all the families or nations of the earth stands, however, in sharp contrast to the way in which the inhabitants of the land of Canaan are to be treated. They are not only to suffer the loss of their territory but are themselves targeted for destruction. This raises the question: why does God specifically promise to give Abraham the land of Canaan, a land already occupied by others? This issue takes on added significance when we observe that in Deuteronomy 2 the Israelites are directly prohibited by God from taking land that belongs to other nations. What distinguishes the land of Canaan from the land of Edom or Moab?

Any attempt to answer this question must begin with Genesis 9:18–29, the account of Noah's shameful treatment by his son Ham. At the start of this passage the reader is alerted to the fact that Ham is the father of Canaan (v. 18), and this is repeated in verse 22. Neither verse by itself requires the reader to know the identity of Ham's son. The significance of this relationship becomes apparent, however, when Noah pronounces judgment upon Ham for what he has done. He states, 'Cursed be Canaan! The lowest of slaves will he be to his brothers' (Gen. 9:25). This is then followed by another pronouncement which also refers to Canaan's being a slave in relation to Shem and Japheth, the brothers of Ham.

The inclusion in Genesis of Noah's malediction upon Canaan must surely anticipate God's promise of the land of Canaan to Abraham.[27] The author could hardly have included these elements without intending the reader to make some connection between them. This is not to say, however, that Noah's curse requires the later annihilation of Canaan's descendants. Nothing in Genesis 9:18–29 demands this; the emphasis is rather upon Canaan's descendants as submissive to those of Shem. Nevertheless, attention is drawn to the immorality of Ham, and the expectation is created that his descendants are likely to act in a similar way. According to

[27] Several factors point in this direction. First, there is the repeated use of the expression 'land of Canaan' as a designation for the region promised to Abraham. This title is striking because the Canaanites are only one of a number of peoples living in the region. Secondly, Gen. 10:15–19 lists various nations descended from Canaan and also a number of towns associated with them. The former includes most of the nations mentioned in subsequent lists relating to the promised land (e.g. Hittites, Jebusites, Amorites, Girgashites, Hivites). The latter mentions, alongside others, Sodom, Gomorrah, Admah and Zeboiim. The divine destruction of the first two of these cities is recorded in Gen. 19.

Genesis 10:15–19, Canaan's descendants include those who live in Sodom and Gomorrah. In the light of this it is noteworthy that in Genesis 19:4 *all the men* of Sodom, 'both young and old', gather around Lot's house in order to have improper sexual relations with the two strangers sheltering there.

The portrayal of some of Canaan's descendants as especially wicked is consistent with another theme developed in Genesis–Kings. The gift of the land of Canaan to Abraham and his descendants is associated with the divine punishment of its original inhabitants. As Genesis 15:16 reveals, the Israelites were to take possession of the land only when the sin of the Amorites had reached its full measure. In a similar fashion Leviticus 18:25 states that the expulsion of Canaan's descendants is due to the land's being defiled by them. In the light of this, Israel's seizure of the land of Canaan is a vivid reminder of the reality of divine judgment.

A further dimension to the process by which the Israelites were to take possession of the land of Canaan is the divine command to destroy completely those nations living there (e.g. Deut. 20:16–17). This process of 'ethnic cleansing' strikes the modern reader as particularly problematic. How could a righteous and loving God sanction such activity? Does this lend justification to similar actions today?

A detailed response to these issues lies beyond the scope of this chapter. However, several considerations may be usefully introduced into any discussion of this topic. As we have already noted, the dispossession of the inhabitants of Canaan by the Israelites is presented as an act of divine judgment. In particular, by worshipping other gods they failed to give to Yahweh the honour and recognition which were due to him alone. Yet this by itself does not adequately explain why the nations of Canaan were subjected to harsher treatment than those living outside the promised land (contrast Deut. 20:10–15 with 20:16–17). Two further factors may be significant. First, the total removal of the nations of Canaan is presented as necessary in order to prevent the Israelites from worshipping other gods (Deut. 20:18). The Israelites are to purge the land of anything that might cause them to sin against God. This, however, ought not to be interpreted as being directed only against the foreign nations living in Canaan; the same attitude was to be adopted towards fellow-Israelites (Deut. 13:1–18; 18:9–22; cf. Exod.

22:20). Secondly, various terms are used to describe the process by which the Israelites were to remove the other nations from the land of Canaan. The most striking of these are the verb *'ḥāram*, meaning 'to devote something to sacred use', and the related noun *'ḥērem*, 'devoted thing(s)'. When these terms are used everything that is captured in battle is to be given over to God; this involves the death of everyone: men, women and children (e.g. Deut. 2:34; 3:6). While the concept of *'ḥērem* comes frequently in Joshua (Josh. 2:10; 6:17–18, 21; 7:1, 11–13, 15; 8:26; 10:1, 28, 35, 37, 39–40; 11:11–12, 20–21; 19:38; 22:20), Weinfeld (1993: 76–78) observes that earlier passages speak of the Israelites 'dispossessing' or 'expelling' the nations of Canaan, without necessarily implying that the nations are to be destroyed completely. In the light of this, it is noteworthy that the concept of *'ḥērem* in war is first introduced in the context of the Israelites' being attacked by the Canaanite king of Arad (Num. 21:1–3). Later, Deuteronomy 2:34 and 3:6 apply the same concept to Sihon king of Heshbon and Og king of Bashan, both of whom deliberately attack the Israelites. A survey of the book of Joshua also suggests that the concept of *'ḥērem* is applied only to those who are actively hostile towards the Israelites. Since such hostility is viewed as being directed against Yahweh, all those involved forfeit their right to life.

In the light of this, it is noteworthy that the book of Joshua gives special attention to those non-Israelites who do not come under the *'ḥērem*. For assisting the Israelite spies to escape from Jericho, Rahab and her family are rescued when the city and its inhabitants are destroyed (Josh. 2:1–24; 6:25). Similarly, the people of Gibeon are not put to death even though they deceive the Israelites in order to establish a treaty with them (Josh. 9:1–27). Interestingly, the book of Joshua contrasts the non-destruction of these groups with the destruction that befalls the Israelite family of Achan (Josh. 7:1–26).

While the destruction of the inhabitants of Canaan by the Israelites raises ethical questions, we should not lose sight of the fact that the Israelites themselves eventually suffer a similar fate at the hand of the Assyrians and Babylonians. So Yahweh can hardly be accused of adopting double standards. Here again we are reminded of the intimate relationship between obedience, divine blessing and the provision of land.

Conclusion

The preceding survey has explored briefly a variety of interrelated themes which are closely associated with the concept of land in the books of Genesis–Kings. Undoubtedly the promise of land to Abraham has to be viewed as part of a much broader matrix which involves the restoration of harmonious relationships between God and some human beings. While the divine provision of land alone may bring certain advantages, land by itself does not supply God's blessing in all its fullness. As the narrative in Genesis–Kings reveals, it is the related aspects of rest and access to the divine presence that are of greatest benefit to people. In the light of this we must ensure that any consideration of the role of land in God's purposes does not get reduced to the issue of ownership of territory alone.

Two other general factors also need to be considered. First, compared with the Old Testament portrait of the Israelites' time in the land of Canaan, the modern State of Israel clearly lacks those elements which we have noted as prominent in Genesis–Kings. There is no temple to provide a sacred location, the population cannot be viewed as the covenant people of God, and there is no rest. Secondly, the New Testament writings look beyond the limited fulfilment of the promises associated with land in the Old Testament to a much greater fulfilment. Thus, for example, Hebrews 4 anticipates 'a Sabbath rest for the people of God', and the final chapters of Revelation look forward to the creation of a new earth where human beings will have direct and intimate access to God.

These observations are offered, not as the final word on this complex topic, but with the prayer that they may help Christians come to a better understanding of the contemporary relevance of the divine promise of land to Abraham.

Bibliography

Alexander, T. D. (1995a), *From Paradise to the Promised Land: An Introduction to the Main Themes of the Pentateuch*, Carlisle: Paternoster.

——— (1995b), 'Messianic ideology in the book of Genesis', in P. E. Satterthwaite, R. S. Hess & G. J. Wenham (eds.), *The Lord's Anointed: Interpretation of Old Testament Messianic Texts*, Carlisle: Paternoster: 19–39.

——— (1998a), *The Servant King: The Bible's Portrait of the Messiah*, Leicester: IVP.

——— (1998b), 'Royal expectations in Genesis to Kings: their importance for biblical theology,' *Tyndale Bulletin* 49.2: 191–212.

Brueggemann, W. (1978), *The Land: Place as Gift, Promise, and Challenge in Biblical Faith*, London: SPCK. US edn 1977.

Dumbrell, W. J. (1985), *The End of the Beginning: Revelation 21–22 and the Old Testament*, Homebush West: Lancer.

Gowan, D. E. (1986), *Eschatology in the Old Testament*, Philadelphia: Fortress.

Habel, N. C. (1995), *The Land is Mine: Six Biblical Land Ideologies*, Minneapolis: Fortress.

Houston, W. (1993), *Purity and Monotheism: Clean and Unclean Animals in Biblical Law*, Journal for the Study of the Old Testament Supplement Series 140; Sheffield: JSOT Press.

Janzen, W. (1992), 'Land', in D. M. Freedman et al. (eds.), *Anchor Bible Dictionary* 4, Garden City: Doubleday.

Kaiser, W. C. (1973), 'The promise theme and the theology of rest', *Bibliotheca Sacra* 130: 135–150.

Martens, E. A. (1994), *God's Design: A Focus on Old Testament Theology*, Leicester: Apollos.

Mathews, K. A. (1996), *Genesis 1–11:26*, New American Commentary, Nashville: Broadman and Holman.

McKeown, J. (1997), 'The theme of land in Genesis 1–11 and its significance for the Abraham narrative', *Irish Biblical Studies* 19: 51–64, 133–144.

Smith, G. V. (1977), 'Structure and purpose in Genesis 1–11', *Journal of the Evangelical Theology Society* 20: 307–319.

Soler, J. (1979), 'The semiotics of food in the Bible', in R. Forster & O. Ranum (eds.), *Food and Drink in History*: 126–138, Baltimore: Johns Hopkins University Press.

Weinfeld, M. (1993), *The Promise of the Land: The Inheritance of the Land of Canaan by the Israelites*, Oxford: University of California Press.

Wenham, G. J. (1981), 'The theology of unclean food', *Evangelical Quarterly* 53: 6–15.

——— (1986), 'Sanctuary symbolism in the Garden of Eden story', *Proceedings of the World Congress of Jewish Studies* 9:19–25.

Wright, C. J. H. (1990), *God's People in God's Land: Family, Land and Property in the Old Testament*, Exeter: Paternoster.

——— (1999), 'Theology and ethics of the land', *Transformation* 16.3: 81–86.

2. THE LAND IN THE PROPHETS

2A
Five prophetic snapshots of the land

Deryck Sheriffs

Addressing this topic means choosing a camera, film and lenses for the job. There is either a fixed-lens automatic compact that will deliver the goods postcard-size, wide-angle view, sharp from front to back. Or there is a complicated gadget-bag of lenses from macro to telephoto and options of manual override of exposure and depth of field. Considering the massive bulk of the collected words of the prophets, and their spread across centuries, not to mention the prophetic oracles in the narrative books, for simplicity's sake we shall start with five historical snapshots that feature the prophets and land issues. The five snapshots range in date from about 1050 BC to 165 BC. They are taken at the beginning and end of the Israelite monarchy, during the exile in Babylon, in post-exilic Jerusalem under the Persian empire, and during the Maccabean war against Antiochus Epiphanes. When we have looked at these snapshots we shall step back and ask what issues they raise for us as viewers.

Snapshot 1: Samuel looks forward to monarchy

Samuel, of course, is renowned as a prophet and, like the canonical prophets, he speaks into the specific social moment. In his times, as later, there are two forms of threat to life in the land – the internal and the external. The Israelites were looking at the external threat to their life in the land, the military and economic pressure from surrounding nations such as the Philistines. Samuel saw things differently. He perceived an internal threat to life in the land and exercised his prophetic critique.

> [The king] ... will take your sons and appoint them to his chariots and to be his horsemen, and to run before his chariots; and he will appoint for himself commanders of thousands and commanders of fifties, and some to plough his ground and to reap his harvest, and to make his implements of war and the equipment of his chariots. He will take your daughters to be perfumers and cooks and bakers. He will take the best of your fields and vineyards and olive orchards and give them to his courtiers. He will take one-tenth of your grain and of your vineyards and give it to his officers and his courtiers. He will take your male and female slaves, and the best of your cattle and donkeys, and put them to his work. He will take one-tenth of your flocks, and you shall be his slaves. And in that day you will cry out because of your king, whom you have chosen for yourselves; but the LORD will not answer you in that day (1 Sam. 8:11–18).

The sixfold repetition of the phrase 'he will take' adds a sonorous and ominous note. The list of royal requisitions is impressive: sons, daughters, fields, vineyards, olive orchards, grain, vineyards, male and female slaves, cattle and donkeys. It is not only quantity but quality – the king will take 'the best of' the livestock and fields. A good deal of this will be redistributed to his favourites, namely, 'his officers and his courtiers'.

Now, 'democratic' as this speech is in its denunciation of the hierarchical and acquisitive nature of the royal court, this is *Realpolitik* that appeals to self-interest – Israelites will be reduced to servant status. The NRSV aptly prefers the stronger nuance – 'you shall be his slaves'.

This speech anticipates a series of prophetic confrontations with the state and the king, but its most obvious sequel is Elijah's confrontation with Ahab over his appropriation of Naboth's vineyard. Naboth says: '[Yahweh] forbid that I should give you my ancestral inheritance' (1 Kgs. 21:3). The 'ancestral inheritance' principle reflects a completely different understanding of land ownership from ours. This principle precluded exchange of vineyards, or monetary compensation; King Ahab had offered Naboth either a better vineyard, or a fair price, before Naboth's point-blank refusal. A Yahwistic theology of land energizes Elijah's fierce denunciation of the Ahab dynasty. Samuel's and Elijah's prophetic denunciations rest on the predicates of an initial divine allocation of land, on kinship, clan, tribal and genealogical identity, and probably on a Jubilee concept of land occupation, meaning Israelite tenancy under Yahwistic ownership and reversion by law to the original distribution pattern (Lev. 25).

This pre-monarchy Samuel snapshot sits on its own page in the album on land, but his social critique is picked up by Amos, Isaiah of Jerusalem and Micah, all of whom denounce the exploitation of the poor and the acquisition of plots of land by the powerful, the adding of field to field (Is. 5:8).

Snapshot 2: Jeremiah takes up the plot

The tape has rolled on five hundred years from the time of Samuel. There is only a southern Jewish population left. The northern tribes are long gone into exile under the Assyrians, and now Nebuchadnezzar's army is laying siege to Jerusalem. Jeremiah is under arrest for his public denunciation of the authorities and his prediction that the populace will be deported to Babylon. At this point, God commands Jeremiah to buy a field in an outlying village. His cousin wishes to dispose of the land, but to buy now is financial folly. Jeremiah, never one to keep quiet for long, questions the sanity of his instructions. God replies that his plans extend beyond the imminent political doom to a restoration to the land and a renewal of the covenant relationship after this judgment.

> See, I am going to gather them from all the lands to which I drove them in my anger and my wrath and in great indignation; I will bring them back to this place, and I will settle them in safety. They shall be my people, and I will be their God. I will give them one heart and one way, that they may fear me for all time, for their own good and the good of their children after them. I will make an everlasting covenant with them, never to draw back from doing good to them; and I will put the fear of me in their hearts, so that they may not turn from me. I will rejoice in doing them good, and I will plant them in this land in faithfulness, with all my heart and all my soul (Jer. 32:37–41).

The language and the theology echo Deuteronomy, which itself envisaged apostasy, invasion, siege and deportation, but beyond that a hope of restoration (Deut. 30). What happened after the seventy years predicted by Jeremiah for exile from the land?

Snapshot 3: Dead men walking

Jeremiah's younger contemporary, Ezekiel, a deportee in Babylonia, is given a tough preaching assignment. He has to address a congregation of disarticulated skeletons. The results are surprising. The bones reassemble and stand up, prepared for the long march home to Palestine: 'I will bring you back to the land of Israel' (Ezek. 37:12). But Ezekiel's vision is for more than a long walk back from Babylon. It is for a return to national life as a united nation under King David, with God, temple and covenant relationship permanently restored:

> They shall live in the land that I gave to my servant Jacob, in which your ancestors lived; they and their children and their children's children shall live there for ever; and my servant David shall be their prince for ever. I will make a covenant of peace with them ... and I will bless them and multiply them, and I will set my sanctuary among them for evermore. My dwelling-place shall be with them; and I will be their God, and they shall be my people. Then the nations shall know that

> I the LORD sanctify Israel, when my sanctuary is among them for evermore (Ezek. 37:25–28).

In Ezekiel's mind all these components belong together in a coherent package – spiritual renewal, national unity, permanent occupation of the promised land, dynastic revival, and a reconstructed temple as a focal point for the presence of God. It scarcely seems a coincidence, then, that in 573 BC Ezekiel is transported 'in visions of God, to the land of Israel' (40:2) and sees the temple in great detail. It is as though he has clicked on the paragraph above and it has opened a window of graphics in virtual reality. He can tour the model, zooming in and zooming out, from inner courtyards to aerial views of Jerusalem, the tribal territories and the Dead Sea. Ezekiel's vision of the future is a promised-land vision – yet it is even more a temple-centred vision (Ezek. 40–48).

Snapshot 4: A look back in lament

If we fast-forward the tape about double the seventy-year period of Judean exile to the middle of the fifth century BC, we can listen to a communal lament that reviews what has happened to Israel between empire, exile and a Judean return. It highlights the role played by the prophets.

> For many years you were patient with them, and warned them by your spirit through your prophets; yet they would not listen. Therefore you handed them over to the peoples of the lands ... Here we are, slaves to this day – slaves in the land that you gave to our ancestors to enjoy its fruit and its good gifts (Neh. 9:30, 36).

Between Samuel and the work of Ezra and Nehemiah lies a period of six centuries, in round figures, from 1050 to 450 BC. During this time, a series of prophets visualized the irrevocable division into northern and southern kingdoms, denounced a creeping syncretism traced from Solomon to Manasseh that had introduced the worship of foreign deities into Jerusalem and into the temple itself, and predicted the deportation of the northern and southern tribes to Mesopotamia under the Assyrians and Babylonians. In holiness vocabulary, the land vomited them out (Lev. 20:22).

Prior to Ezra's and Nehemiah's lifetimes, a group of Judeans returned in the second part of the sixth century under Cyrus. Three generations later, Ezra and Nehemiah – who came from a Judean group that had not returned to the promised land – came on separate missions to reconstitute the worshipping community in Palestine and to rebuild and repopulate Jerusalem. Yet the net effect of the hundred years between 540 and 440 BC, including the renewals under Ezra and Nehemiah, was one of disappointment. The lyrical promises of the prophets contrasted with the harsh reality of life in the land and the post-exilic subservience to the Persians evoked these words of communal lament. The new exodus to the promised land had proved to be unspectacular. Instead of liberation, autonomy and empire, there were heavy taxes and local threats to security.

Snapshot 5: Vision, dream and nightmare

If we fast-forward the tape yet another three hundred years from the renewal under Ezra and Nehemiah and freeze-frame it at 165 BC, we are watching the effects of Hellenism in Jerusalem in the wake of Alexander's conquests. The Jewish community is divided again. Some are apostate (Dan. 11:30, 32) while others turn to armed resistance in Yahweh's name when Antiochus Epiphanes sets up an altar to Zeus Olympus in the Jerusalem temple (1 Macc.). Soon a Jewish alliance with Rome will open the door to another imperial occupation and yet further experience of life in the land as foreign domination.

Daniel's prayer, like Nehemiah's, reviews the history of the covenant and the role of the prophets using these words: 'we have not listened to your servants the prophets, who spoke in your name to our kings, our princes, and our ancestors, and to all the people of the land' (Dan. 9:6). The book of Daniel does not stop with a review of the past, but raises the stakes on a glorious future. It adds an apocalyptic dimension while still talking in terms of the physical land of Palestine and foreign invading armies passing through Palestine, 'the beautiful land' between Syria and Egypt (11:41; cf. 11:45, 'the beautiful holy mountain', i.e. Zion). There is no dragon in Daniel, but angels and archangels are involved in the battle for national survival (12:1), and there is talk of 'the end' and of resurrection from the dead after martyrdom. The visionary Daniel expects decisive political intervention by the 'Ancient of Days' (7:21–22 mg.), but remains baffled by the disclosures from the heavenly realm (12:8).

During the Maccabean crisis in 165 BC, there was apparently no prophet to consult (1 Macc. 4:46), and we too are pretty much in the dark about the activity of prophets and prophecy for another two hundred years. Apocalyptists dream dreams and write intertestamental works like *Enoch* and the *War Scroll* that are read at Qumran. The Jews in Palestine are now monotheists, but as if to compensate for that agreement on adherence to the first commandment, the Jews in the land are divided among themselves into parties and sects. The Qumran priests, the Sadducees, the Pharisees, the Essenes, the Zealots and the pro-Roman accommodators like Josephus are those best known to us. Kingdom and dominion have not passed to 'the people of the holy ones of the Most High' (Dan. 7:27). Instead, the 'ships of Kittim' (11:30) have sailed in and Rome is in occupation of the promised land. Rome crucifies Zealots and subversives. John the Baptist appears on the scene preaching the kingdom of God and national renewal. He is beheaded by internal politicking before the Roman authorities take an interest. Jesus is caught in the web of politicking and passed to and fro between the Sanhedrin and Herod before Roman crucifixion. He has spoken of the meek inheriting the earth (Matt. 5:5, echoing Ps. 37), but his followers were not meant to fight for power (John 18:36).

The Jesus movement ushers in a major reinterpretation of what constitutes the community of faith, the kingdom of God, true worship and the dynasty of David. This is linked with the institution of a new covenant and a radical re-reading of the Hebrew Scriptures. What changes did it bring to the understanding of the prophets' words about land?

The snapshots on the coffee table

What do these five snapshots tell us when we spread them out on the tabletop? First, like photographs returned from the high-street processor, they are date-stamped. The natural way for us to lay them out is in historical sequence: 1050, 587, 573, 450, 165 BC – not forgetting AD 2000 for the tabletop itself. Through the six dates, a story has unfolded that is interwoven with the politics of the Near East. A series of Gentile powers use Palestine as a land bridge in pursuit of their own economic and imperial designs.

Secondly, the series underlines the fact that sociological dynamics play a major role in ownership, occupation and access to land. Each setting is different. Power is differently located and expressed. The marginalized and the élite are differently characterized. Moral and spiritual force emanates differently. Prophets such as Samuel and Nathan exercised immense influence on national leaders, whereas other prophets, Jeremiah for instance, are marginalized. The Davidic dynasty arrives new, along with a capital city, a harem, mercenaries as bodyguards, civil war, international alliances and trade, chariotry and naval enterprise, organization of Levitical guilds and the intention of housing the ark permanently in the state capital in an opulent temple. Later, the dynasty and the Jewish social élite disappear. What is the role of the land? It is the stage for the dynamics of power, a dynamic subjected to prophetic critique.

Thirdly, the prophets and visionaries are not mystics. Their critique of land-occupation and power invokes a set of criteria.[1] This set of criteria includes theological beliefs and moral evaluations, and these are rooted in covenant stipulations. Explicitly and implicitly they invoke God's covenant with the ancestors, and the most obvious of the stipulations of this covenant is the first commandment: exclusive loyalty to Yahweh. Hence, this covenant theology of loyalty or disloyalty to Yahweh permeates the historical reviews embedded in Nehemiah 7 and Daniel 9, and we have the interpretation of Israel's ejection from the land framed thus: 'the curse and the oath written in the law of Moses, the servant of God, have been poured out upon us, because we have sinned against you' (Dan. 9:11). The most obvious expectation arising from covenant

[1] Notice the criteria of justice and compassion by which Daniel evaluates Nebuchadnezzar's rule: 'break with your sins by doing justice, break with your errors by showing favour to the needy, in case there might be a prolonging of your success' (Dan. 4:27 in the translation of Goldingay 1989: 79).

theology is material blessing for covenant loyalty and political punishment for breaking the covenant stipulations.

Fourthly, in this series of snapshots, faith in Yahweh survives organizational and institutional disruption. The national, tribal and cultic institutions are shattered. National life never reverts to the 'norm', if by the 'norm' we are thinking of the ideal of twelve tribes living in unity on ancestral territory, under a single leader anointed by Yahweh, and worshipping at a centralized shrine that houses the ark of the covenant. God moves on, and in the process proves to be somewhat of an iconoclast.

Finally, we see that an apocalyptic worldview emerges as something in continuity with and yet distinct from earlier prophetic perspectives: continuous in its land-, nation- and temple-centredness; distinct in its global and cosmic scale, and its hope of a new age that is qualitatively different, including resurrection from the dead. Prophets modelled martyrdom for covenant loyalty, instead of blessing and prosperity. Their suffering and executions were, in the first instance, at the hands of their own kings and courts, Jeremiah and Zechariah being prime examples (2 Chr. 24:20–22; Jer. 20:2; 32:3; 37:15; 38:1–6). Apocalyptic extends this horizon to the persecution and martyrdom of the loyal under Gentile powers (Dan. 11:33). With Old Testament apocalyptic, a global and cosmic perspective on the kingdom of God emerges from Palestinian soil.

In this glance at the snapshots on the table, we notice straight away that land is a key factor in the picture – but only one factor among several. We cannot talk coherently about territory without talking about the Israelite tribes. Nor can we talk about the land without talking about local plots of land. Plots of land in turn provoke a discussion of crops. In covenant theology as Deuteronomy 28 spells it out, spiritual disobedience has repercussions for land. Covenant-breaking will set off drought and crop diseases that will produce famine. The 'land of milk and honey' will turn into a barren and depopulated land. Hosea invokes this correlation between breaking the commandments and the land languishing (Hos. 4:1–3). Haggai explains the miserable crops in post-exilic Jerusalem as the consequences of neglecting the temple, a state which God would reverse dramatically if given his due. Malachi concurs, focusing on the right offering of tithes and unblemished animals as the remedy for post-exilic malaise (Mal. 1:6–14; 3:8–12). All this underlines the impossibility for us of speaking about the land in the prophets without speaking about the covenant, about national identity, tribal structure, ruling dynasty and cultic focus.

We can picture these entities as concentric circles. The focal point of covenant is Yahweh, and the focal point of Yahweh's presence among his people is the space above the ark of the covenant in the holy of holies in the temple in Jerusalem.[2] The reality of this central focus on the Jerusalem temple is underlined by the shock of its destruction, the insistence on its being rebuilt, and the role of Zion in the casting of prophetic eschatology. There is no discussion of the land in the prophetic books without reference to the capital city, the palace and the temple. The prophets do not speak about spiritual renewal, about renewal of the covenant, without speaking about the land, the capital city, the palace and the temple. Land, capital, palace and temple are all thoroughly physical entities. We could pinpoint them on a surveillance-satellite photo taken from above the Holy Land. On the whole, though, in the prophetic scenario, the land takes second place to Zion for the simple reason that Jerusalem since the time of David is the focal point of Yahwism. This is true historically and politically, and it is equally true eschatologically.

For instance, Isaiah 2 and Micah 4 speak about the mountain of the house of the Lord becoming the highest mountain in the world. The water that brings fertility and life to the land and to the nations in Ezekiel 47 flows from under the temple doors. Zechariah 14 describes continuous light replacing normal daylight and seasons, the land being levelled but Jerusalem elevated, water flowing from it, and nations flowing to it to acknowledge Yahweh's kingship at the feast of Tabernacles. Daniel foresees the removal of 'the appalling horror' – the termination once and for all of foreign invasions and the desecration of the temple by paganism. In this way, we could go on adding passages that demonstrate the Zion-centredness of the prophetic hope, but it is simpler to point to Daniel in exile,

[2] 'Zion theology' is the shorthand term for the cluster of imagery that relates Yahweh's presence to the Jerusalem temple and access to him there. It comes to expression in a number of psalms that celebrate the kingship of Yahweh in Zion and the role of the Davidic dynasty: Pss. 2; 24; 48; 87; 99 and 132, to mention the most obvious ones. See Ollenburger 1987.

on his knees three times a day, with his casement windows open. He is facing towards Jerusalem (Dan. 6:10).

These date-stamped snapshots from the prophets tell a story. The film has been wound on from empire to exile with the land as background and Jerusalem in the frame. The film begins as history and ends as apocalyptic. We have talked about the snapshots laid out on the coffee table of AD 2000 as though there were no process of development between the press of the shutter and the print we are looking at. Photography is more complicated than that, and so is biblical interpretation. These snapshots, in reality, do not involve historical moments captured on camera, but theological concepts, emotions and ways of looking at things. These theological concepts and ways of looking at things may change between the press of the shutter and the print on our table.

In fact, the Hebrew text that records the snapshot is more like the photographic negative. Before the negative yields a print for us to view, there are processes of chemistry and filtration to apply. We can think of these processes as the chemistry and filtration of hermeneutics, aided by the spectacles and lenses that we wear to see the snapshots in clear focus. In the next chapter, we shall need to ask questions about how best to see the prints in their true colours and in focus. We shall need to pay attention to the issues of hermeneutics.

Bibliography

Goldingay, J. E. (1989), *Daniel*, Word Biblical Commentary, Dallas: Word.

Ollenburger, B. C. (1987), *Zion, City of the Great King*, Journal for the Study of the Old Testament Supplement Series 41, Sheffield: JSOT Press.

2B
Hermeneutical spectacles and the return to the land

Deryck Sheriffs

The snapshots discussed in the previous chapter, the sequence of developments between them, and the conceptual categories on their surface confront us with several issues. The snapshots are situation-specific and culture-bound. Moreover, the prophets met with scepticism in their original audiences and may generate cognitive dissonance now. In addition, the utterances were augmented and reapplied in other scriptures. Daniel 9, for instance, reinterprets Jeremiah, while Daniel 10 – 12 recycles material from the Assyrian invasion as portrayed in Isaiah.[1] Engaging these issues will demand of us that we make explicit our own hermeneutical standpoint and reading strategies. I discover my need to put on spectacles to see the snapshots in focus. The spectacles place the lenses of a Christian re-reading of the Old Testament between the print on the coffee table

[1] The reinterpretation of 'the foe from the north' who invades the land is one example of intertextuality, reapplication and development within the Hebrew canon. See, for instance, the comments of Goldingay on the allusions to other prophetic utterances and the developments of them in Dan. 10 – 12 in Goldingay 1989: 284–285.

and my brain. The urgency to don the New Testament pair of glasses is driven by my fundamental hermeneutical assumptions and principles. This shifts my focus from what the prophets might originally have been saying about the land to how I understand what they said in the light of the New Testament. That is a radical shift – from the craft of Hebrew exegesis to debating worldview and hermeneutical frameworks.

Let me illustrate the difference between exegetical endeavour and a radical Christian re-reading of the Old Testament by reference to the opening words of the second so-called Servant poem: 'Here is my servant, whom I uphold, my chosen, in whom my soul delights; I have put my spirit upon him; he will bring forth justice to the nations.' In Isaiah 42:1–4 we hear Yahweh publicly present an agent through whom he will bring justice to the world, and we might recall the denunciation of Judean kings for injustice. Exegesis will endeavour to pinpoint the kind of language that is being used by looking for parallels in Old Testament poetry. What exegesis will never uncover in the words quoted is a fully fledged trinitarian theology. It is simply not there, despite the fact that the speaking voice is God's, and he is presenting a figure who is endowed with his spirit. This language cannot be forced into making a statement of Christian systematics. It is the voice of Yahwistic monotheism as much as the rest of these chapters. Nevertheless, with Christian hindsight and with the Gospel accounts of the baptism of Jesus as another packet of photos spread on our coffee table, we could re-read Isaiah 42:1 as a glimpse into God's purpose through Jesus. Indeed, we could re-read Isaiah 42:1 as God the Father speaking of God the Son interacting with God the Holy Spirit, played out centuries later next to the Jordan river.[2] That re-reading is a radical interpretation of the prophet's language: its radicalness is underlined by its obvious offensiveness to Jewish readers.

In the light of the fuller Christian revelation, I would want to argue that my radical re-reading is both a necessary reconstrual of the prophet's language, and yet, paradoxically, is loyal to the original thrust of the prophet's message. The 'thrust' spoken of here is the

[2] Luke 3:22 has the Spirit descending on Jesus in the form of a dove and a voice from heaven saying, 'You are my Son, the Beloved; with you I am well pleased.' This combines allusions to Is. 42 and Ps. 2.

dynamic, the direction, the impetus that carries God's purpose to fruition. In the metaphor of a trajectory, a force is imparted to the announcement like an arrow leaving the bow. Conceptually, there is an origin for an idea, a highpoint in which it comes to fullest articulation, and a place where the arrow embeds. Hence, God's promises about land originate before the prophets, arc to a climax in the prophets, but may embed beyond the prophets in new-covenant terrain.

What I shall do now is put on my hermeneutical glasses, unroll the fifteen chapters from the Isaiah scroll with their vision of a return to the land and a return of the land to fertility, and ask what a Christian re-reading of them might disclose. I may try to listen to the oracles of Isaiah 40 – 55 imaginatively as a Judean deportee in Babylon, but in the end I am not a tribally defined Judean, I am not a deportee, and I do not belong in the Sinai covenant community. Abraham, Sarah and Jacob are not my ancestors, and I have access to information that the Judean exiles did not have when they listened to the prophet. This information includes the facts that the dynasty of David was never restored, that the twelve tribes never returned to tribal life in Palestine, that Jerusalem never became the centre of an international empire, and that the peoples of the world have never acknowledged Yahweh as the only true God. Nevertheless, and somewhat paradoxically, I see myself as responding in a fundamental way to the message of Isaiah 40 – 55 rather than rejecting it as irrelevant or as false prophecy. In doing so, I believe that I am responding to the same God, but I am also aware of meeting him on different terms from the Judeans, and in a different place in several senses. I understand the words of exilic Isaiah historically, culturally and theologically, but, of necessity, in radically redefined conceptual categories as well. It is not a reading of exilic Isaiah, but quite consciously and deliberately a re-reading through New Testament spectacles.

We can set out the alternative reading strategies as follows: (a) a reductionist reading; (b) a literalist reading; (c) a contextualist reading; or (d) a radical re-reading. None of these hermeneutical operations is plain sailing, and their application divides both Jewish and Christian communities of faith to this day. Clearly, the theological position and the faith community of the interpreter come into play as factors that energize a reading strategy. There may well be a variety of life experiences that colour our interpretation, some of which we can easily retrieve but others of which may be outside conscious awareness. It will help matters to make the process of choosing between reading strategies explicit and transparent, although some of our reading assumptions become so automatic that we are not conscious of the processes that underlie them.

The common ground between the reductionist, contextualist and literalist readings is that the oracles of exilic Isaiah are read in their primary categories: as utterances addressed to Judean exiles as deportees, as Jacob-Israel, as citizens of Jerusalem and the cities of Judah, as inhabitants of Palestine. The oracles were not addressed to Gentiles, or to the Christian church. They speak in terms of the people of Israel over against other nation states and people groups: Babylonia and the Chaldeans, the Persians, the Egyptians, the Assyrians, the Ethiopians and the Sabeans, to mention only those named specifically,[3] and not to mention the many passages that use general terms such as 'the nations', the 'coastlands' and the desert regions. It is always wise to state the obvious before adding anything more sophisticated.

Reductionist lenses and the illegibility factor

An example of a reductionist reading is that of Föhrer. He reduces what the prophet claims for his utterances, the claim to speak reliably in God's name (Is. 44: 25–26; 48: 3ff.). For Föhrer, exilic Isaiah reads as a Zionist nationalism that is so utopian that it must be labelled as an 'optimistic illusion'. Föhrer concluded that 'eschatological prophecy was based on a misunderstanding of the message of the great individual prophets and on the optimistic illusion of God's exclusive will to save Israel' and that 'Deutero-Isaiah's preaching, in consequence of its reliance on the optimistic message of the earlier professional prophets, also contained questionable nationalistic and materialistic elements' that 'marked the beginning of [true prophecy's] decline'.[4] So Föhrer thinks that the work of exilic Isaiah is a

[3] Is. 43: 3, 14; 45:1, 14; 47:1; 48:14; 48:20 and 52:4 all refer to specifically named national groups.

[4] Föhrer 1972: 353, 327. Föhrer specifically frames Deutero-Isaiah for corrupting the purer ethical message: 'Therefore this prophet did not stand at the apex of Israelite prophecy, but marked the beginning of its decline' (1972: 327).

mixed and flawed product. Although it has a somewhat loftier message than a naked nationalism sustained by theological legitimation, it has absorbed utopian and national elements and conceived of salvation in material terms.

Föhrer's reading is robustly reductionist. The beatific vision is an optimistic illusion, not a revelation from God. No doubt the prophet sincerely believed his message, but he believed it because he was nationalistic and materialistic in his assumptions. The prophet, indeed a succession of prophets, put the Jews, their God and their fortunes at the centre of the world and the centre of the map. They did not, and could not, think of a future without their God, or of a future with their God without their being a nation, or of their nation without a land, or of their nation-state and God without political autonomy. We could, with justification, call this ideology a form of nationalism. Ethnic identity was linked with a Yahweh monotheism, so the one reinforced the other. No future without Yahweh, no Yahweh without worship, no proper worship without a temple. No temple without a city, indeed without the former capital city, Jerusalem, and its citadel, Zion. There is no way one can read Isaiah 40 – 55 removing all references to Jerusalem, Zion and the ancestral land while retaining its message intact. The message embraces the future of the nation.

Föhrer typifies an era of scholarship that imagined that it was always speaking rationally and objectively, and could survey and evaluate all of reality from some detached vantage point, secure in its developmentalist framing of Israel's faith. Brueggemann has characterized this era and its shortcomings well, and as an alternative has opened Old Testament scholarship to the rhetorical, imaginative ways in which the poetry of the Old Testament sings reality into existence.[5] This said, there is enough of the unreconstructed modernist left in all of us, and enough of a shudder at the sales pitch of the television evangelist or the extravagant claims of healing crusades, for us to applaud Föhrer for wanting to pop any bubbles of 'optimistic illusion'. Whether that is the right phrase for describing exilic Isaiah's oracles we might dispute, but we would affirm

[5] Brueggemann 1997. See his remarks on modernity and the historical-critical enterprise (pp. 6–15) and on the contemporary scene (especially pp. 67ff.).

that his message is not of a universal monotheism that fits comfortably into post-Enlightenment Europe. It is a Judean prophet's message to Jacob-Israel about return to the land of Palestine and a national future with Yahweh. New-exodus language of national liberation runs right through it (e.g. Is. 43:14–21; 48:20–21; 52:11–12, to mention the obvious allusions).

Credibility is indeed an issue in the face of flowery rhetoric and the failure of what is advertised to match up to its rather grandiose advertising campaign, so we can thank Föhrer for drawing our attention to issues in exilic Isaiah that we cannot ignore. Moreover, the credibility issue is not a modern or a modernist issue. It seems that we are not the first to compare the promise with the eventuality and to notice a huge gap. The words of Snapshot 4 register the full weight of the dissonance and the disappointment: 'Here we are, slaves to this day – slaves in the land that you gave to our ancestors to enjoy its fruit and its good gifts' (Neh. 9:36). This was not what devout Israelites in the post-exilic period were expecting – or there would have been no lament. What were they expecting, in the light of exilic Isaiah?

We can lay this out in list form and then go on to offer some comments on the literalist and contextualist readings. A Judean exile who was a devout and responsive Yahwist listening to the oracles of Isaiah 40 – 55 would have had every reason to expect the following things to happen, and to happen in his or her lifetime:

- a dramatic theophany comparable to the exodus;
- the conclusive refutation of polytheism;
- the humiliation of Babylon, or even its complete destruction;
- a glorious new exodus return of Jewish exiles from Babylonia to Palestine;
- international recognition of Yahweh as the only true God;
- the rebuilding of the temple and Jerusalem, surpassing even former glories;
- an Eden-like fertility and prosperity in a repopulated land;
- permanent military security against all invasion or attack;
- an international empire focused on Jerusalem;
- the material produce of the nations brought to Zion as vassal tribute; and

- a renewed permanent covenant of Yahweh with Israel.[6]

What actually happened between exilic Isaiah's message and the liturgical lament in Nehemiah, as far as we can reconstruct it, was that, after Cyrus took over Babylon relatively peacefully in 539 BC, the Jewish exiles requested permission to return to their homeland and restart their temple worship. This request was granted; it was in line with a general policy of Cyrus to reinstate the captives of Babylon and their religious observances. Sheshbazzar led about 42,000 Judeans back to Palestine, and was apparently appointed a governor of Yehud province (2 Chr. 36:22–23; Ezra 1 – 3). The foundation of the Jerusalem temple was laid amid rejoicing – or weeping for former splendours – but no major headway was made on the rebuilding.

Subsequently, post-exilic prophets such as Haggai and Zechariah stirred up expectations of the restoration of the Davidic dynasty under Zerubbabel (Hag. 2:20–23; Ezra 5:1; 6:14), and building work on the temple restarted. It was completed in 515 BC, though ominously for national aspiration this is dated 'in the sixth year of King Darius' (Ezra 6:15). There is then a hiatus of information until the reforms of Ezra and Nehemiah in the middle of the next century, when Nehemiah acts as governor of Yehud province. What we do know about Nehemiah's time is that the walls of Jerusalem are in a tumbled-down state and that the Jewish governors and administrators before Nehemiah had exacted taxes from the populace and attached their fields and orchards in exactly the manner that Samuel had predicted of the monarchy. This sad state of internal economic enslavement is rectified by Nehemiah after legal charges, a public indictment and a bound oath accompanied by a dramatized curse (Neh. 5).

Apart from the fact of a return of part of the Jewish population, a return of the temple vessels (though not the ark of the covenant) and the restart of cultic worship, nothing of exilic Isaiah's glorious programme materialized. The exodus from Babylonia was inglorious compared with the exodus from Egypt, for it

[6] Specific passages illustrating these points include 40:5; 41:8–20; 43:14–21; 44:25 – 45:7; 45:13–17; 45:20–25; 48:20–21; 49:6–13; 49:22–26; 51:1–3; 51:11; 52:7–10; 54:1–3, 10, 11–17; 55:3–5.

was not marked by miracles or theophany, and was not accompanied by a pillar of cloud and fire (Is. 52:12), nor was there miraculous water in the wilderness. We could take the fountains, springs and burgeoning growth promised as metaphors of spiritual renewal (41:17–20; 42:14–16; 43:14–21), but we cannot be sure that there was an outburst of faith, trust, praise and creativity among those who returned. It certainly did not translate into temple-building. There was no descendant of David on the throne, no political autonomy, no fertility and prosperity – in fact, the opposite. Pagan polytheism continued as ever both in Babylonia and Persia and in Palestine, where Jews, including priests and Levites, intermarried with Moabites, Ammonites and Phoenicians (Ezra 9 – 10; Neh. 13:23).

So what do we do with the utopian vision of exilic Isaiah? Before we answer that, we had better note that the reaction of devout Judeans was to canonize the oracles of Isaiah 40 – 55, to canonize their reaffirmation in Isaiah 60 – 62, and to canonize the complementary prophecies of exilic and post-exilic prophets such as Ezekiel, Haggai and Zechariah. One example will suffice to illustrate the process of the recycling and elaboration of the exilic material in subsequent prophecies.[7] In Isaiah 45:14 the Egyptians, Ethiopians and Sabeans are pictured travelling to Zion in chains, converting to Yahwism and bringing their wealth and merchandise as tribute. In Isaiah 49:22–23 Israelite deportees are carried home, and foreign kings and queens prostrate themselves and lick the dust at the exiles' feet. This material from Isaiah 40 – 55 is recycled in Isaiah 60. There the silver, gold, spices and building wood of foreign nations flow into Jerusalem. The nations that do not become subservient will be annihilated. The Israelite population will witness a population explosion and will possess the land for ever. In similar vein, Haggai goes on to speak about the overthrow of all foreign nations and their military powers, and the prestige and election of Zerubbabel by way of contrast (Hag. 2:20–23).

[7] For a fuller discussion of the intertextuality, see Williamson 1998: ch. 5 and the related footnotes that deal with the recycling of exilic Isaiah's message in Is. 60 – 62. Williamson postulates a background to Is. 60 – 62 in these terms: 'In the face of what may at first have seemed like a denial of the promise – a disappointment that the new age did not arrive quite as suddenly as Deutero-Isaiah had envisaged – this prophet nevertheless keeps faith with that promise and reaffirms it without qualification for a new generation' (p. 171).

Literalist lenses and the millennial magnifying-glass

Confronted with the complete failure of any such reversal of international and religious affairs to materialize either then or since, we are confronted with 'the failure of prophecy'.[8] If we do not wish to embrace 'the failure of prophecy' option, what move can we make? The futurist option is simply to reaffirm all that the Isaiah scroll says about a global empire centred on Jerusalem with nations paying tribute to Jews and acknowledging Yahweh as God. This means affirming Isaiah 40 – 55 in its own factual terms, which are political, economic, geographical and demographic – but to shift its realization into the unpredictable and indefinite future. This futurist manoeuvre is the mainstream of the literalist reading strategy and is usually linked with a form of Christian millennialism.

What might motivate the literalist futurist form of re-reading? Probably a spectrum of factors contribute to the literalist agenda. We suggest the following ones for consideration. Some literalists might hold to a doctrine of scriptural inerrancy that perceives non-literal fulfilment as fatal to it, or to a form of empirical positivism that requires factual-physical verification because alternatives are adjudged as insubstantial. This might be linked with an unsophisticated understanding of literary genre, figures of speech, metaphor and intertextuality that prefers the literal reading as 'the common-sense, plain meaning of the Bible'. Perhaps there is an 'American dream', a can-do optimism for utopian possibility and global empire, and an 'evil empire' perspective on those outside the church, which in turn fans an Armageddon mentality that anticipates a conflagrational annihilation of all human resistance to God. Or there could be a preference for Paul and Romans as a canon within the canon, combined with the particular understanding of Romans 9 – 11 that foresees a future global conversion of Jews to faith in Jesus, inseparable from a political future for ethnic Israel. There might be a pro-Israeli perception of contemporary middle-eastern politics coupled with a demonizing perception of Islam as a world threat to Christian faith. There might be the weight of tradition written into the theological training institution and its doctrinal declaration that

[8] The phrase has become linked with the work of R. P. Carroll; see Carroll 1978, 1979.

could not easily be altered without the institution losing its ethos and funding, or without its graduates experiencing a form of alienation in the process of changing their mind about eschatology.

What weighs against the literalist reading – apart from the fact that this future has not materialized so far? The simple answer is: the cogency of the combined contextualist and radical re-reading strategies. We shall develop this point much further, but are content here with this succinctly stated claim. An alternative claim, that God could never reconstitute Israel and reign from Jerusalem in a literalist way at some point in the near or remote future, is not as cogent. After all, God can raise the dead.

Contextualist bifocals

The contextualist option starts exegetically with what the prophet has said, but then makes allowance for its thought categories by explaining the prophecy's terms of reference situationally and contextually. Some of these conceptual categories are then understood as artefacts of the times, as the phenomenology of the Judaism of that era, rather than as the essence of the message. For example, the ark of the covenant that seemed so central to Israel's national covenant proved to be a physical artefact that disappeared in Jeremiah's day. Likewise the succession of Judean kings: Yahwistic faith continued without them. We shall argue later that covenant relationship with Israel's God is the essence, while ark, priesthood, dynasty, tribal structure and all the ideas associated with them in their specific forms are artefacts of their era.[9]

In the contextualist reading it is self-evident that the culture-specificness of prophetic utterance will entail a degree of culture-boundness, and the reader must distinguish between the culture-bound specifics and the essential message. This is analogous to understanding the gist of what someone said, independent of the exact vocabulary and syntax of the sentence he or she actually spoke. If I wanted to pass on this person's message, I could substitute my

[9] An artefact in this sense is a metaphor borrowed from archaeology for something that is left behind that reflects the culture of its times.

own preferred vocabulary and sentence structure for those of the original speaker, yet still convey what he or she said.

As the label suggests, the contextualist reading is aware of the context, and understands that context as the world of the ancient Near East. Bifocal lenses allow us to read the Hebrew manuscript on the desk and glance up at documents from the ancient Near East displayed on the OHP screen. There were alternative forms of religious nationalism to Israel's in her contemporary world. The Moabites had their version of theological nationalism, a theology of people, land and god, with Moab and god Chemosh.[10] The Edomites would have had theirs, with Edom and god Quas. The Babylonians certainly had theirs, complete with map and charter myth. In fact, as I have argued elsewhere with detailed substantiation from indigenous Babylonian documents, we cannot really appreciate the message of exilic Isaiah without hearing it as a polemic against Marduk, Babylon and the divination experts.[11] This is both explicit and implicit in Isaiah 40 – 55.

We find explicit satire on idolatry (44:9–20), the mocking of the omen experts and astrologers (44:25; 47:12–13) and the lampooning of Marduk and Nabu by name (46:1). More than that, Babylon has its counterpoint in Jerusalem. The two cities represent competing theological interpretations of the creation of the world, the flow of history, the sovereignty of God and the destiny of the nations. Either Babylon and its ziggurat, 'the foundation of heaven and earth', are the centre from which the world is run, or Zion is. The two claims cannot coexist without resolution. Either Marduk made the universe, setting its features in place and regulating its times and seasons with the moon, sun and constellations, or Yahweh did. Either Marduk founded Babylon, where the gods meet at New Year to decree the destinies for the next twelve months, as the Babylonian creation myth *When above* ... has it, or Yahweh founded

[10] Few inscriptions have survived from Israel or the surrounding nations, but the one royal Moabite inscription describing wars that we do have carries a Chemosh theology expressed in nationalistic terms. The Moabite king Mesha recaptured a town from Israel and slaughtered its entire population 'for Chemosh and for Moab' (line 12). See Dearman 1989.

[11] See my 1986 Tyndale Old Testament Lecture (1988) for the details and the supporting translations from the Babylonian texts themselves. A colour photo of the Babylonian map of the world is published in N. Hillyer et al. (eds.), *The Illustrated Bible Dictionary* (IVP, 1980), 1:168.

Zion and rules the nations. Either Marduk is warrior king, the cosmic dragon-slayer, or Yahweh is the supreme champion (51:9).

We may read the prophetic future contextually in this manner, carefully delineating the alternative worldviews that orthodox Yahwism was engaging. We then understand the terms of engagement as partly indigenous and Yahwistic, and partly generated by the struggle with polytheism. Both worlds of discourse, the biblical and the Babylonian, use the language and concepts of their times: for instance, the colourful and dramatic language of cosmic battle with a monster.[12]

There would seem to be a great deal of authenticity in this contextual and culture-specific reading strategy applied to exilic Isaiah. The contextualist reading is sympathetic and loyal to the text, substantiates its assertions with detail rather than with bland generalizations, and makes sense of the material within its own original horizon. Moreover, it is open to the central theological truths of what the prophet affirms, and in particular to his affirmation of Yahweh as sole creator who offers forgiveness of sin and covenant relationship, first to Jacob-Israel, and then, by extension, to the nations (Is. 49: 6). This would be the essence of the message, while the rebuilding of the Jerusalem temple is the culture-specific artefact of God's presence among his people in this era (44:28; 45:22–23; 54:7–8).

How does the contextualist reading fare with the non-fulfilment issues? On that count, the contextualist reading might point to the rhetorical and persuasive features of the message. The poetry of exilic Isaiah is lyrical, even hymnic. The mountains and hills break forth into singing, and the trees of the field clap their hands (55:12). The heavens are invited to shower down righteousness, and the earth to cause it to spring up (45:8). Jerusalem is rebuilt with antimony, rubies, sapphires and precious stones. The gates are made of jewels (54:11–12). This is hyperbole. Elsewhere, figurative and symbolic language appears: for example, the streams of life-giving water on dry ground parallel the outpouring of the spirit of God on Israel's offspring (44:3). The whole message of Isaiah 40 – 55 builds

[12] Babylon's most celebrated version of the combat myth is its charter myth called *Enuma elish* (*When above* ...), which is translated in Dalley 1991. The Old Testament's counterpoints are scattered throughout its poetry from the Pentateuch to the Psalms to Job and the prophets. For a study of this motif, see Longman & Reid 1995.

a symbolism into the physical. Thus the return from Babylonian exile is the symbol and sign of return to Yahweh. The very Hebrew word for 'return', *šûb*, also does duty for 'repent', and in the epilogue the prophet's concluding appeal is: 'let the wicked forsake their way, and the unrighteous their thoughts; let them return to the LORD, that he may have mercy on them, and to our God, for he will abundantly pardon' (55:7). This inward spiritual reorientation is expressed through walking out of Babylon back home to Jerusalem (52:11–12), encouraged by the promise that God himself will 'return' to his house there (52:8).

All this is true, and is very much part of the style of Isaiah 40 – 55. But what does a contextualist reading do with a land statement such as the following?

> For the LORD will comfort Zion;
> he will comfort all her waste places,
> and will make her wilderness like Eden,
> her desert like the garden of the LORD;
> joy and gladness will be found in her,
> thanksgiving and the voice of song.
>
> (Is. 51:3)

This is hyperbole, no doubt, for it pictures a return to Paradise. It could hardly offer a starker contrast between the ruined Judean cities set in derelict land and its future as an 'Eden' and 'garden of God'.[13] How much transformation of the devastated land is enough to fulfil this utopian vision? The temple vessels were restored to a rebuilt temple, as Isaiah 52:11, 44:28 and 45:13 anticipate, but this, and whatever else happened, was evidently not enough fulfilment by Nehemiah's time for life in the land to seem comforting, joyous, filled with thanksgiving, and like living in Paradise. The Judean community of 450 BC were not satisfied that a contextualist reading resolved matters. Their community had returned to the land, had repented, and had renewed

[13] This recycling of the Eden tradition is all the more striking because references to the Garden of Eden are so rare in the Hebrew canon. On the Paradise motifs in eschatology, see Cornelius 1988 and Fishbane, 'The "Eden" motif: the landscape of spatial renewal' (1979: 111–120).

their covenant allegiance, yet their expectations were disappointed rather than contextually fulfilled. The limited transformation of nature, towns and populace did not match the lyrical picture of the new things to come. It did not match up to, let alone excel, the high points of Israel's previous national experience in the times of David and Solomon.

So how did a reading that hung on to the nationalism, the scale and the utopian features of the exilic hope linger on in the faith community? Partial factual fulfilments, deep theological conviction about Yahweh as the sole God, a sense of covenant relationship with him, and human longings for a better national future may have combined to keep faith in a utopian future alive despite its dissonance with political reality. The overcoming of dissonance is, after all, a survival strategy, and the need to survive draws on the most powerful urges that our biology has built into us. In a social and territorial species like ourselves, group identity accompanies the biological drive for survival. Perhaps it has a survival advantage to defer hope, rather than to abandon it and face the consequent loss of identity and the deconstruction of the belief system.

R. P. Carroll has devoted a book to the study of the processes of reinterpretation that are brought into play in order to overcome cognitive dissonance. This does not mean that he is sympathetic with these reinterpretational stratagems. In fact, he strongly disapproves of the reinterpretations that rationalize away the lack of fulfilment. He thereby aligns himself with a reductionist reading of eschatological prophecy. He is even so bold as to ascribe this reductionist-reading stance to the early Judeans themselves: 'many Israelites must have regarded most, if not all, prophets as false deceivers of the community' (Carroll 1979: 219).[14] Moreover, he considers that exilic Isaiah 'provides the best paradigm for dissonance analysis', because 'the proclamation of a salvation so vivid in its details and so absent in its realisation constitutes the essence of dissonance arousal' (1979: 151–152).

[14] Carroll lays the charge against reinterpretation that 'it avoids dissonance by emptying the original terms of their content'. It involves 'redefinition of all the ground rules', 'for meaning is manipulated by such conventionalist stratagems' so that 'the spectre of Humpty Dumpty stalks all interpretation' (1979: 216).

Radical-re-reading glasses and image resolution

The irony is that since the late 1970s, when Carroll was studying dissonance theory, postmodernism has arrived and generated its own version of redefining all the ground rules of interpretation. We must choose our own starting-point and develop reasons for bypassing reductionist assessments such as Carroll's, for disentangling ourselves from the deferment strategy of literalists, and for moving beyond contextualist explanations that stop short of recontextualizing the message of the prophet. Granted that we shall convince only those who belong to the community of faith in any case, and only some within this, we can at least be explicit about how this radical-re-reading procedure operates and what is driving it. The results will be that much more transparent, and if there is a certain coherence and consistency to them, so much the better.

The step beyond a contextualist reading is to give the material a radical Christian re-reading. This is to prefer and privilege the Christian vocabulary over against the prophet's or, to alter the analogy a little, it is to opt for dynamic equivalence instead of a wooden translation. A radical Christian re-reading also involves arguing for a fruition, an outcome or fulfilment of God's intentions in terms and conceptual categories that could be radically different from the original announcement, and yet would be applicable to covenant with the same God. This re-reading would rescue the utopian national empire of exilic Isaiah from 'optimistic illusion' by abandoning those concepts that are deemed to be contextual artefacts and by recoding and recontextualizing its message. Of course, this would require agreement about fulfilment and fruition.

Without going into detailed discussion, we may list the key factors in the radical Christian re-reading as follows:

- Jesus' own interpretation of himself and his significance in terms of the suffering Servant;
- the permanent replacement of the temple, its priesthood and sacrifices by Jesus himself;
- the non-geographical nature of the kingdom of God that Jesus proclaimed;

- Jesus' institution of a new covenant in the upper room at Passover in Jerusalem;
- the significance of Pentecost and the outpouring of the Spirit in Palestine;
- the emergence of a trinitarian understanding of God from Yahwistic monotheism;
- the redefining of who belongs within the covenant of faith in Pauline theology;
- the Christianizing of Jewish apocalyptic in the New Testament; and
- the conspicuous absence from the New Testament of the land promises in their original terms.

The reasons for the radical re-reading of concepts in exilic Isaiah are fundamentally Christological. If Jesus understands himself as fulfilling the Servant role, especially in his death and its significance (Luke 22:37, quoting from Is. 53), this provides a hermeneutical key for a re-reading of the whole of Isaiah 40 – 55. This re-reading would not discount a measure of fulfilment during the lifetime of the Judean exiles who were the original audience. In particular, the renewal of covenant by God's initiative (Is. 40:1; 54:9–10 and 55:3–4) came to a first fruition before the upper room. The return to the land by some exiles was a step of faith. Yet there is a radicalness to the Christian re-reading that cannot be denied. On our re-reading of exilic Isaiah, the temple was rebuilt factually by Judeans, but rebuilt radically differently by Jesus in his replacing it as the focal point for encounter with God (John 2:19–22). With the replacement of the temple as a physical meeting-point go Zion, Jerusalem and the land as well. They are concentric circles. Remove the centre-point, the Holy of Holies, and the surrounding circles come away with it. People will no longer worship on that mountain, or on Mount Gerizim, or on the mount of transfiguration, or the Mount of Olives near Bethany, but in spirit and in truth (John 4:23–24), anywhere Jesus is present among his disciples.[15]

[15] For an understanding of Jesus in his first-century setting that takes his acts and attitudes to the temple as a key, see Wright 1996. Without endorsing all of Wright's re-reading strategies for the Old Testament language of exile and for apocalyptic imagery, I consider that his case for Jesus' re-reading of Is. 40 – 55 is a strong one, combined with Jesus' symbolic prophetic acts. See his index for page references to Isaiah 40 – 55, esp. pp. 597ff. Note his summary statement: 'Nor ... did he envisage the rebuilding of the Temple, whether by

This radical re-reading would want to claim that it is loyal to the thrust of exilic Isaiah's message while leaving behind its contextually embedded features. The contrast now is not between Zion and Babylon but more broadly between the kingdom of God and 'the world' (in its 'present evil age' sense). In other words, the Babylon of Isaiah 40 – 55 is updated by its appearance in the apocalypse of John, where it may code for Rome and where 'Rome' represents all ideological manifestations that are hostile to the gospel for moral, economic and religious reasons. Palestine, Babylonia and the Middle East are too small a canvas for the outworking of this ideological struggle. Competing nationalisms no longer define the combatants, nor are the gains territorial.

What might be driving this radical Christian re-reading? It is not springing to the defence of an inerrancy position, or wanting to deny that the prophets expected things to happen in their own generation. Nor is it trying to deny the nationalism and the other culturally conditioned and contextually embedded features of Old Testament prophetic utterances.[16] Avoidance of reductionist readings and of the charges of 'false prophecy' no doubt come into the picture, but proponents of the radical re-reading would say that it is not so much avoidance as, positively, the hermeneutic of Jesus himself that drives the reading. Perhaps the lack of fruition for hundreds of years before Jesus and the two thousand years of non-literal fulfilment since then play a significant part as well. Nothing much happened to the prophecies about the land by way of fulfilment before Jesus. It was Jesus and his resurrection that rescued Jewish eschatological faith from the category of wishful thinking, from 'optimistic illusion'. Yet the majority of Jews missed the point and were devastated by subsequent defeats in the national struggle for autonomy from the Romans.

The radical Christian re-reading can afford to listen to the reductionist and dissonance discussion quite calmly because it can allow

---

humans or by supernatural agency. Rather, he announced ... the reconstruction of the people of YHWH on a basis that would leave no future role for the Temple' (p. 594). Compare Wright 1992: 269ff. in the section on the beliefs of Israel.

[16] Of course, the radical re-reading might, in theory, be driven by anti-Semitism, by reaction against modern Zionism and Jewish settlement, or by a pro-Palestinian perspective on human rights and land issues in Israel today.

that the prophets were bound, in a certain sense, to have got it wrong, not simply on the timescale, but as regards the form that the fulfilment of their visions would take: namely, via the abolition of temple, sacrifice, national autonomy and empire. Notice, for instance, how the 'conversion' of Gentiles in Isaiah 56:1–8 involves Sabbath-keeping, temple worship and animal sacrifice – all rendered obsolete by new-covenant concepts of conversion. Jeremiah, Ezekiel, exilic Isaiah, Haggai and Daniel would surely have been as surprised as most first-century Judeans that the coming of Jesus and his preaching of the kingdom took the form that it did, rather than the national form of liberation that they were expecting.[17] The necessity for a radical Christian re-reading is driven by Jesus' self-understanding, but also by the realization that without Jesus, and without resort to manoeuvres to sidestep cognitive dissonance, the reality of the world as it was and is would endorse a reductionist conclusion. What we see historically is a problem land, not a promised land. There was and is nothing like the Eden of Isaiah 51:3, of Hosea, Joel, Amos and Zechariah. A land with covenant relationship, justice, peace and fertility has remained utopian, a Never Land.

In the end, the snapshots on the coffee table are not the scenery itself. With a choice of the right hermeneutical spectacles we may view the snapshots in focus, but we shall not want to confuse snapshots from the family album with a living reality outdoors, especially if there have been a change of scenery and a whole new ecology since the snapshots were taken. The land in the prophets is not the same as the kingdom of God proclaimed by Jesus and demonstrated by his resurrection. Ezekiel himself might have concluded that skeletons walking back to Palestine are no match for the terrain of the new kingdom.

Bibliography

Brueggemann, W. (1997), *Theology of the Old Testament: Testimony, Dispute, Advocacy*, Minneapolis: Fortress.

[17] One has only to note the form of expectancy expressed in the disciples' post-resurrection question: 'Lord, is this the time when you will restore the kingdom to Israel?' (Acts 1:6). See Hos. 2:14; Joel 3:18; Amos 9:14; Mic. 4:4; Zech. 8:9–17; 9:16 – 10:1; 14:8; and the discussion of them in Cornelius 1988: 41–83.

Carroll, R. P. (1978), 'Second Isaiah and the failure of prophecy', *Studia Theologica* 32: 119–131.
———— (1979), *When Prophecy Failed: Reactions and Responses to Failure in the Old Testament Prophetic Tradition*, London: SCM.
Cornelius, I. (1988), 'Paradise motifs in the "eschatology" of the minor prophets and the iconography of the ANE. The concepts of fertility, water, trees, and "Tierfrieden" and Gen 2 – 3', *Journal of Northwest Semitic Languages* 14: 41–83.
Dalley, S. (1991), *Myths from Mesopotamia*, Oxford: Oxford University Press.
Dearman, A. (ed.) (1989), *Studies in the Mesha Inscription and Moab*, Atlanta: Scholars.
Fishbane, M. (1979), *Text and Texture*, New York: Schocken.
Föhrer, G. (1972), *History of Israelite Religion*, London: SPCK.
Goldingay, J. E. (1989), *Daniel*, Word Biblical Commentary, Dallas: Word.
Longman, T., & Reid, D. G. (1995), *God is a Warrior*, Carlisle: Paternoster.
Sheriffs, D. C. T. (1988), '"A tale of two cities" – nationalism in Zion and Babylon', *Tyndale Bulletin* 39: 19–57.
Williamson, H. G. M. (1998), *Variations on a Theme: King, Messiah and Servant in the Book of Isaiah*, Carlisle: Paternoster.
Wright, N. T. (1992), *The New Testament and the People of God*, London: SPCK.
———— (1996), *Jesus and the Victory of God*, London: SPCK.

3. THE LAND IN THE NEW TESTAMENT

3A
The land in the apostles' writings

Peter W. L. Walker

Introduction

Many people have cherished notions concerning both Jesus and the land of Israel/Palestine. A paper such as this, which seeks to tackle both of them, is inevitably heading into some deep water, both in scholarly circles (because of the 'historical Jesus' debate) and in popular circles (because of what the land of Israel means to so many today, both in the Middle East and in the West). Yet it cannot be avoided. A Christian approach to the land that somehow bypassed Jesus Christ would be a contradiction in terms. So the task must be done. But how?

The precise point at issue is this: how did Jesus and the New Testament writers view the covenant promises found in the Old Testament concerning the land? If they saw this as a divine gift in times past, how was that gift now to be understood in the light of God's activity through Jesus? If, as a result of what God had accomplished in Jerusalem through Jesus and the Spirit, the time had come for the Gentiles to be brought into the 'people of God', what did this do to these land-promises that had been an integral part of God's elective purposes towards Israel as his people? And if many of the Old Testament promises described not simply the original gift of the land but also the promise that God would one day 'restore' his exiled people to that land (in an act that would in some ways repeat the deliverance of Israel from Egypt into the promised land), how did the New Testament writers understand this theme of 'restoration'?

To answer these interconnected questions requires a multifaceted approach. We shall need not only to look at explicit references to the land in the teaching of Jesus and the apostles, but also to set these references within a much larger framework which takes note of how the New Testament writers understand other related concepts, such as election and fulfilment, exodus and restoration, temple and city.

This wider matrix proves its value immediately, for, as is frequently observed, explicit references to the land in the New Testament are remarkably rare.[1] The numerous references to the land in the Old Testament caused Brueggemann (1978: 3) to describe it as 'a central, if not *the central theme* of biblical faith' (his italics). In the New Testament, by contrast, there are fewer than fifty references, and scholars struggle to find more than a handful of these that unambiguously refer to the land of Israel rather than to the world in general. An analysis that examined only these few references and failed to see the interconnection that exists between the land and other themes would be brief indeed – and almost certainly wrong.

The method we propose to employ here is as follows. In the present chapter we shall examine various New Testament writers to see if we can establish their understanding of the land and other related themes. In chapter 3B we shall then ask if their approach to the land can be traced back to Jesus himself; a final section in that chapter will draw together some suggestions for developing an overall 'biblical theology' of the land in the light of our analysis.[2]

[1] See e.g. Ateek, p. 201 below.

[2] A similar method was pursued in Walker 1996, which focused primarily on the issues of the city and the temple. The sections below on Paul, Hebrews and John are extracted and abbreviated from that book (chs. 4, 5, and 6 respectively), to which the reader is referred for a fuller discussion.

In fact, the New Testament has more to say on this issue than has been previously supposed. Some interpreters, noting the comparative silence of the New Testament, presume that this issue was of no essential importance to the apostles and they therefore had no distinctive opinion about it. As a result, even if one acknowledges the important function of the New Testament as being the apostolic interpretation of the Old, on this issue this is all quite irrelevant – precisely because there is no such apostolic interpretation! So when it comes to making contemporary applications, the Old Testament material is deemed to be left entirely unaffected by the New Testament. In other words, the Old Testament can be read today entirely as if the New Testament had never been written.

But this argument is incorrect. For a start, the very contrast in number of references to the land in the two Testaments tells in the opposite direction, demanding some explanation other than apostolic indifference or occupation with other issues. How could such a major biblical theme be screened out from their attention? No, it is far more probable to suppose that this major theme was consciously in their sights – and not just because it was so prevalent in their Bibles, but also because it was one of the key issues of first-century Judaism.

Why else was Palestine such a hotbed of unrest in this period, if not because the divine promises relating to the land seemed so blatantly unfulfilled? There was far too glaring a contrast between the biblical ideal and the political reality, and people urgently wanted to see the situation changed. In such a context a 'Messiah' or 'apostle' who was ignorant of this land issue would simply be dismissed as out of touch, floating on some ethereal cloud that bore no connection with 'where people were at'. No, interest in the biblical promises relating to the land is not a modern pastime; it was an ancient one. It forms part of the essential life-setting in which the gospel was first proclaimed, and the New Testament writers were therefore well aware of the fact.

But the consequence is this: if the New Testament writers not only knew of this issue but offered a response to it, then that dominical and apostolic response must determine our own response to the essentially similar issue in our own day.

The New Testament suddenly leaps back into the centre stage, inviting our respect and demanding our response. The complicated intricacies of this issue are immense, both in academic biblical theology and in contemporary middle-eastern politics. Could it be that this tiny volume that we call the New Testament might be able in this area (as in so many others) to speak a word of profound and liberating insight? Could it cut through this particular Gordian knot and shine its light into dark places? If so, it is high time we tuned in to its 'still small voice'.

Paul

Paul's attitudes to the land have been extensively studied by W. D. Davies in *The Gospel and the Land* (1974). This is probably the most significant study of the New Testament data to appear in recent years. Davies's detailed analysis (1974: 166) confirms our contention: the land would have been a key issue in the first century, keenly felt by a Jewish writer such as Paul. Yet Paul, he argues, came to view these things quite differently in the light of Christ. Paul speaks of the land rarely, if at all, despite its contemporary importance; other theological motifs have taken its place.

Davies builds his argument upon two initial observations. First, that in Romans 9:4 (when Paul lists Israel's privileges) there is no mention of the 'promise' of a land for Israel, but only a general concluding reference to 'the promises'. Secondly, that in all Paul's discussions concerning the Abrahamic promise (e.g. in Rom. 4 and Gal. 3) he omits one of its central themes, namely God's promise to give to Abraham and his 'offspring for ever' 'all the land that you see' (Gen. 13:15; cf. 17:8, 21:17). Paul concentrates instead on the more universal promise that in Abraham all the families of the earth will be blessed (Gen. 12:3; cf. 17:5, 21:18; see Gal. 3:8). This is especially noteworthy in Galatians, we may add, where much of the argument turns on the use in Genesis of the word 'offspring' or 'seed'. This does not occur in this 'universal' promise, but *does* appear in each of the three promises relating to the land. So Paul can hardly have been unaware of this question. In Romans, Davies suggests, there might be tactical reasons why Paul omitted this more 'political' issue of the land, but in Galatians it would have been particularly apposite.[3] Concerning this 'territorial aspect of the promise', Davies (1974: 179) concludes: '...his silence points not to the absence of a conscious concern with it, but to his deliberate rejection of it. His interpretation of the promise is a-territorial.' Davies therefore comes to the following conclusions about Paul's attitude to the land:

> Paul ignores completely the territorial aspect of the promise ... In the christological logic of Paul, the land (like the law, particular and provisional) had become irrelevant ... The people of Israel living in the land had been replaced as the people of God by a universal community which had no special territorial attachment ... The land has for him been 'christified'. It is not the promised land (much as he had loved it) that became his 'inheritance', but the Living Lord, in whom was a 'new creation' ... To be 'in Christ' ... has replaced being 'in the land' as the ideal life (1974: 178, 179, 182, 213, 217).[4]

This was a remarkable attitude, which flew directly in the face of the increasing Jewish nationalism of Paul's day.

The following observations confirm Davies's conclusions:

1. Paul passes over the issue of the land again in Romans 15:8–9.[5] The original inclusion of the land within the patriarchal promises has been either ignored or radically redefined.

2. Paul's statement in 2 Corinthians 1:20 (that in Christ every one of God's promises is a 'Yes') suggests he would indeed have redefined the land-promises in Genesis through Christ. The fulfilment had evidently come about in a different, non-territorial way.

3. The word for 'gospel' (*euangelion*) is derived from Isaiah's proclamation of 'good news' to Israel that Jerusalem had been

[3] On the possible nationalistic assumptions of the Judaizers in Galatians, see Jewett 1970–1, Longenecker 1990: xcv; George 1994: 60.

[4] Giving Paul's frequent phrase 'in Christ' this 'locational' sense gives important new meaning to such texts as Phil.1:1; Eph. 1:1, 11; 2:13.

[5] The same pattern can be observed on the other occasions when he refers to God's promises (in 2 Cor. 7:1; Eph. 1:13; 2:12; 3:6). In none of these instances is any reference made to the 'land'.

'redeemed' (Is. 52:7–9).[6] Terminology that had originally applied to Jerusalem and to the land was now applied instead to the salvation experienced in Christ.

4. Paul also understood such concepts as redemption, exodus and Passover in new ways, which would then affect his view of the land. Within the Old Testament these motifs had their origin in God's act of bringing his people from Egypt into the promised land. Paul now applied them to what God had done for his people through the cross and resurrection of Christ. The logical development of this would be that through Christ's work believers had now been ushered into the promised land, albeit a quite different 'land' from the former one. This may have been in Paul's mind in 1 Corinthians when he speaks of Christ as the 'Passover lamb' (1 Cor. 5:7), and especially when he compares the believers' experience in conversion to that of the people of Israel under Moses (10:1ff.). As a result, the Corinthians will 'inherit the kingdom of God' (6:9; cf. 3:21). In other words, through Christ's act of redemption (cf. also 1:30; 6:20) they had been brought into all that the promised land had been intended to signify: the true inheritance, the 'kingdom of God'.[7]

5. Paul's reworking of the exodus motif can be seen in other places: for example, in Romans 5 – 8. The four stages of redemption (from Egypt, through the Red Sea, via Sinai to the promised land) are now transposed in four successive chapters into a Christian key. The argument proceeds from redemption from sin (ch. 5), to baptism (ch. 6), to the issue of law (ch. 7) and on to the renewal of the cosmos (ch. 8). On this view, the analogue of the promised land is the whole *kosmos* renewed in Christ. The goal of redemption is not limited to the promised land but is widened out to include the renewal of God's whole creation.[8]

[6] See Bruce 1982b: 81–82; N. T. Wright 1994: 223ff.

[7] Cf. also the use of 'redemption' in Eph. 1:7 (leading to 'blessing in the heavenly realms', 1:3) and in Col. 1:14 (resulting in being 'rescued ... from the dominion of darkness and brought ... into the kingdom of the Son he loves', 1:13). The concept of 'kingdom' for Paul was clearly universal, even if not 'other-worldly', and no longer related exclusively to the people of Israel in Palestine (e.g. 1 Cor. 15:24; Gal. 5:21; Col. 1:13; 4:11; 1 Thess. 2:12; 2 Thess. 1:5; Eph. 5:5). Note too his similar understanding of the Christian's 'inheritance' and 'hope' (Gal. 3:29; 4:7; 1 Cor. 6:9–10; Col. 1:5, 12; 3:24; cf. Eph. 1:3, 14, 18; 5:5).

[8] I am grateful to N. T. Wright for this insight, which he will be developing in his forthcoming commentary on Romans.

6. Paul therefore understood the land in a more universal way, because he was convinced that Christ was Lord over the whole world. He is the Messiah of Israel, but his rule also extends far beyond the borders of the original promised land (e.g. Phil. 2:10; cf. 1 Cor. 3:22–23; Eph. 1:10). The ethical commands that previously pertained to Israel's life in the land are therefore applicable to all who seek to live under Christ's rule. Hence when Paul quotes the fifth commandment (Eph. 6:3), he omits the phrase 'that the Lord your God is giving you'; instead, the reference to 'land' is left undefined and comes to refer to the 'earth' in general. God's rule over the promised land is now extended through Christ to the whole world, and his true 'people' are a worldwide community, not an ethnic group associated with a particular land.

7. This makes sense of the otherwise puzzling reference in Romans 4:13 to Abraham's receiving 'the promise that he would be heir of the world'. In Genesis the promised 'inheritance' applied onlyto the promised land. Contemporary Jews may have aggrandized the promise in their belief that Israel would inherit the 'world'.[9] Paul, however, has a different reason for giving the promise a new twist. Instead, he is asserting that behind the promise of a particular land to Abraham there lay God's prior purpose to use this as a means of blessing 'all the nations of the earth'. That divine purpose had now come to pass in Christ, the one who as Abraham's 'seed' was indeed the 'heir of the world'.

The land, like the Torah, was a temporary stage in the long purpose of the God of Abraham. It is as though, in fact, the land were a great advance metaphor for the design of God that his people should eventually bring the whole world into submission to his healing reign. God's purpose now goes beyond Jerusalem and the land to the whole world (Wright 1994: 67).

Davies's analysis can therefore be confirmed. There is good evidence that Paul saw the land and the promises associated with it in a quite new way. 'The real centre of his interest has moved from the

[9] So Dunn 1988: 213; this assumption that Israel's inheritance is really the whole world is seen in e.g. *4 Ezra* 6:59 ('if the world had indeed been created for us, why do we not possess our world as an inheritance?').

land, concentrated in Jerusalem, to the communities "in Christ"' (1974: 182). Or, as Holwerda (1995: 104) summarized it:

> The horizons of the land have been shaped by the revelation of Jesus Christ. [Paul's] previous Jewish focus on a particularistic fulfillment has been transformed into a Christian universalism focused on the new creation. Just as in Christ the Temple had become a universal dwelling-place and the seed of Abraham had been transformed into a universal people, so the promise of the land already embraces the world.

God's purposes now have their focus in Christ, in his rule over the earth and in his ultimately renewing the cosmos with his resurrection power. This is what the land signified.

This is all the more remarkable if, before his conversion, Paul's Pharisaism had been of the Shammaite variety, with its probable emphasis on a nationalistic 'zeal' for the land (see Wright 1997). Paul speaks of this 'zeal' in Philippians 3:6 and Galatians 1:14, but within his own lifetime this same word was becoming associated with a very particular form of zeal – that of the Zealots, who desired the dismissal of the Romans from their land. After his conversion all this changed.

It was not that he was disloyal; several times he went up to Jerusalem, at personal risk to himself (Acts 11:30; 18:22; 21:17). It was not that he had suddenly forgotten or dismissed the teaching of the Old Testament. It was that he had met with Christ. If previously there had been a biblical tradition of the joys and blessings of being 'in the land', Paul now saw this as fulfilled in the possibility of being 'in Christ' (his favourite phrase). That was the blessed location; that was where he longed to be and that was the place to which he wanted to lead as many people as possible while he was alive.

Hebrews

The book of Hebrews is perhaps the most Jewish of the New Testament books. It also plays a key role in formulating any Christian theology of the land. For it deals not just with the issues of the temple (chs. 7 – 10) and Jerusalem (chs. 11 – 13), but expressly with the issue of the land: first in chapters 3 – 4, and then later in chapter 11. In both these sections the author reveals some significant assumptions concerning the land.

The force of the argument in the earlier section (3:1 – 4:13) depends on the assumption that the divine warning in Psalm 95:11 (that the rebellious Israelites would 'never enter my rest') is applicable to his audience as well. This in turn requires that this divine 'rest', which originally referred to entrance into the promised land, must now be understood as a reference instead to eschatological salvation in 'heaven'. This then entails the further conviction that the entrance into the promised land under Joshua was not the only rest God had had in mind; what happened under Joshua was also a pointer to a greater, heavenly reality. These ideas come to the fore in 4:8–9. But we notice in these verses that the author takes the argument one stage further. He effectively denies that the historical entrance into the promised land gave the people rest at all: 'For if Joshua had given them rest, God would not have spoken later about another day. There remains, then, a Sabbath-rest for the people of God.'

Our task is to consider the consequences of such a view for the author's understanding of the contemporary land. For, if he was asserting that the whole concept of the promised land was really an advance metaphor for the heavenly rest enjoyed by God's people, then the significance of the physical land would indeed be severely undercut.

To be sure, the author of Hebrews does not develop this at the time, reserving the full force of his argument concerning shadows and fulfilment until his discussion of the temple (chs. 7 – 10). Yet it can hardly be illegitimate to see how the pattern of his thinking, as revealed in those later chapters, would cause him to view the land in the same way. Just as the temple was now eclipsed by the revelation of the 'heavenly sanctuary',[10] so the land was eclipsed by the new focus on the heavenly 'rest'.

Both the temple and the land had had a real significance in times past, yet there had always been something about both of them that

[10] For full argument, see Walker 1996: ch. 6.

was incomplete. The temple could not fully effect the forgiveness of sins (10:4), nor could the land give complete rest. With the coming of Christ, what was lacking had now been revealed. So the time had now come to shift one's focus away from those physical entities. The promised inheritance, which once upon a time had indeed focused upon the land, was now consciously transferred by this author to a quite different entity: the heavenly rest.

Further indications of this can then be discerned when the theme of the land reappears in chapter 11, the list of those who practised faith (the majority of them, interestingly, while they were living outside the land). In his analysis of the faith of Abraham and his sons (vv. 8–16), the writer reiterates his distinctive view of the promised land. He uses the actual phrase 'land of promise' in verse 9 (literally), and in the previous verse he has identified this as the 'place he would later receive as an inheritance'. These positive descriptions of the physical land, however, are then immediately eclipsed by his insistence that the real focus of the promise to which Abraham 'looked forward' was the 'city with foundations, whose architect and builder is God' (v. 10). This eschatological focus is then repeated in verse 16: 'Instead, they were looking for a better country – a heavenly one. Therefore God is not ashamed to be called their God, for he has prepared a city for them.'

So the patriarchs were looking forward, not so much to the day when their descendants would inherit the physical land, but rather to the day when they would inherit the heavenly country (or city) which the physical land signified. In a sense they 'saw through' the promise of the land, looking beyond it to a deeper, spiritual reality.

In imputing such an attitude to the patriarchs, the author once again had to draw implicitly on the assumptions of typology, whereby the promise concerning the land, while real and valid in its own terms, was now to be seen as a pointer to something far greater. Moreover, it was this ability to see beyond present realities to their true heavenly fulfilment that was precisely one of the hallmarks of the attitude of faith described in this chapter. Inevitably, then, if the readers of this letter were ever to manifest an enthusiastic attitude towards the contemporary land, the author's response would have been decidedly negative: the whole essence of the faith he was trying to encourage was one that looked *beyond* such things.

There is nothing in Hebrews, therefore, to suggest that the author would have himself maintained any theological attachment to the promised land.[11] Moreover, as with Paul, this negative attitude towards the physical land would be merely endorsed by his conviction that Christ had accomplished a new exodus. Thus he compared his audience to the 'people of Israel' in the desert (3:7ff.); Jesus himself was greater than Moses (3:3).[12] Jesus was leading his people to a new promised land, the place to which he himself had gone ahead as the pioneer, namely the 'heavenly Jerusalem' (12:22; cf. 12:2). This is the place where God's promises are fulfilled.

In this way he would have dismissed any aspirations of a more political kind. Instead, in a climactic, concluding sentence he fixes his audience's attention on the 'kingdom that cannot be shaken' (12:28). Other, earthly kingdoms will prove to be part of the 'created things' which will not 'remain' (12:27). The land, however important as a theme within previous biblical faith, has now been caught up into a new understanding. It is given a quite new meaning, one that fulfils and yet eclipses its former role within God's purposes.

If, as argued elsewhere (see Walker 1996: 227–230), the author of Hebrews was writing this crucial work at a critical time – in the years leading up to AD 70 – the issue of a proper evaluation of Jerusalem, the temple and the land would have been especially relevant. The issue of how Jewish believers in Jesus should now view their ancestral commitments was almost certainly an integral part of the very issue he was seeking to address. And his message was that this was a time for siding decisively with Jesus. 'Let us go out to *him*' (13:13, my translation).

Jewish believers in Jesus were to turn away from a focus on such things, because in Jesus they had the solid reality to which those other things merely pointed. This message might go against their own natural preferences and might well lead to opposition when their fellow-Jews looked for signs of solidarity with the land, the

[11] This is confirmed by noting his non-territorial understanding both of the 'inheritance' (1:2, 4, 14; 6:12, 17; 9:15; 11:7) and of the 'promise' (6:13–15; 9:15; 10:36; 11:39). Both are now focused on and through Christ.

[12] On this, see e.g. Jones 1979. See also 12:18ff. (references to Sinai) and 13:20ff. (with its exodus language of 'leading up' applied to the resurrection and its description of Jesus the 'great shepherd' – like Moses).

temple and Jerusalem at this critical juncture. It was a prophetic call based on faith (for the temple was still operational) and it was an urgent call (for there were large issues at stake).

The question is: is it also a timeless call, directly applicable to today? Or was it very much a child of its time, influenced by the looming fall of Jerusalem? Would the same author have counselled his fellow Jewish believers quite differently if he were writing in the year 2000? Do recent events make his theology irrelevant? Or do they make it all the more vital?

John's Gospel

John too has come to view the land in a new light. This can be seen in at least three ways. First, like Paul and the author of Hebrews, John clearly sees Jesus as a latter-day Moses,[13] who of course is even greater than Moses (1:17–18; cf. Num. 12:18).[14] For John, the 'time of Moses has returned' (Jansen 1985: 136). What then is the promised land to which this new Moses has brought them? Or, to put it another way, if John presents Jesus as the Passover lamb (1:29; 18:28), what is the new exodus that has been achieved?

The second half of the Gospel, and in particular the Farewell Discourse, provides an answer. For here there are also clear allusions to Moses and his 'farewell discourse' to Israel as contained in the book of Deuteronomy.[15] Unlike Moses, Jesus would return after his death to be with his disciples, but what was the promised land that the disciples were about to enter? Interpreters have offered various answers. Some suggest that it is 'heaven' (as portrayed in 14:1–3): 'The disciples, no less than the Israelites, have a home promised to them, the possession of which is imminent' (Lacomara 1974: 78). Some focus on the whole experience of the disciples being 'in the truth': 'What Jesus surveyed on the eve of his death was a domain

[13] So, for example, the three gifts given by God in connection with the ministry of Moses (manna, water from the rock, the fiery pillar) are all now offered by Jesus (John 6 – 8). Note too the bronze snake (3:14), Jesus as the great 'shepherd' (10:11ff.) and John's description of Jesus' death (19:18; cf. Exod. 17:21). Cf. Glasson 1963, Meeks 1967; Enz 1957, Schillebeeckx 1980: 312–321, and, most recently, Motyer 1997: chs. 5–6.

[14] Jesus *himself* is the manna, 'the bread of life' (6:32ff.); he is also 'greater than Jacob' and Abraham (4:12; 8:56–58). See further Meeks 1967: 319; Ashton 1991: 470ff.; Pryor 1992: 120–121).

[15] See Lacomara 1974; cf. Brown 1966–70: 625.

which held out more promise than the land of Canaan did to the Israelites: it was "the truth", a territory whose boundaries had already been clearly defined as the revelation of Jesus, but the extent of whose riches had yet to be discovered' (Ashton 1991: 476).

A third possibility, however, is that the promised land is effectively the world into which Jesus' disciples are about to be sent (see e.g. 17:18). Just as Moses had addressed the Israelites on the point of their entry into Canaan, so Jesus spoke to his disciples about their mission in a hostile world (15:18ff.; cf. Lacomara 1974: 66).

Whatever the precise application, the emphasis on this Moses–Jesus parallelism strongly suggests that John would have seen the theme of the promised land as something that had now been typologically fulfilled in a way that no longer related to the physical land of Palestine. If the Johannine Jesus emphasized not the slavery of Israel in Egypt but the slavery (even of his contemporary Israel) 'to sin' (8:34–35), then those who were set free by the Son were even now in the promised land. Jesus thus offers 'a new exodus from sin and deliverance from death' (Motyer 1997: 197).[16] 'The 'promised land has been reached' (Smith 1962–3: 144).

Secondly, John's presentation of Jesus as the fulfilment of the Feast of Tabernacles ceremonies (7:37–39; 8:12) points to the same conclusion. This festival did not just look back nostalgically to Israel's wanderings in the wilderness; it had also become a vehicle for channelling Jewish hopes for a second exodus, when the many prophecies relating to the Jerusalem of the new age would come to fulfilment (see Brown 1966–70: 326). Jesus' words were therefore a challenge to many contemporary messianic ideas. Those hopes were to be focused not on God's doing a new thing for Jerusalem in the promised land, but upon what God was doing for them in Jesus.

The Feast of Tabernacles also fuelled the expectation that there would be an 'ingathering' of Jewish exiles to Jerusalem and the promised land.[17] However, for John this gathering process did not involve geographical relocation. On the contrary, it took place as men and women were brought into the 'people' of Jesus: Jesus

[16] Cf. Morgan 1957: 159; Beasley-Murray 1989: 76.

[17] So Smith 1962–3: 143, following the ideas of R. H. Lightfoot: Tabernacles looked forward to the 'ingathering or harvest of the nations in the days of the Messiah'.

would die 'for the *scattered* children of God, to bring them together and make them one' (11:52).

For John, this work of Jesus in gathering his people was also implicit in his being the 'good shepherd' who would 'bring others also' (10:14–16). In the light of Ezekiel 34, where the imagery of the shepherd is used to describe the way God will restore the flock of Israel from their exile, John may have been indicating that the restoration promised then would now fully come to pass in Jesus. 'Those who ... are "found" by Jesus and come to worship him are caught up in a restoration of exile on the Ezekiel 34 model, with Jesus as the "Shepherd" of Israel' (Motyer 1997: 138). Jesus, not the promised land, is now the focus of this long-awaited ingathering.

John's Gospel thus acts as a corrective to any Jewish nationalism which, through its convictions about the role of the promised land within God's purposes, would seek a political freedom. The Johannine Jesus talks about a different kind of 'freedom' (8:32–36) and a different kind of 'kingdom' (3:3–5; 6:15; 12:14; 18:33ff.; 19:15). The messianic kingdom has been manifested in a way quite different from that which was expected. The hermeneutic that led to that way of thinking was wrong. In fact, Israel's whole notion of kingship 'belongs to the realm of the world' (Pryor 1992: 77).

Thirdly, John's identification of Jesus with the 'true vine' (15:1ff.) may tell in a similar direction. Burge argues that, in the light of its use in the Old Testament (e.g. Is. 5:1ff.), the vine was understood as the 'people of Israel' and the vineyard as Israel's land (Burge 1994: 393; cf. Jaubert 1967).

> The crux of John 15 is that Jesus is changing the place of rootedness for Israel. The commonplace prophetic metaphor (the land as vineyard, the people of Israel as vines) now undergoes a dramatic shift. God's vineyard, the land of Israel, now has only one vine, Jesus ... And the only means of attachment to the land is through this one vine, Jesus Christ ... He offers what attachment to the land once promised: rootedness and life and hope ... The Fourth Gospel is transferring spatial, earthbound gifts from God and connecting them to a living person, Jesus Christ (Burge 1994: 393–394).

> In a Gospel replete with the motif of Jesus as the replacement of central Jewish symbols, this final 'I Am' saying thus suggests that the promised land too needs to be seen as fulfilled in Christ. As a result, the land as holy territory should now recede from the concerns of God's people. The vineyard is no longer an object of religious desire as it once had been (1994: 395).

Thus, although the theme of the promised land has not been given any major prominence in his Gospel, there are evident features in John's presentation of Jesus which reveal his re-evaluation of this concept. Those features include his understanding of Jesus as one who in his person and in his achievements offers his people something greater than Moses, and his reflection on Jesus as the 'true vine', as the true fulfilment of the festival of Tabernacles, and as the one in whom God's 'scattered' people truly are 'gathered' to himself. If John's readers included those who still wished to emphasize the importance of the promised land, John's message would be plain.

John's message would be similar if any of his readers (ancient or modern) were tempted to emphasize Palestine on the quite different grounds that it was now the Holy Land visited by the 'Word made flesh' (1:14). Despite his clear incarnational emphasis, John sets the incarnation against a universal backdrop: Jesus comes not to Palestine but 'into the *world*' (see e.g. 1:10; 3:17; 6:14; 9:5, 39; etc.). John also replaces 'holy places' with the person of Jesus, and this new 'Holy Place' (Jesus) is made accessible to all by the Spirit – 'the presence of Jesus when Jesus is absent' (Brown 1966–70: 1141). So the places where Jesus walked are no longer theologically significant, since his Spirit is no longer tied to any place or land, but rather 'blows wherever it pleases' (3:8), enabling people to worship 'in spirit and truth' in *any* location (4:21–24).[18]

Davies (1974: 334) therefore concluded that John now had little 'emotional attachment' to Jerusalem and Palestine; he had left his homeland behind. Despite the necessary focus of his Gospel story upon Jerusalem, the ultimate direction of the Gospel is outwards,

[18] See extended discussion in Walker 1996: 190–194. Cf. Davies 1974: 289–318, 334, and 1981: 65; Burge 1987: 195–197; Schillebeeckx 1980: 318.

and the particularities are subsumed in a comprehensive emphasis upon the universal implications of what had transpired in Palestine for the sake of the world.

Luke-Acts

This new understanding of the land is seen in other writers too. When we turn to Luke-Acts, we note that its author, although probably a Gentile himself, sympathizes with the longings of the Jewish people. His opening chapters reveal the desire for restoration among God's people, that they should be 'set free from the hands of their enemies' (1:71). Yet the story of his Gospel soon takes a surprising twist: Jesus pronounces instead an imminent judgment upon Jerusalem (13:33–35; 19:41–44; 21:6ff.; 23:27–31); instead of the Romans' being removed, it is their armies who will surround Jerusalem (21:20–24). Something paradoxical has occurred. 'We had hoped that he would be the one to redeem Israel', sigh the Emmaus disciples (24:21). Indeed he had, implied Luke, but not in the way you expected.[19]

The overall structure of Luke-Acts makes a similar point. The Gospel goes up to Jerusalem, but Acts goes out from Jerusalem through Judea and Samaria to the 'ends of the earth' (Acts 1:8). This embodies the truth that God's purposes are no longer tied to the land as once they had been. Significantly, the story of Jesus ends up in Rome with Paul preaching there the very Jewish notion of the 'kingdom of God' (28:31).

Some have even wondered if the book of Acts is modelled on the book of Joshua, noting, for example, the parallels between Achan's fate and that of Ananias and Sapphira (Josh. 7; Acts 5:1–11; see e.g. Chapman 1989: 141–142)). The story of the Israelites taking over the promised land was punctuated in Joshua by frequent references to the land having rest from war (Josh. 11:23; 14:15; 21:44; 23:1); in Acts, the story of the gospel going out to the nations is similarly punctuated by references to the peace of the church (9:31) and the growth of the 'Word' (6:7; 2:47; 12:24; 13:49; 19:20). If this was in Luke's mind, then the land is now analogous to the world.[20]

[19] See ch. 3B, p. 106.

Further confirmation of this general Lukan approach to the land is seen in his extended portrait of Stephen (Acts 6:8 – 7:60), whose speech highlights the way God had revealed his holy presence and divine activity outside the land and prepares the way thematically for the dispersal of the believers from Jerusalem recorded in the next chapter (8:1ff.).

Revelation

Finally, turning to Revelation, we find a similar shift of focus from the land to the world. To be sure, some interpreters understand many of the seventy-seven references to the 'earth' or 'land' as referring narrowly to the land of Israel (Gentry 1989: 121). Yet the frequent references to 'the kings of the earth' (e.g. 1:5; 6:15; 16:14; 17:2; 18:3, 9; 19:19) and 'the four corners of the earth' (7:1; etc.) strongly suggest that the seer is thinking instead of the whole world. Hence his several references to the inhabited world (*oikoumenē*: see 3:10; 12:9; 16:14).

The focus of Revelation is cosmic, not parochial. Jewish apocalyptic is now seen to be the basis for an interpretation of the world as a whole, and imagery that previously related to the exodus and the deliverance from Egypt is now applied to the deliverance won by Jesus. Once again, this means that Christians are concerned with a quite different promised land.

> Moses celebrated a deliverance by the Lord which adumbrated a greater deliverance to come. The greater redemption eclipsed the former by a similar degree as the second redeemer transcended the first. Moses and the Lamb are no more to be bracketed than the promised land of Israel is to be equated with the kingdom of God (Beasley-Murray 1974: 235).

For the author of Revelation, the coming of Jesus signals the end of a narrow focus on the land.

[20] Note too how Jesus' words in Luke 24:44 are a direct quotation of the opening words of Deut. 1:1 (literally, 'These are the words that I spoke…'). As Deuteronomy was the book of Moses prior to Israel's entrance into the land, so the gospel of Jesus preceded the apostles' going out into the world.

Conclusion

The above survey suggests that there is a whole new approach to the issue of the land in the New Testament. The coming of Jesus, in the interpretation of the apostles, has not reinforced the land-promises. Nor has it led simply to those promises being put temporarily 'on hold', awaiting fulfilment at another time. On the contrary, the New Testament writers are well aware of this important theme, which was of vital importance to their Jewish contemporaries. They offer an alternative way of understanding the divine purpose relating to the land. In the gospel God had at last fulfilled his covenant promise that through Abraham all the nations of the earth might be blessed (Gen. 12:3); God's light could now lighten the Gentiles (Luke 2:32). The universal purpose that had always undergirded the particular promises was at last capable of being realized, and in that new reality the land became subsumed under God's purposes for the world as a whole.

Bibliography

Ashton, J. (1991), *Understanding the Fourth Gospel*, Oxford: Oxford University Press.

Beasley-Murray, G. R. (1974), *The Book of Revelation*, New Century Bible, London: Marshall, Morgan and Scott.

Brown, R. E. (1966–70), *The Gospel According to John*, 2 vols., Anchor Bible, Garden City: Doubleday.

Bruce, F. F. (1982), *The Epistle to the Galatians*, New International Greek Testament Commentary, Grand Rapids: Eerdmans.

Brueggemann, W. (1978), *The Land: Place as Gift, Promise, and Challenge in Biblical Faith*, London: SPCK. US edn 1977.

Burge, G. M. (1987), *The Anointed Community*, Grand Rapids: Eerdmans.

——— (1994), 'Territorial religion, Johannine Christology and the vineyard of John 15', in J. B. Green & M. Turner (eds.), *Jesus of Nazareth: Lord and Christ*, Carlisle: Paternoster.

Chapman, C. (1989), *Whose Promised Land?*, rev. edn, Tring: Lion. First edn 1983.

Davies, W. D. (1974), *The Gospel and the Land: Early Christianity and Jewish Territorial Doctrine*, Berkeley: University of California Press.

Dunn, J. D. G. (1988), *Romans*, 2 vols., Word Biblical Commentary, Waco: Word.

Enz, J. J. (1957), 'The book of Exodus as a literary type of the Gospel of John', *Journal of Biblical Literature,* 76: 208–215.
Evans, C. A., & J. A. Sanders, (1993), *Paul and the Scriptures of Israel,* Journal for the Study of the New Testament Supplement Series 83, Sheffield: JSOT Press.
Gentry, K. L. (1989), *Before Jerusalem Fell: Dating the Book of Revelation,* Texas: Tyler.
George, T. (1994), *Galatians,* New American Commentary, Nashville: Broadman and Holman.
Glasson, T. F. (1963), *Moses in the Fourth Gospel,* London: SCM.
Holwerda, D. E. (1995), *Jesus and Israel: One Covenant or Two?* Leicester: Apollos.
Jansen, H. L. (1985), 'Typology in the Gospel of John', in P. Borgen (ed.), *The Many and the One,* Trondheim: Tapir: 125–143.
Jewett, R. (1970–1), 'Agitators and the Galatian congregation', *New Testament Studies* 17: 198–212.
Jones, P. R. (1979), 'The figure of Moses as a heuristic device for understanding the pastoral intent of Hebrews', *Review and Expositor* 76: 95–102.
Lacomara, A. (1974), 'Deuteronomy and the Farewell Discourse', *Catholic Biblical Quarterly* 36: 65–84.
Longenecker, R. N. (1990), *Galatians,* Word Biblical Commentary, Dallas: Word.
Meeks, W. A. (1967), *The Prophet-King: Moses Traditions and the Johannine Christology,* Novum Testamentum Supplement 14, Leiden: Brill.
Morgan, R. (1957), 'Fulfilment in the Fourth Gospel', *Interpretation* 11:155–165.
Motyer, S. (1997), *Your Father the Devil? A New Approach to John and 'the Jews',* Carlisle: Paternoster.
Pryor, J. W. (1992), *John: Evangelist of the Covenant People,* London: Darton, Longman and Todd.
Schillebeeckx, E. (1980), *Christ: The Christian Experience in the Modern World,* London: SCM.
Smith, C. W. R. (1962–3), 'Tabernacles in the Fourth Gospel and Mark', *New Testament Studies* 9: 130–146.
Walker, P. W. L. (1996), *Jesus and the Holy City: New Testament Perspectives on Jerusalem,* Grand Rapids: Eerdmans.
Wright, N. T. (1994), 'Gospel and theology in Galatians', in L. A. Jervis and P. Richardson (eds.), *Gospel in Paul,* Journal for the Study of the New Testament Supplement Series 108: 222–239, Sheffield: Sheffield Academic Press.

3B
The land and Jesus himself

Peter W. L. Walker

'No smoke without fire,' they say. If the argument of the previous chapter approximates to the true teaching of the New Testament on the issue of the land, then the crucial question becomes: how much of this is dependent on the teaching of Jesus? Were the apostles coming up with new ideas quite out of keeping with the intentions of Jesus, perhaps because they were encountering new situations in the wider pagan world? Or were they taking their lead from Jesus himself?[1]

Jesus' express teaching on the land is fairly minimal, with Matthew 5:5 often being cited as the only place where the theme is explicitly mentioned. In the statement that the 'meek ... shall inherit the *gē* [land/earth]', does this refer (as in the original, Ps. 37:11) to the land of Israel, or has it now got the universalized

[1] Of course, at this point, we encounter all the problems associated with discovering the mind of the historical Jesus. For the present, it will be assumed that the Gospels do indeed accurately recount his teaching. For a defence of this position from a sound historical perspective see most recently N. T. Wright 1996. I am greatly indebted to him for his ideas in this area, and the following analysis draws out the implications of his overall framework for this one particular issue.

meaning, referring to the 'earth' as a whole? In view of the subsequent references to Jesus' followers being 'the light of the world', there is a *prima facie* case that at this point the more universal theme is in Jesus' mind, and also in Matthew's (cf. 28:19). Others would disagree, however, seeing this as still a reference to the particular land of Israel. If so, it would still be significant that Jesus redefines who will inherit this land: not necessarily those who are ethnically Jewish, or those who fight for the land's freedom, but rather those who are 'meek'. Nevertheless, we clearly need some more general pointers to Jesus' mindset than this one slightly ambiguous text. Below we highlight four key aspects of Jesus' ministry which may give us the information we need.

Jesus and the symbols of Judaism: temple, city and land

Jesus may not expressly have said much about the land, but he did speak frequently about both Jerusalem and its temple. Within a first-century Jewish worldview the temple, the city and the land were understood as three interconnecting theological *realia*. They were like concentric circles. So a new approach to one aspect of this triad might well signify a new attitude towards the others as well.[2]

A full analysis of Jesus' approach to the temple and the city has been offered in *Jesus and the Holy City* (Walker 1996).[3] In sum, Jesus was outspoken about both. Concerning the temple, he warned that Jerusalem's 'house' would soon be left desolate (Luke 13:35; cf. Matt. 23:38). By forgiving the paralytic his sins, he implicitly set up a challenge to the temple as the unique place for the assurance of sins forgiven (Mark 2:1–12), and, according to Matthew, he saw himself as 'one greater than the temple' and 'greater than Solomon', the builder of the temple (Matt. 12:6, 42).

[2] See e.g. Davies 1974: 152: 'just as Jerusalem became the quintessence of the Land, so the Temple became the quintessence of Jerusalem'. See also Holwerda 1995: 101–112, who helpfully suggests that 'the New Testament is more interested in the promise of the land than it appears at first glance', because it 'focuses on Jerusalem as the essence of the promise of the land' (p. 111). Cf. Kreider n.d.: 7: 'already in the Hebrew Bible as well as in Judaism, Jerusalem had come to symbolise all that the land stood for', and 'just as Jerusalem became the symbol of the land, so the Temple became the symbol of the City'. A similar pattern, we note, can be detected in the book of 2 Chronicles.

[3] On Jesus' attitudes, see esp. ch. 8.

The so-called 'cleansing of the temple' (Mark 11:12–21) was then more truly a portent of its imminent destruction. Although some see this as little more than a call for the temple's reformation, far more likely is the interpretation offered in Mark's Gospel. Here the incident is couched within the episode of the cursing of the fig-tree, an event which effectively gives to the disciples a private interpretation of what the public action in the temple really signified. God was looking for fruit in his temple, had found it lacking, and was consequently acting in judgment towards it.[4]

This is then confirmed by Jesus' various predictions that the temple would indeed be destroyed: the abomination of desolation will stand where it should not (Mark 13:14); 'not one stone ... will be left on another' (Mark 13:2); 'Destroy this temple, and I will raise it again in three days' (John 2:19; cf. Mark 14: 58; Acts 6:14). Jesus was preparing his disciples for an almost unimaginable future: that time when the temple would come crashing down. He was also hinting that this event would in some strange way be connected with himself, and with something that would occur 'after three days'.

Jesus had a similar view of Jerusalem as a whole. Although it was 'the city of the Great King' (Matt. 5:35), it was the city which was about to reject its true king. In fulfilment of Zechariah's prophecy concerning Zion's king, this king entered his capital city on a donkey. This was truly the moment of the city's visitation by God, but the city missed its moment: 'if you ... had only known on this day what would bring you peace – but now it is hidden from your eyes' (Luke 19:42). Jerusalem's children were in danger of being led astray by a false mother, but Jesus had longed to be that true mother, 'as a hen gathers her chicks under her wings' (Luke 13:34). Instead the city would be encircled, not by Jesus' protective arms, but by the Roman armies (Luke 19:43). Just as Jesus prophesied that Capernaum would be judged for its lack of repentance (using language formerly applied to proud Babylon: Matt. 11:23–24, reflecting Is. 14), so too Jerusalem would be trampled on by the

[4] Of the vast literature on this episode, see e.g. Bauckham 1988; Evans 1989, 1993; N. T. Wright 1996: 333–336, 490ff.

[5] If Luke's final version of his Gospel was published after the fall of Jerusalem in AD 70, his language might reflect recent events. Dodd (1947), however, argued convincingly that there is nothing in his language which is not culled from the Old Testament. It is probable therefore that these oracles are pre-70, and that they are consistent with other aspects of Jesus' teaching.

Roman overlord (Luke 21:20–24).[5] So what he had predicted concerning the temple would prove equally true of the city: not one stone would be left upon another (Luke 19:44).

Not for nothing, then, was Jesus likened to Jeremiah (Matt. 16:14), that former prophet of doom. Nor was it a coincidence that Jesus quoted from the famous Temple Sermon of Jeremiah in his cleansing of the temple: 'you have made it "a den of robbers"' (Mark 11:17; cf. Jer. 7:11). What had happened in Jeremiah's day would happen again.

In bringing this prophetic word to Israel, Jesus was thus standing in a thoroughly Jewish tradition, warning Israel of what Yahweh would do when he visited his people. He was not being anti-Semitic, nor was he implying that Jerusalem and its temple had not been genuinely God-ordained aspects of Israel's past. Instead he was saying that judgment was a solemn reality, and also that Israel's defining moment had come in his own person. He was, in other words, an *eschatological prophet*, announcing that the new age for which Israel had long awaited was now breaking in upon her, but also warning that when it came it would have surprising and alarming consequences for Israel herself.

Our point is this. If Jesus could treat in this radical way the many hopes associated in the minds of his contemporaries with Jerusalem and its temple, then in principle he could easily have done the same with their cherished hopes towards the land. Indeed, the interconnection between these three *realia* makes this more likely than not.

This is then confirmed by the way Jesus evidently re-evaluated the other key symbols of Jewish identity: Sabbath, food, nation (or family) and land (see N. T. Wright 1996: 383–384).[6] Wright argues cogently that we can see in each of these areas how Jesus offered a radically new understanding – again, not because these former 'boundary markers' of Israel were bad, but because God was now both redefining his people *and* doing a new thing in and through Jesus.

Of these four symbols, 'land' is admittedly the one Jesus mentioned least. Nevertheless, Wright may well be correct to see Jesus'

[6] For Jesus' attitude to these, see e.g. Mark 2:23–28 (Sabbath), 3:34–35 (family/nation), 7:17ff. (food).

challenges on the issue of possessions as speaking to this issue. For the most basic of all possessions is land, and for Israel the land was an inheritance given by God. Not surprisingly, the revolt of Judas the Galilean was triggered by Roman registration of the land. In such a tense climate, Jesus' warnings concerning possessions may have had a contemporary application missed by modern materialists: 'Someone in the crowd said to him, "Teacher, tell my brother to divide the inheritance with me". Jesus replied, "... life does not consist in ... possessions"' (Luke 12:13–15). 'Do not store up for yourselves treasures on earth ... where thieves break in and steal' (Matt. 6:19).

> Family and property both functioned symbolically within the total Jewish worldview. Those who followed Jesus, who were loyal to his kingdom-agenda, would have to be prepared to renounce them, God-given though they were. [Jesus' coming] will not reaffirm Israel's symbolic, and zealously defended, territorial inheritance and possession. On the contrary: the unfaithful tenants will have their vineyard taken away... (N. T. Wright 1996: 405).

> Among the sacred things that would have to be sold was the traditional symbol of sacred land itself. It was swallowed up in the eschatological promise. YHWH was now to be king of all the earth (1996: 429).

Jesus' radical approach to possessions, to other Jewish symbols, and to the great central realities of Jerusalem and its temple all suggest that his approach to the issue of the land was similarly provocative – thoroughly Jewish but radically distinct and surprising.

Jesus and prophetic fulfilment: Israel restored

The above may seem to cast Jesus' message in an overly negative light, as though he was intent on overturning centuries of Jewish tradition for the sake of it. Yet, as already hinted, this message of judgment needs to be seen within the positive context of fulfilment.

Israel's defining moment had come. After sending many servants to his vineyard, the owner was now sending 'last of all' his 'son' (Mark 12:6). The message of Jesus was fully in keeping with the prophets, but he was the last prophet, the one who introduced the new age of the kingdom. In this respect Jesus *was* different from Jeremiah and the other prophets. Hereafter things will never be the same again. Matters will not return to the *status quo ante.* The new age of fulfilment has arrived.

Preserving this focus on fulfilment is also vital because it forces us to ask the question: what were the Jews of Jesus' day longing to see fulfilled? Israel's hope is summarized by Wright under three headings, each rooted in Isaiah 52: the longing for a return from exile, the conquest of evil and the arrival of the king.

> How beautiful upon the mountains
> are the feet of those who bring good news,
> who proclaim peace,
> who bring good tidings,
> who proclaim salvation,
> who say to Zion,
> 'Your God reigns!' . . .
> When the LORD returns to Zion,
> they will see it with their own eyes.
> Burst into songs of joy together,
> you ruins of Jerusalem;
> for the LORD has comforted his people,
> he has redeemed Jerusalem.
> The LORD will lay bare his holy arm
> in the sight of all the nations;
> and all the ends of the earth will see
> the salvation of our God.
>
> (Is. 52:7–10)

Since this prophecy had evidently not yet been fulfilled, Wright argues that Israel saw itself as still 'in exile'. Evil had not been dealt with, the king had not come. Those who *had* returned from exile felt the incongruity of being slaves in their own land (Neh. 9:36), and the promised land was now once again under the rule of the pagans. In one way the exile had come to an end, but in almost all the ways that mattered it had not.

This longing for the end of exile inevitably raises the issue of the land and its significance. 'Exile' and 'native land' belong together conceptually. It then becomes vital to know how Jesus viewed this issue of the return of Israel from exile, for implicit within that will lie his understanding of the land.

For Wright, we cannot understand Jesus without recognizing this background. His was not a timeless message of ethereal truths, but one that made strong connections with this urgent situation, one that was simultaneously religious *and* political in nature. When therefore Jesus proclaimed the imminence of God's kingdom, this was not a vague hope (attractive to liberal Protestantism), but a startling announcement that the age of fulfilment had arrived. These Jewish hopes were about to be realized: the king was coming, evil was going to be overthrown and *Israel's exile was about to end.*

Another way of expressing the same cluster of hopes is to talk of the 'restoration of Israel'. Wright argues that Jesus was claiming in his public ministry to be *himself* the one through whom Israel was now being restored in his own person. John the Baptist's ministry was imbued with this restoration eschatology, preparing God's people for the time of fulfilment.[7] Then when John the Baptist began to have doubts about Jesus, Jesus sent back a message based on Isaiah 35, a passage where great healings are seen as a sign of the longed-for end of exile (Luke 7:20–23).

The disciples did not understand all this at the time, reckoning still on a political restoration for Israel, no doubt with themselves in positions of authority (cf. Mark 10:37). Hence their agitated question in Acts 1:6. Now that Jesus was raised from the dead, surely *now* was the time when this Messiah would do the one thing he was expected to do! 'Lord, are you at this time going to restore the kingdom to Israel?' (Acts 1:6). This question reveals a great deal about what was uppermost in the minds of first-century Jews, including the disciples. They longed to see the prophecies of Israel's restoration fulfilled and the exile concluded.

The answer of the New Testament to this urgent Jewish question appears to be this: the longed-for restoration of Israel has indeed taken place, but in a most unexpected way – through the coming of Messiah Jesus and in particular through his being raised from the dead.

[7] See e.g. Meyer 1979, Sanders 1985, and N. T. Wright 1996: 160–162.

Thus when the Emmaus disciples express this same hope (that Jesus would have been the one to 'redeem Israel'; Luke 24:21), their doubts are answered as the risen Jesus explains that the suffering and resurrection 'on the third day' of Israel's Messiah are 'written' in the Scriptures. This may possibly allude to a general pattern of suffering and glory in the Old Testament, or to the sign of Jonah in the whale for three days, but the only clear prophecy which speaks about something happening on the third day is Hosea 6:2: 'on the third day he will restore us'. If this passage from Hosea is indeed what underlies this teaching, then a prediction which ostensibly concerned the restoration of *Israel* has now been applied by Jesus to his *own* resurrection. Thus Dodd (1952: 103) could conclude: 'the resurrection of Christ *is* the restoration of Israel of which the prophets spoke' (his italics).

Further confirmation of this may be found in Acts 15. When it is remembered that within popular Jewish expectation the 'ingathering of the Gentiles' would take place only *after* Israel had been restored, we can sense that one of the key issues in the apostolic council was: what does the conversion of Gentiles to faith in Messiah Jesus mean concerning the restoration of Israel? Has the order been reversed, or has the restoration of Israel in fact taken place, though in an unexpected manner? The definitive intervention of James is therefore intriguing: he quotes from Amos a passage which says that Gentiles may seek the Lord after the restoration of 'David's fallen tent' (Amos 9:11–12 in Acts 15:16ff.). The clear implication is that James believed that with the coming of Jesus and his resurrection the longed-for restoration of Israel had indeed already taken place. They should therefore have no qualms in welcoming the ingathering of the Gentiles.[8]

The writer of Luke-Acts, therefore, is almost certainly working with this understanding that in Jesus Israel has been restored. These were the very hopes which he highlighted on the lips of faithful Jewish people at the beginning of his Gospel. Simeon and Anna had been longing for the 'consolation of Israel' and the 'redemption of Jerusalem' (Luke 2:25, 38); and Zechariah believed the time was now come when God would rescue his people 'from the hand of

[8] See further C. J. H. Wright 1994: 16.

[their] enemies' (1:74). Strangely, of course, these hopes, if understood in a literal sense, would be dashed very soon in the same Gospel, as the adult Jesus predicts that those Gentiles enemies will in fact destroy Jerusalem (Luke 19:41–44; 21:20–24). Yet that is precisely the evangelist's point. The hopes of restoration *have* been fulfilled, but not in the expected way. Hence when he records Jesus' answer to the disciples' agitated question in Acts 1, he almost certainly intends us to hear this as meaning: 'Your understanding of restoration is wrong; Israel has been restored in my resurrection, and you will be witnesses of this fact from Jerusalem to the ends of the earth. The restored kingdom of Israel is the world coming under the rule of Israel's true king.' The throne of David is no longer empty, but in accordance with God's promise it has now been occupied by the risen Jesus (Acts 2:30–31). Israel's kingdom has therefore been restored through the resurrection of her king – the one whom God has made both Lord and Messiah (2:36).

If this portrait of Luke and of Jesus himself is correct, then a strong claim is being made that the restoration of Israel has occurred through the agency of Jesus. Restoration proves to be far from straightforwardly political. It does not concern the 'kingdom of Israel' (Acts 1:6), but the 'kingdom of God' (Acts 1:3). Israel has been restored in principle through the resurrection of her Messiah. Hence she will be restored in practice only when she bows the knee before her Messiah.

The relevance of all this to our primary issue concerning the land should by now be clear. For on this reading of the Gospels and Acts, restoration is not a Jewish return to the land, but rather a coming to the Messiah and an acceptance of his rule. The cluster of hopes for which 'the restoration of Israel' is shorthand was based on texts that included references to the exiles returning to the land. If Jesus and the apostles saw this as fulfilled *completely but not literally*, this must have had enormous repercussions for the way they viewed the significance of the land. If the importance of the land had previously been dependent on those texts which spoke about the return of exiles to the land, then that importance was now brought severely into question. And those texts could no longer be interpreted in that literalistic manner. The God of Israel had indeed come to help his people Israel (Luke 1:54), there had indeed been divine fulfilment of biblical promises, but not in the expected manner. In other words, the essential fulfilment of the prophecy outstripped the precise, external form of the prediction.

One striking confirmation of this new pattern of thought can be found in Matthew 8:10–12. Jesus refers to many people coming 'from the east and the west'. This evokes such passages as Isaiah 43:5–7 and Psalm 107:2–3, which seemingly referred to a future 'restoration' of Jewish people to the land from the four quarters of the globe. Jesus interpreted it differently. As R. T. France (1975: 73) rightly observed: 'Jesus took Old Testament prophecies that had that connotation and applied them instead to the ingathering of the Christian community, in this case, to the exclusion of some Jews.' The longed-for 'end of exile' was thus brought about when people of all nations came into the kingdom of God through Jesus.

Jesus and God's universal purposes: through Israel to the world

One of the conundrums in considering the historical Jesus is getting the appropriate blend of particularity and universality. Some portraits of Jesus, influenced by later Gentile Christian theology, have produced an image of Jesus which makes little sense within the real Judaism of Jesus' day. Other portraits, in reaction, have produced a credibly Jewish Jesus, but one who leaves a big question-mark as to how Gentiles could ever come to faith in him. One of the advantages of Wright's scheme is precisely that it has Jesus being concerned with a task that was thoroughly Jewish (the fulfilment of Israel's national hopes rooted in the Scriptures) yet one which *by its own inner logic* inevitably has repercussions for the world beyond Israel. For when God has done for Israel that which he promised to do for Israel, the time has come for the Gentiles to be brought into the picture. Gentiles approaching this event retrospectively might of course miss some of the original layers of meaning, but they would not be wrong about the divinely intended result.

Wright's scheme is thus able to see the New Testament's radical re-evaluation of concepts such as the land *as a thoroughly Jewish phenomenon*. A vital Gordian knot is thereby cut. A theology that plays down the land is often dubbed un-Jewish; but if Jesus was authentically Jewish, then surely, so it is argued, he must have endorsed the land emphasis of his fellow-Jews? Now it becomes clear how Jesus could truly have wrestled with all the hopes of Israel, including that of the land, but could also have given a quite distinctive answer. He was engaging with the Jewish issues in an authentically Jewish manner; but what emerges is quite different from what Judaism would have expected. And what emerges is the New Testament emphases we highlighted above (in chapter 3A).

The resultant picture is of a Jesus who focused on the issues of Israel, while having in his sights the blessing that would thereby come to the Gentiles. Israel consumed his attention (because that was where God had to work), but the ultimate goal lay beyond Israel. So the Syro-Phoenician woman learns that Jesus' ministry has to be focused on the 'lost sheep of Israel' (Matt. 15:24), but blessing is promised for those outside. Thereafter Jesus, loyal to his mission, returns to Galilee and then up to Jerusalem. Why? To do the task that could be done only there, but which once accomplished would bring blessing to the waiting world. The 'word of the LORD' would then be able to 'go out from Jerusalem' (cf. Is. 2:4) because God had now done in Israel and for Israel what he had promised.

Luke is therefore not wrong to draw out the universal implications and intentions of Jesus – even though it takes little guesswork on our part to know why he as a Gentile had an interest in emphasizing them.[9] Jesus' welcome to the outsider within Israel and to the Samaritan located within Israel's own borders is symptomatic of a mindset that is looking beyond the confines of Israel, even though the primary task must always remain firmly within Israel.

Jesus' choice of Capernaum for his base of operations may reflect this more universal goal.[10] Matthew describes Galilee as 'Galilee of the Gentiles' and makes reference to 'the way of the sea' (Matt. 4:15). So he too may have sensed that the choice of Capernaum (a key border post on the 'way of the sea' from the Mediterranean to Damascus and beyond) reflected Jesus' 'international' intentions. His ministry might seem Israel-focused in some ways, but Jesus was putting down a marker that it would also have repercussions way beyond the confines of Israel.

[9] See e.g. Luke 3:38; 4:24–27; 7:1–10; 9:55; etc.

[10] See Robertson 1996: 116, and below, p. pp. 137–138.

It is then quite in keeping with this mindset of Jesus that his reference to the meek inheriting the earth (Matt. 5:5, see above) could have both an Israel-focused meaning and also, simultaneously, a wider resonance. Similarly, the perspective of the Fourth Gospel is also entirely credible in its portrait of Jesus' conversation with the Samaritan woman (John 4:19–26). Jesus breaks across the national boundaries, yet he simultaneously insists without apology that 'salvation is from the Jews' (v. 22). He then goes on to say that one key result of his coming to Israel as its Messiah is that the previous geographical focus on Jerusalem (or Mount Gerizim) will come to an end. Because of what God is doing for Israel through her Messiah, things will look quite different in the future. The previous focus on the temple and the city (and indeed the land?) had been entirely correct and necessary, but a new age was dawning, and in that new age these physical *realia* of Judaism would come to be relativized.

So Jesus placed a necessary emphasis on Israel, but his sights were not limited to Israel. Even as he remains totally Jewish, Jesus is able to take the Jewish tradition in a surprising new direction. It is that sudden unexpected 'twist' which stares at us from the pages of the New Testament and which has to be given some adequate explanation. And the thesis of this chapter is that it is rooted in none other than Jesus himself, reflecting how he saw himself, Israel and the world.

Jesus and contemporary politics: his critique of Jewish nationalism

Finally, what about Jesus' response to the growing tide of Jewish nationalism in his day? Again, this will be helpful in building up a picture of Jesus' understanding of the land.

After the uprisings associated with Judas the Galilean, a lid was kept on the situation, but the tension was mounting throughout the time leading up to the outbreak of the first Jewish Revolt. Even if the name 'zealot' was coined in subsequent decades, political 'zealotry' was already a powerful phenomenon.

Few have followed Brandon in seeing Jesus as a proto-Zealot, going to Jerusalem with an anti-Rome agenda and being crucified by the Romans for so doing. As N. T. Wright (1996: 370) says, this portrait of Jesus might explain the crucifixion, but it makes no sense of his earlier controversies in Galilee, and can be upheld only 'at the expense of most of the evidence of Jesus' ministry'. In other words, Jesus did not share the convictions of what later became the Zealot party: namely, that Rome was the real enemy and that she needed to be rooted out of the promised land. Instead, we see Jesus praising the faith of a Roman centurion (Luke 7:9), telling his disciples to go the extra mile when requisitioned by a soldier, and encouraging and practising an ethic of turning the other cheek and forgiving one's enemies (Matt. 5:44; Luke 23:34). When presented with the awkward question about paying tribute, his skilful answer reveals no hostility towards the emperor (Mark 12:17). He may disapprove of Pilate's treatment of some Galileans, but he takes it as an opportunity to warn people of what will happen to them if they do not repent (Luke 13:1–3). There is political realism here.

More than that, he appeared to see the nationalistic cause as destined for failure: Jerusalem would be surrounded by Rome's armies (Luke 17:37; 20:20ff.). In some ways this was simply cool-headed *Realpolitik*: any causal observer might conclude that if tiny Israel rose up against colossal Rome, it would stand little chance of success. Yet Jesus overlaid this assessment of the political situation with an alarming theological conviction. When Rome defeated Israel, this would need to be seen as an indication of divine judgment (Luke 19:43; N. T. Wright 1996: 332ff.).

Jesus disagreed with the nationalist agenda. There was another way of being Israel. Israel was called to be a light to the nations, but there were other ways of achieving this than through going to war against those nations. Indeed, Jesus is almost certainly claiming that the true way of being Israel is to follow him (see N. T. Wright 1996: 472–474).

For our purposes this may be sufficient. For the nationalistic cause was motivated (at its best) by the vision held forth in the prophets of an Israel restored to her land and enjoying God's rule. And other messianic claimants would all be motivated by a clear political agenda: freedom from Rome. So when Jesus advanced a different, non-nationalistic model of messiahship, it was not only radical and prone to misunderstanding. It must also have involved *an implicit critique of the theological tradition drawn from the Old Testament concerning the land.*

Jesus knew the Old Testament passages which gave rise to this nationalistic hope, but he evidently interpreted these passages differently. He had an alternative hermeneutic. Although the nationalistic hermeneutic was attractively straightforward and 'literalistic', it was a false interpretation. For Jesus there was another way of being faithful to the prophetic vision. Israel would be 'restored', as we have seen, in quite a different sense.

The paradox in this is then revealed in the crucifixion. Although Jesus was not a proto-Zealot, in his love for his fellow-Jews he was prepared to end up on a Roman cross, on the false charge of being just such a nationalist. It was Barabbas who was the nationalist insurrectionist, but Jesus took his place. As N. T. Wright (1985: 87) has well said, 'Jesus could not preach the zealot's cause, but he could die for it.' In other words, Jesus had diagnosed the disease of Jewish nationalism and publicly distanced himself from it, but at the last he allows the consequence of that disease to fall upon him. He takes the place of the Zealot and identifies with Israel precisely where he has highlighted Israel's sin and God's judgment upon her.

So Jesus experienced the fate of the rebel strung up on a Roman cross. This then warned his contemporaries that such would be the fate of all who took the rebellious route against the Roman overlords. His going out to Golgotha was, as he said to the weeping women, only a vignette of what would happen within a generation when their children rose up to fight against Rome. 'Do not weep for me; weep for yourselves ... If men do these things when the tree is green [i.e. I am innocent of the charge], what will happen when it is dry [i.e. when the Zealots reveal their true colours]?' (Luke 23:28–31). Jesus had warned that when that time came, this would be the moment of God's judgment upon Israel.

The love of Jesus and the mercy of God are seen in the fact that Jesus suffered in advance the very judgment that he himself had predicted would come upon Israel and Jerusalem. This was no criticism thrown from a distance, but a radical love, highlighting the disease, identifying with it, indeed suffering for it, but also showing an alternative, 'more excellent' way. The resurrection of Jesus then shows that there is a way through judgment to life. The way of nationalism was broad and would lead to death, but the narrow way of Jesus would take one through judgment and lead to resurrection life (cf. Matt. 7:13).

The resurrection had another vital consequence. It could be taken as a divine confirmation that Jesus' alternative hermeneutic was indeed correct. Jesus' interpretation, risky and distinctive as it was, was vindicated. It endorsed his vision for Israel, his understanding of 'restoration', and his concept of how the Scriptures would be fulfilled. Ever since then, his followers have been given the challenge to read those same Scriptures in the same way as he did and in the light of what he achieved in and for Israel.

Some of this may have been sensed by Paul in the years after his conversion. N. T. Wright (1997: 25–37) argues that Paul, as a Pharisee, would quite likely have himself been an ardent nationalist. Our picture of Pharisaism before AD 70, he argues, has been distorted through the lens of the less politically concerned Hillelite party. Before that date the Shammaite party was far stronger, and in their grouping political nationalism was high on the agenda. The fact that Paul describes his earlier life as marked by 'zeal' (Gal. 1:14; Phil. 3:6) may well indicate that he was not so far removed politically from the later Zealot party. If so, the resurrection of Israel's Messiah after crucifixion on a Roman cross would be devastating in its impact.

Far from endorsing the nationalist agenda, this startling event revealed the poverty of that agenda; it showed that God's purposes for Israel were quite other than what Paul had expected. His fellow-Jews might look for the 'miraculous signs' (1 Cor. 1:22) – possibly signs of Israel's political restoration – but they would be disappointed. They would be presented instead with a crucified Messiah. Their hope was now cruciform. And they would have to go back to the Scriptures to see how this death and resurrection of Israel's Messiah were paradoxically the fulfilment of their prophetic hope in accordance with the Scriptures (1 Cor. 15:3). Paul himself became convinced that all the promises of God find their 'Yes' in Christ (2 Cor. 1:20). So as he looked at those scriptural promises he realized that each now needed to be understood in the light of Christ. The promise of God's blessing to the seed of Abraham was now accessible through Christ, himself the 'seed' (Gal. 3:8–22).

And the promise of the land could now be seen as a necessary stage in God's purposes (just as were the other symbols of Israel, such as the Torah) which could now be fulfilled as the gospel went out into all the world.

At this point we have come full circle in our argument – from Paul's theology back to Jesus' and out again to Paul's. The key point to note here, however, is that both Jesus and Paul were working in a climate of articulate Jewish nationalism, which drew much of its rationale from the prophetic scriptures concerning the restoration of Israel and the land. If this is so, it becomes impossible to suggest that the issue of the land passed them by, that they were hardly aware of it. On the contrary, this would have been an integral part of the theological map with which they needed to wrestle. If then their teaching gives to some the initial impression of dealing little with the land, this is far more likely an indication that they have now consciously processed this issue such that it appears in different forms – not that they have never considered it in the first place.

Our thesis is that the New Testament writers were well aware of this issue and that their distinctive views were a natural development of the direction which Jesus himself in his ministry had given to the debate. In his role as a Jewish eschatological prophet, Jesus had announced the time when God was at work to fulfil his ancient promises of restoration from exile and of blessings to the nations, of the conquest of evil and the coming of the King; he had also in his own person embodied the coming of God's kingdom. In this new age, however, Israel would experience judgment, and former Jewish symbols of identity would come to be redefined as the gospel of the kingdom went out to all nations. The divine purpose, in keeping with its original universal intention, now broke forth from the confines of Jerusalem and the land towards the world.

Conclusion: pointers towards a biblical theology

This argument for a biblical theology of the land clearly has some important consequences.

1. No biblical theology of the land is possible which bypasses Jesus on this issue. If it is acknowledged in other areas of biblical theology that Christ is the centre of the Bible, the same must apply

here. Christian biblical theology must be rightly and unashamedly Christological. And the Old Testament must be read through the lens of the New.

2. On this particular issue, this means acknowledging not only that Christ is the centre of the Bible in some spiritual sense, but also that the historical Jesus of Nazareth effected a dramatic turning-point in the scriptural narrative. In other words, we shall have the confidence to see the New Testament emphasis, not as a new 'spiritualizing' system which has jettisoned the physicality of the Old Testament promise and has arbitrarily imposed its own categories on the subject matter, but as rooted in the story. This is what Jesus of Nazareth did to the storyline; this is how he read the story so far; this is how the story worked itself out in the New Testament period; this is how that same story works itself out today. The systematic categories make sense and have validity because they reflect a true story. The so-called 'spiritual' approach is in fact rooted in history.

3. At work beneath this New Testament concept of the land is an awareness that the Old Testament's particularity, and its focus on the land, must be set against the wider backdrop of God's purposes for all humanity. The call to Abraham (Gen. 12) is the divine answer to the sin of Adam (Gen. 3), and the election of Israel always has the ultimate goal of the blessing of the nations (Gen. 12:3). The focus on the land of Israel was effectively a bridgehead within God's long-term purpose of reclaiming the *whole world* to himself and of bringing in his 'new creation', the restored Eden. The land can then be seen either as a temporary phase within God's eternal purposes or (perhaps more properly) as an eternal aspect of those purposes – but one which in the era of the new covenant is opened out to include all those who are in Christ, the true 'seed' of Abraham (Gal. 3:16). It thereby loses its physical particularity, but it still functions as a potent vehicle for God's purposes of blessing in his world.

4. Another aspect which our study has highlighted is the probable interrelationship within biblical theology of the three themes of land, city and temple. If this is correct, we can begin to see a pattern emerging in the New Testament's use of the Old. For there is explicit New Testament teaching concerning the fulfilment of the

temple in Christ. We can then work out from the clear to the less clear, from the temple through the city to the land, to see how the same phenomenon of fulfilment in Christ affects the issue of the land. It is worth noting that if one works in the reverse direction, from the land to the temple (i.e. from the less clear to the more clear) one might reach some quite different results. Many dispensational treatments fail to allow the New Testament teaching concerning the temple adequately to shape their thinking about the land.

5. Further work will need to be done on how exactly the various New Testament understandings of the land interrelate. On the basis of Hebrews it is often thought that 'land' in the Old Testament corresponds almost entirely to 'heaven' in the New Testament.[11] Yet, as we have seen, there are other outworkings of this theme in the New Testament writers.

A strong argument, for example, could be made for saying that the prime analogue of 'land' in the New Testament era is not 'heaven' but the inhabited world over which the rule of Israel's God is now to be known. Hence Paul's language in Romans 4:13.[12] Hence too the possible parallelism between the books of Joshua and Acts, with the apostles' going out with the gospel to 'the ends of the earth' corresponding to the Israelites' entrance into the promised land.[13]

Moreover, Davies's argument that for Paul the concept of being 'in Christ' has effectively replaced the blessings of being 'in the land' also needs to be taken into consideration. If John's Gospel presents Jesus himself as the true temple and the true 'holy place',[14] then in some senses *Christ himself* is the fulfilment of the land.

Yet another suggestion comes from C. J. H. Wright (1983: 84), who argues that in some instances the New Testament equivalent of land is the Christian fellowship (or *koinōnia*) – the place of shared commitments, the place where God's rule is to be recognized.

We can already see at least four different New Testament analo-

[11] See e.g. Goldsworthy 1991: 303, though for Goldsworthy the first application is in fact to Christ himself; cf. Goldsworthy 1981: 92.

[12] See above, p. 100.

[13] On this, see further Chapman 1989: 141–142.

[14] See above, p. 111.

gues for the land: heaven, the world, Christ himself and Christian fellowship. A creative biblical theology will have room for each where it is appropriate, and will not force the biblical material into only one channel to the exclusion of the others.

6. Nothing in our argument need militate against also seeing some appropriate applications of biblical land-theology in the realms of modern society and economics. Our argument has focused on how Jesus and the New Testament writers might understand the ongoing significance of the particular physical land of Israel. Yet the land also functioned in the Old Testament in a quite different way: as the arena in which the divine pattern for human communities was gradually revealed. In Hebrew, concrete expressions are often preferred to abstract ones (e.g. 'sword', to 'war'). So in this case 'land' might on some occasions be better translated by 'society'. An application of biblical land-theology to modern society (such as espoused by C. J. H. Wright) need not therefore be excluded. The New Testament points to a Christ-focused interpretation of the *promise* of the land, but some of the *principles* about life in the land may well be carried over into the New Testament era.[15] The 'spiritual' interpretation of the 'promise' does not necessarily require an otherworldly approach to these principles. The two can complement each other.

7. Finally, concerning the issue of helping Christians to view the modern State of Israel biblically, our analysis highlights the following points:

- Jesus and the resurrection remain central.
- The Old Testament must be interpreted in the light of the New.
- Jesus must be acknowledged as both thoroughly Jewish and yet critical of Israel, daring to take the story of Israel in a new direction focused around himself.
- The apparent silence of the New Testament must not be construed as tantamount to its ignorance or lack of concern about the unfulfilled promise concerning the land.
- The Christological approach can be seen not as mere 'spiritualizing' but rather as rooted in Jesus of Nazareth (the second point

[15] See further C. J. H. Wright 1990, and Armerding, below, p. ch.6A.

in this list), giving Christians confidence to uphold this traditional, classical and apostolic hermeneutic in the face of modern dispensational approaches.

- The New Testament blessings, which are found now 'in Christ' and not 'in the land', must be presented to *all* those in the Holy Land.
- And (most importantly) we can see that those prophetic texts which inspire people today were having the same effect in the first century, but also that Jesus and the apostles rejected the literalistic (or, we might even say, 'Zionist') approach. If this was correct then, is it not equally valid today? Or are we to believe that we live in quite different 'days'?

It need hardly be said that the Holy Land today is raising profound issues for the Christian church – both about its past and about its vision for the future. A good measure of the conflict within Christian circles emanates from different approaches to this very topic addressed here in these two chapters. They are offered in the hope that they might take some of the heat out of this debate by bringing in some light. In particular we have sought to hear again the living voice of the New Testament, set within its proper historical context, and to highlight the importance of Jesus as a historical figure in the story.

Jesus is also a living reality, the one who alone is our true peace, the one in whom the 'dividing wall' between Jew and Gentile has been broken down (Eph. 2:14). Only through focusing on him can our various theologies concerning the land ever find a measure of reconciliation. And he alone, through his incarnate ministry, can set us a true example of how to walk amid the confusing agendas of the Holy Land, swayed neither by theologically defended nationalism nor by the desire for revenge. He offers us an alternative, seldom tried, but well worth following. And into this situation he speaks with a refreshingly different voice, which we need to obey.

Bibliography

Bauckham, R. J. (1988), 'Jesus' demonstration in the temple', in B. Lindars (ed.), *Law and Religion*, Cambridge: Cambridge University Press: 72–89.

Chapman, C. (1989), *Whose Promised Land?*, Tring: Lion. Rev. edn.
Davies, W. D. (1974), *The Gospel and the Land: Early Christianity and Jewish Territorial Doctrine*, Berkeley: University of California Press.
Dodd, C. H. (1947), 'The fall of Jerusalem and the abomination of desolation', *Journal of Roman Studies* 37: 47–55, repr. in his *More New Testament Studies*, Manchester: Manchester University Press: 69–83.
——— (1952), *According to the Scriptures*, London: Nisbet.
Evans, C. A. (1989), 'Jesus' action in the temple: cleansing or portent of destruction?', *Catholic Biblical Quarterly* 51: 237–270.
France, R. T. (1975), 'Old Testament prophecy and the future of Israel', *Tyndale Bulletin* 26: 53–78.
Goldsworthy, G. (1981), *Gospel and Kingdom: A Christian Interpretation of the Old Testament*, Exeter: Paternoster.
——— (1991), *According to Plan: The Unfolding Revelation of the Bible*, Leicester: IVP.
Holwerda, D. E. (1995), *Jesus and Israel: One Covenant or Two*? Leicester: Apollos.
Kreider, R. (n.d.), 'The covenant and the land' (unpublished paper).
Meyer, B. F. (1979), *The Aims of Jesus*, London: SCM.
Robertson, O. P. (1996), *Understanding the Land of the Bible: A Biblical-Theological Guide*, Phillipsburg: Presbyterian and Reformed.
Sanders, E. P. (1985), *Jesus and Judaism*, Philadelphia: Fortress.
Walker, P. W. L. (1996), *Jesus and the Holy City: New Testament perspectives on Jerusalem*, Grand Rapids: Eerdmans.
——— (ed.), (1994), *Jerusalem Past and Present in the Purposes of God*, Carlisle: Paternoster. Rev. edn.
Wright, C. J. H. (1983), *Living as the People of God: The Relevance of Old Testament Ethics*, Leicester: IVP.
——— (1990), *God's People in God's Land: Family, Land and Property in the Old Testament*, Grand Rapids: Eerdmans.
——— (1994), 'A Christian approach to Old Testament prophecy concerning Israel', in Walker 1994: 1–19.
Wright, N. T. (1985), 'Jesus, Israel and the cross', *Society for Biblical Literature Seminar Papers*, Atlanta: Scholars.
——— (1996), *Jesus and the Victory of God*, London: SPCK.
——— (1997), *What Saint Paul Really Said: Was Paul of Tarsus the Real Founder of Christianity?* Oxford: Lion.

4. THE LAND IN CHRISTIAN THEOLOGY

4A
A new-covenant perspective on the land[1]

O. Palmer Robertson

Introduction

It has been rightly observed that the idea of land as a theological factor has been largely overlooked both by Judaism and by Christianity.[2] Except for eschatological speculations concerning the return of Israel to the land, the whole concept of land as presented in Scripture has been generally neglected. The reasons for this hiatus in theological thinking might be variously evaluated.[3] But unquestionably the significance of land as a theological idea needs fuller

[1] This is a slightly revised version of a paper delivered at the first consultation on 'The Theology of the Land' sponsored by the Levant Study Center and held in Droushia, Cyprus, in July 1996.

[2] Cf. Davies 1974: 3–5. One significant work is Brueggemann 1978, which involves many stimulating proposals. However, he allows his sociological perspective undue influence, e.g. in appeal to a lesson from Marxist philosophy (p. 111).

[3] Davies (1974: 3–4) faults Christianity's concentration on abstract ideas about God and the world rather than on the concrete significance of the land-promise as it would relate to an ongoing Israel. Cf. also Davies 1991: xvii–xviii.

exploration.[4] This study proposes to consider one aspect of the subject of 'land' as it appears in Scripture. Attention will be focused specifically on the topic of land as promised in the old covenant and as fulfilled in the new.

Preliminary to a proper understanding of the relation of old-covenant promise to new-covenant fulfilment is a recognition of the fact that the administration of the old covenant came in the limited form of temporal shadow, type, image and prophecy, in contrast to the categories of reality, substance, fulfilment and permanence as found in the new covenant. These contrasting categories come to expression in various ways in the writings of the New Testament. Throughout Matthew's Gospel, significant events in the life of Jesus are explained as occurring so that old-covenant anticipations might be fulfilled (Matt. 2:15, 17, 23; 13:14, 35; 26:54, 56; 27:9). John declares that God now 'tabernacles' with his people in a way that far surpasses the dwelling of God with Israel in the days of their wilderness wandering (John 1:14), that the angels of God now ascend and descend on the Son of Man rather than on Jacob's visionary ladder (1:51), that the lifting up of the Son of God supersedes the lifting of the serpent in the wilderness (3:14), and that the manna from heaven given by Moses has been transformed into 'living bread' given by Christ (6:49–51). Paul speaks of the religious festivals of the old covenant as 'a *shadow* of the things that were to come' (Col. 2:17) and the events of Israel's redemptive history as *types* for the believers of the new-covenant age (1 Cor. 10:6). All these authors of new-covenant documents develop a significant aspect of their theology by contrasting old-covenant shadows with new-covenant realities.

But it is particularly in the epistle to the Hebrews that this contrast between anticipation and realization, between shadow and reality, finds its fullest and most distinctive expression. According to the writer to the Hebrews, the administration of redemption under the law of the old covenant was 'only a shadow' of the good things that were coming (Heb. 10:1). These shadowy images of redemptive reality are not represented as having their origin merely in the

[4] Cf. von Rad 1943: 79–93: 'In the whole of the Hexateuch there is probably no more important idea than that expressed in terms of the land promised and later granted by Yahweh . . .' (p. 79).

context of the old-covenant experiences. Instead, these prophetic shadows are presented in Hebrews as having their origin in the abiding realities of heaven itself. Because Melchizedek, the priest/king, was made 'like' the Son of God in his eternal relationship to the Father, he could anticipate the priestly role of Jesus (7:1, 3). Only because the tabernacle of the wilderness was constructed precisely 'according to the pattern' shown to Moses on the mount could its worship pattern provide insight into the realities of a proper approach to God under the provisions of the new covenant (8:5).

This principle has great significance when it is applied to the idea of land as experienced by Israel under the administration of the old covenant. For the land-promise also had its origin in the heavenly realities and not merely in the temporal experiences of Israel. According to the writer to the Hebrews, Abraham and the patriarchs longed for a 'better country – a *heavenly* one' (11:16, my emphasis). They understood, though only dimly, that the land promised them actually had its origins in the heavenly, eternal reality that yet remained before them. As a consequence, it is unthinkable that once the people of God have tasted of these eternal, heavenly realities they should somehow be thrust back into living with the old-covenant forms that could only foreshadow the realities of new-covenant fulfilments. Instead of moving toward a worship centre localized in modern-day Jerusalem, the new-covenant believer joins with the angels to worship at the 'heavenly Jerusalem, the city of the living God' (12:22).

According to all these different documents of the new covenant, the mode of administration of redemption under the old covenant was prophetically typological in nature, anticipating the substantial realities of the new covenant. Other examples may be cited to substantiate this same principle. The sacrifice of animals and foodstuffs anticipated the offering of the body of Jesus under the new covenant. A temporal priesthood anticipated the permanent priesthood of Christ. The mobile tabernacle foreshadowed the abiding presence of God's glory in the person of Jesus. As the Israelites journeyed through the desert, God provided them manna from heaven, water from the rock, and a serpent on a pole. All these images found their new-covenant fulfilment not in more manna and water, or a larger serpent on a taller pole, but in the redemptive realities that these old-covenant forms foreshadowed (see e.g. John 3:14; 6:51; 7:37; Rom. 15:16). The very nature of the old-covenant provisions requires that they be viewed in terms of prophetic shadows instead of permanent realities.

This relation of prophetic shadow to substantial fulfilment becomes increasingly evident as the theme of the land is traced throughout Scripture: first in the actual history of Israel, then in the psalms and prophets, and finally within the documents of the new covenant itself. In reviewing this material, it will be helpful to note that the idea of land in Scripture centres particularly on two basic concepts, one broad and one focused: (1) the totality of the area known as the land of the Bible, and (2) the city of Jerusalem with its locale at Mount Zion.[5]

The land in Israel's historical experience

The theological idea of land as a framework for experiencing the blessing of God originates in Paradise.[6] This simple fact, so often overlooked, plays a critical role in evaluating the significance of the land in terms of its consummate fulfilment. Land as a factor of theological significance did not begin with the promise given to Abraham (Gen. 12). Instead, the patriarch's hope of possessing a land arose out of the prospect of restoration to the original state from which humanity had fallen (Gen. 3).[7] The idea of land as originating in the Paradise of creation had a specific significance in shaping the expectations associated with redemption. As the locale of blessedness arising from unbroken fellowship and communion with the one true living God, the land of Paradise became the goal toward which redeemed humanity was returning.

Land as Paradise was lost in the fall. The sinful couple was expelled from the land of exclusive blessing. But the idea of Paradise

[5] The centrality of Jerusalem in the land-experience of Israel is developed extensively in Holwerda 1995: 106–112. For a thorough analysis of the significance of Jerusalem for New Testament theology, see Walker 1996.

[6] Cf. the stimulating article of C. J. H. Wright 1993: 153–167: 'Reflections on land obviously have to begin with the biblical theme of creation . . .' (p. 153).

[7] Cf. Alexander 1995: 25: 'whereas the early chapters of Genesis focus on the loss of land as a result of disobedience, Abraham is portrayed as gaining the land due to obedience and trust in God'.

was renewed in the imagery of the promise concerning the land in the commitment God made to redeem humanity from its fallen condition. As Adam and Eve had known God's blessing in Eden, so God would bless his people in a new land. This idea of restoration to Paradise provides the proper biblical context for understanding God's promise of a land to Abraham (Gen. 12:1).

This divine promise was restated to Moses in terms of a 'land flowing with milk and honey' (Exod. 3:8, 17; 13:5; 33:3; Lev. 20:24; Num. 13:27; etc.). This description of the promised land intentionally reflects the nature of Paradise. Yet the reality of the condition of the land as experienced by Israel was quite different, as can be sensed from an old Jewish fable. According to this, God at creation commissioned two storks to scatter stones all over the face of the earth. The stones had been divided into two bags so that the two storks could distribute them across the earth's surface. But one stork's bag broke over the land of the Bible, so half the world's stones are located in Israel!

In the time of David and Solomon the full extent of the land was described as stretching from the Tigris-Euphrates to the River of Egypt. In this restored Paradise of the kingdom, every man would sit under his vine and his fig-tree (1 Kgs. 4:25; Mic. 4:4; Zech. 3:10). Yet from the beginning, the actual experience of the people with reference to the land was quite different. From Solomon's day onwards, the people experienced oppression rather than Paradise, which had the effect of placing this promise firmly within the category of an old-covenant shadow that would have to wait for the arrival of new-covenant realities for the actual fulfilment of the promise.

The possession of the land under the old covenant, therefore, did not realize the final goal of God's purposes in redemption. Instead, land-possession always fitted within the category of shadows, types and prophecies characteristic of the old covenant in its presentation of redemptive truth. Just as the tabernacle was never intended to be a settled item in the plan of redemption, but rather was designed to point to Christ's tabernacling among his people (cf. John 1:14), and just as the sacrificial system could never atone for sins, but could only foreshadow the offering of the sacrifice of the Son of God (Heb. 9:23–26), so in a similar manner the patriarch Abraham received the promise of the land but never experienced the blessing of full possession. By this non-possession, the patriarch learned to look forward 'to the city with foundations, whose architect and builder is God' (Heb. 11:10). Abraham and his immediate descendants never returned to the fatherland which they had left, because 'they were longing for a better country – a heavenly one' (Heb. 11:15–16). As a consequence, even the denial of the realization of the promise to the patriarchs served the purposes of God by forcing them (and also us) to look beyond their present experience to the future reality. According to one analysis,

> ... the patriarchs were looking forward, not so much to the day when their descendants would inherit the physical Land, as to the day when they themselves would inherit the heavenly country which the physical Land signified. They 'saw through' the promise of the Land, looking beyond it to a deeper, spiritual reality. The promise concerning the Land, whilst real and valid in its own terms, pointed typologically to something greater (Walker 1996: 212).

At this early stage, the central role of Jerusalem as a focal point in the land-promise is also foreshadowed. Abraham paid tithes to Melchizedek, the priest/king of (Jeru)Salem (Gen. 14:20). At this important place, Abraham also presented his son Isaac as an offering to God (Gen. 22:2; 2 Chr. 3:1). But in both these cases, the events associated with Jerusalem pointed to the greater realities of the new covenant: namely, the heavenly priesthood of Christ after 'the order of Melchizedek' (Heb. 7:15–17) and the once-for-all sacrifice of the Son of God, a better offering than of Isaac (cf. Heb. 7:26–27).

Subsequent to the life of Abraham, the nation of Israel moves in and out of the land. As a landless people during the bondage instituted by Pharaoh, they suffer with the 'reproach of Egypt' (Josh. 5:9). This condition prevails for four hundred years until the conquest of Joshua. The people then possess the land during the period of the judges and the kings, but their possession is never perfected. A restored paradise in the land remains as a tantalizing possibility which never comes to full realization. Solomon ruins his prospects for enjoying the full blessing of the land by importing foreign gods and tolerating the worship assemblies of his heathen wives on the 'Hill of Corruption', just across the valley from the temple mount (1 Kgs. 11:7–8; 2 Kgs. 23:13). During this period, invading armies sent by the Lord repeatedly chastise the people for living in unfaithfulness while in the land (1 Kgs. 11:14, 22–25). Finally, the people are dispossessed from the land altogether (2 Kgs. 17:22, 23; 25:21). They are driven out, exiled from the promise that had been given to their ancestors.

Of course, Jerusalem could not possibly be dispossessed so long as the Shekinah, the visual manifestation of God's Glory, dwelt in its midst. This fact underscores the significance of Ezekiel's vision of the step-by-step departure of the Glory from the city (cf. Ezek. 9 – 11). First, the Glory of the God of Israel rises from above the cherubim in the Most Holy Place, where it had resided since the day Solomon dedicated the temple, and moves to the threshold of the temple (9:3; cf. 1 Kgs. 8:10–11). Next, Ezekiel hears the whirling wheels of the cherubim that dwelt above the ark, indicating that they are on the move (10:13). Then the Glory of the Lord departs from the threshold of the temple and moves, along with the cherubim and the whirling wheels, to the east gate of the Lord's house (10:16–19). Finally, the Glory of God along with the cherubim and the wheels rises above the city of Jerusalem and hovers over the mountain east of it, the Mount of Olives (11:22–23).

What are these 'whirling wheels', and what is their significance in the book of Ezekiel? The key to answering these questions appears to be found in the provisions made by David for Solomon's building of the temple. Among other things, David left for Solomon his son 'the plan for the chariot, that is, the cherubim of gold that spread their wings and shelter the ark of the covenant of the LORD' (1 Chr. 28:18). In other words, a 'chariot' with 'wheels' was a portion of the structure of the ark and its paraphernalia. The 'wheels' associated with the ark then came to symbolize the fact that God's presence among his people had a mobile characteristic.[8] It

[8] Cf. Selman 1994: 254: 'A chariot (v. 18) is unknown elsewhere as part of the temple furniture, but its connection with the winged cherubim suggests the idea of God's mobile throne (cf. Ps. 18:10; Ezk. 1:15ff.).' Keil (1976–7: 294) relates the 'chariot' to the cherubim, noting that Ezekiel saw wheels on the throne of God under the cherubim. This interpretation is supported by the rendering of the LXX and the Vulgate.

could not be presumed that he would always remain within the Jerusalem sanctuary. So the chariot with wheels associated with the ark of the covenant proved a fitting symbol that anticipated the message which Ezekiel would bring.

Once the Glory had departed from Jerusalem, the city was as vulnerable as any other place on the face of the earth. Its consecration to the Lord had been lost, and so the city was no longer 'holy'. It was neither dedicated to the Lord nor guaranteed his protection. As a consequence, the exile of Jerusalem's inhabitants could not be avoided.

So the loss of the 'land' was laden with theological significance. When the possession of this land is viewed as a sign of the blessings of the covenant of redemption, its loss must have equally widespread implications. Dispossession and loss of the land must mean the loss of redemptive blessings. Those who once had been God's people may become 'not-my-people' (*lō' 'ammî*, Hos. 1:9).

Yet the history of God's people under the old covenant did not end with exile. At God's appointed time, the chosen of the Lord were graciously granted the privilege of returning to the land (Ezra 1:1–3). They came back, however, as a small body of only 49,000 (Ezra 2:64). In addition, they came to only a tiny territory, and were able to rebuild only a small replica of the original temple (Ezra 3:10–12).

Nevertheless, God's prophets were not distracted from their vision of the greatness of God's redemptive work. On the contrary, they painted a picture of land restoration so glorious that it could not be contained within the boundaries of the old-covenant forms of realization. Jerusalem, they declared, would be a city 'without walls', with 'a wall of fire' about it, and the Glory of the Lord 'within' (Zech. 2:1–5). The reconstructed temple would manifest a greater glory than Solomon's magnificent structure (Hag. 2:9). The language is inspired and inspiring, but once more the reality as experienced under the old covenant remains much less impressive. In fact, this extravagant picture of a city without walls but with a wall of fire about it, with Gentile nations streaming into its confines, breaks the bonds of all the old-covenant images. How can such images find their fulfilment?

The realization of these glorious prospects, as in the case of all old-covenant shadows, must be perceived as occurring in the days of the new covenant, when people worship neither in Jerusalem nor in Samaria, but wherever in the world the Spirit of God manifests himself (John 4:21–24). The redemptive reality that the old-covenant city could only foreshadow finds its consummate realization in the 'Jerusalem above' that is the 'mother of us all' (Gal. 4:26). This 'Jerusalem above', however, is not a merely 'spiritual' phenomenon with no connection to the 'real' world in which we live. Its reality injects itself constantly into the lives of God's people. For every time Christians assemble for worship they join with the host of the 'heavenly Jerusalem' (Heb. 12:22).

Once this stage of consummate fulfilment has been reached, never again will the revelation from God suggest that his people should aspire to the old, typological ways of the old covenant. Progression toward consummation in the new covenant does not allow for a retrogression to the older, shadowy forms.

The land in the teaching of the prophets and Psalms

In both the Psalms and the prophets a full recognition is given to the ongoing significance of a 'land of promise' in redemptive history. Yet the movement toward the new-covenant era presses the conception of land well beyond the geographical limits of Palestine.

In the Psalms, the inheritance of the land is celebrated as one of the greatest blessings of redemption. Psalm 37 encourages the people of God not to despair over the prosperity of the wicked, but to trust the Lord's promises that they will 'inherit the land'. Six times over, an almost identical phrase is used:

> For evil men will be cut off,
> but those who hope in the Covenant LORD *will inherit the land* (v. 9).

> A little while, and the wicked will be no more . . .
> But the meek *will inherit the land* (vv. 10–11).

> . . . those the Covenant LORD blesses *will inherit the land,*
> but those he curses will be cut off (v. 22).

Turn from evil and do good;
then you *will dwell in the land* for ever (v. 27).

... the righteous *will inherit the land*
and dwell in it for ever (v. 29).

Wait for the Covenant LORD
and keep his way.
He will exalt you to *inherit the land* (v. 34).[9]

As this Psalm was celebrated regularly in the assembled congregation of God's people, it must have had the effect of strengthening the concept in the minds of the people that the land of redemption was God's gift to them. Yet this assurance was clearly given not to the wicked and unbelieving from among Israel, but only to the righteous and faithful. This principle regarding the possession of the land has a vital application in the present day. Never can the promise of the land be claimed by those who fail to exercise true faith and faithfulness in the Redeemer provided by the LORD of the covenant.

In this regard, it is sometimes suggested that possession of the land by Israel is a totally unconditional promise that cannot fail. According to one analysis (Davies 1991: 9), the 'Priestly' redaction of the pentateuchal material that occurred in later Israelite history 'changed' the content of the covenant by heightening its promissory character. As a consequence, 'Israel's election, and with it the possession of the Land, can never, for P, become conditional on obedience to the Law; that election, resting upon the Abrahamic covenant, cannot be annulled by human disobedience. Israel, it follows, cannot be destroyed, and the Land *will* be hers.'

This conclusion may be reached only by eliminating significant portions of the biblical witness concerning the covenant that God established with Israel. A proper treatment of the promise in total context cannot deny the conditional elements of the covenant.[10]

[9] NIV translation modified by using 'Covenant LORD' to convey the meaning of the tetragrammaton, the covenant name for God in the Old Testament. My emphasis.

[10] Brueggemann (1998: 419–420) rightly denies the 'unconditional' character of some of the biblical covenants. But he wrongly blames this 'false dichotomy' on Paul's effort to

Abraham was required from the beginning of God's dealing with him to leave his own homeland and family. Subsequently he was told that he must walk before the Lord and 'be blameless' (Gen. 17:1). Indeed, it is quite appropriate to speak of the *certainty of the fulfilment* of the conditions of the covenant, so that the intended blessings will come. But a convincing case cannot be made for the idea that the covenants of God had no conditions. The recognition of the presence of conditions properly forces the student of Scripture to look toward one who would fulfil the conditions of the covenant perfectly on behalf of his people. But this recognition will lead in a direction totally different from one based on the idea that the land belongs to Israel in perpetuity without any regard for their response of faith and faithfulness with respect to the demands of covenant loyalty.

In turning to the prophets, a number of passages may be seen as focusing on the significance of land in the expectations for Israel's future. Perhaps the boldest of the prophetic pictures of the future with respect to the land is found in the prophecy of Isaiah. In a most dramatic reversal of roles, the prophet declares that an 'altar for the Covenant LORD' will be raised up in the land, 'with a monument to the Covenant LORD at its border' (Is. 19:19, my translation). Only in this case, the land of which he speaks is Egypt! The people of this land will cry out because of their oppressors, and the LORD will send them a saviour, a deliverer (v. 20). Indeed, the LORD will strike them with a plague as he did in the days of Moses; but then he will heal them (v. 22). Across the lands will be built 'a highway from Egypt to Assyria' (v. 23). Although this highway will pass directly through Israel, the travellers will continue on their way so they can worship the Covenant LORD in the lands of Egypt and Assyria. It is almost as though the land of Israel is to be bypassed! Yet Israel's land will not be entirely neglected, for 'in that day Israel will be the third, along with Egypt and Assyria, a blessing on the earth' (v. 24).

Isaiah's vision of the Lord's future plans for his land is amazing.

---

distinguish the Christian gospel from its Jewish counterpart, by claiming for Christians the 'gospel beforehand' as proclaimed to Abraham while assigning Moses and the law to his Jewish opponents. Paul plainly states that the law could not add a codicil to the promise previously given (Gal. 3:15), and is in no way opposed to the promises of God (Gal. 3:21).

Israel is not first, but third after Egypt and Assyria. The land of Israel will be a part of God's future plan, but the overall orientation of the lands of nations will be radically altered. In Isaiah's vision, the land characterized as the place of redemptive work by the Covenant LORD will not be the same as it had been previously. New lands will be claimed equally by the Lord.

Ezekiel's message is also vitally important. As previously noted, his message in the first portion of his book concerned the departing of God's Glory from the city of Jerusalem. The end of his book, however, describes the returning of the Glory. But what will be the framework in which this departed Glory of the Lord will return? The circumstance is made plain in Ezekiel's vision of the valley of dry bones:

> This is what the Sovereign LORD says: O my people, I am going to open your graves and bring you up from them; I will bring you back to the land of Israel. Then you, my people, will know that I am the LORD, when I open your graves and bring you up from them. I will put my Spirit in you and you will live, and I will settle you in your own land. Then you will know that I the LORD have spoken, and I have done it, declares the LORD (Ezek. 37:12–14).

Clearly, Ezekiel is talking about a return to the land. But exactly what does his prophecy anticipate? Some interpreters have suggested that the prophet is only using figurative language of bodily resurrection that anticipates nothing more than the return of Israel to the land.[11] But then of course the origin of this imagery must be explained. Where did Ezekiel get the idea of talking about a return from exile in terms of the opening of graves? Certainly he did not derive it from the cultic enactment of the myth of a dying and rising god, as some have proposed.[12]

Previous biblical references acknowledging the power of God to raise the dead support an understanding of the prophet's vision to go beyond merely a wondrous return of exiles to the land of

[11] E.g. Taylor 1969: 236, emphatically, Eichrodt 1970: 509, Zimmerli 1983: 264.
[12] E.g. Zimmerli 1983: 264, citing Riesenfeld.

promise.[13] As one critical scholar has noted: 'that God by a miracle could restore the dead to life no devout Israelite ever doubted'.[14] The scepticism of the Sadducees of New Testament times regarding the prospect of resurrection for the dead would require at least a modification of this all-embracing assertion (cf. Matt. 22:23–32 and par.). Yet Jesus' response to this very scepticism indicates his assumption that testimony to bodily resurrection was a part of Old Testament teaching: 'You are in error *because you do not know the Scriptures* or the power of God' (Matt. 22:29, my emphasis). Only a few cases of actual resurrection from the dead are recorded in the Old Testament (1 Kgs. 17:17–24; 2 Kgs. 4:18–37; 13:20–21). But additional witness to the possibility of resurrection may be found scattered throughout the Scriptures. In reasoning about the relation of Isaac's role in God's promise to the divine command to sacrifice his son, Abraham concluded that if necessary God could raise Isaac from the dead (Heb. 11:19; cf. Gen. 22:5: '*We* will worship and then *we* will come back to you'; my emphasis). Rather than despairing as he grew older without possessing the promise of the land, Abraham began to look for a city 'whose architect and builder' was God, and for a 'better country' that had the characteristics of heavenly realities (Heb. 11:10, 16). Joseph showed his confidence in the upcoming exodus by giving a commandment concerning the disposition of his bones (Gen. 50:25; Heb. 11:22). But why was he so concerned that his bones be transported to the land of promise? It could be that he expressed this concern for purely sentimental reasons. On the other hand, his determination in this matter may indicate that he expected to participate personally in the possession of the land that had been promised. If Abraham had come to look for a heaven-like, eternal realization of the land-promise (Heb. 11:10, 16), then almost certainly this expectation would have been passed on to later generations that would have included Joseph (cf. Gen. 18:17–19). It is not indicated specifically that Moses himself

[13] Cf. Block's extensive treatment (1998: 381–392), noting Jewish and Christian interpretations of Ezekiel's vision as describing an actual resurrection.. Block discusses several resurrection passages that pre-date Ezekiel (pp. 386–387, and n. 97), and concludes: 'In a new and dramatic way, the conviction that the grave need not be the end provided a powerful vehicle for announcing the full restoration of Israel. The curse would be lifted. Yahweh would bring his people back to life' (p. 387).

[14] Skinner, cited and countered in Taylor 1969: 236.

fully grasped all the implications of God's self-revelation at the burning bush. Nevertheless, he heard the Covenant LORD identify himself as the God of Abraham despite the fact that the patriarch had been dead for almost five hundred years; and God is not a God of the dead but of the living (Exod. 3:6; Matt. 22:32). Repeatedly the fulfilment of the land-promise was associated with life beyond death, and the word from the LORD to Ezekiel fits squarely into this expectation.[15] At a minimum, Ezekiel's prophecy of the return to the land involves God's putting his Spirit in people so that they come alive (Ezek. 37:14a). This description of new life generated by God's Spirit appears to be the most likely scripture that Jesus expected Nicodemus to know as they discussed the necessity of being 'born of water and the Spirit' (John 3:5, 10). But the specificness of Ezekiel's language regarding the uncovering of graves, as well as the context of dry, dead bones coming to life, suggests the reality of bodily resurrection. Upon the opening of graves and the coming alive of the dead, a return to the land will be effected.

Often a point of emphasis is placed on the two stages involved in this process of resurrection as described by Ezekiel.[16] First the bones and sinews come together, and then the Spirit of God breathes life. It has been proposed that the two phases represent first Israel's return to the land without the vitality of new spiritual life from God, and then the revival of true faith in the coming Messiah.

But the obvious parallel with the creation account in Genesis 2:7 makes it plain that this return to life, though in two stages, must be viewed as a single event. First God formed a man of the dust of the earth, and then he breathed into his nostrils the breath of life. Only after this second action of the Creator was the man declared a 'living being'. In a similar fashion, the skeleton formed by the coming together of the bones in Ezekiel was a totally lifeless being still lying at the foot of the valley. Only after the breath of life from God entered the skeleton did it come to life.

[15] In spite of serious questioning by many of the presence of resurrection faith in the Old Testament, additional passages deserving careful consideration may be noted: Ps. 16:9–11 (cf. Acts 2:24–32); Ps. 17:15 (cf. 1 John 3:2); Is. 25:6–8 (cf. Rev. 21:4); 26:19; Dan. 12:2–3 (cf. John 5:28–29). Paul's summation of the gospel which he had received and which he passed on includes the affirmation that Christ 'was raised on the third day *according to the Scriptures*' (1 Cor. 15:4).

[16] Cf. Feinberg 1969: 214.

From this perspective on Ezekiel's prophecy, it would seem evident that the minimal return from exile that occured shortly after Ezekiel's own day could not be regarded as the consummate fulfilment of expectations created by his prophecy. Israel's return at that time, as significant for redemptive history as it might have been, served in its turn to point to a greater restoration in accord with the provisions of the new covenant.

The return of the Jews to the land in the twentieth century, eventuating in the formation of the modern State of Israel in 1948, should not be regarded as a fulfilment of this prophecy of Ezekiel. For their re-formation involved no opening of graves, no resurrection of the body, no inpouring of the Spirit of God, and no affirmation of Jesus as the Christ of the consummating covenant. However the restoration of the State of Israel may be viewed, it does not fulfil the expectation of Ezekiel as described in this most vivid prophecy. Instead, this picture of a people brought to newness of life by the Spirit of God naturally leads to a consideration of the role of the land in the new covenant.[17]

The land from a new-covenant perspective

How does this long historical development of land significance under the old covenant translate into the categories of fulfilment within the new covenant? It must be remembered at the outset that transferral between these two eras of God's working in the world inescapably involves a movement from shadow to reality. The old-covenant form of redemption is indeed glorious and appeals to the human longing for a sure and settled land. Yet it cannot compare with the realities of new-covenant fulfilment.

This perspective is confirmed by a number of references in the new-covenant documents. Note first how Abraham is declared to be the heir, not of the land, but of the cosmos (Rom. 4:13). Here the

[17] Similarly Walker 1996: 313, concerning Ezekiel's vision of the restored temple. The New Testament writers 'were presumably not expecting Ezekiel's prophecy to be fulfilled literally at some future point in a physical Temple. Instead this prophecy became a brilliant way of speaking pictorially of what God had now achieved in and through Jesus. Paradoxically, therefore, although Ezekiel's vision had focused so much upon the Temple, it found its ultimate fulfilment in that city where there was "no Temple", because "its Temple is the Lord God Almighty and the Lamb" (Rev. 21:22).'

imagery of land as a picture of restored Paradise has finally come of age. The thing that depicts the consummation of God's redemptive work within a fallen world is no longer merely a portion of the earth. Instead, the whole of the cosmos participates in this glorious rejuvenation.

How does this perspective effect an understanding of the return to the land described by Ezekiel and the other prophets? In the nature of things Old Testament writers such as Ezekiel could employ only the images with which they and their hearers were familiar. In their case, the idea of restoration to the geographical land from which Israel had been deported represented the fulfilment of their fondest hopes. Yet in the context of the realities of the new covenant, this land must be understood in terms of the newly re-created cosmos about which the apostle Paul speaks in Romans. The whole universe groans in its travail, waiting for the redemption that will come with the resurrection of the bodies of the redeemed (Rom. 8:22–23). The return to Paradise in the framework of the new covenant does not involve a return to the shadowy forms of the old covenant. It means a rejuvenation of the entire cosmos. By this renewal of the entirety of creation, the land-promise of the old covenant finds its new-covenant realization.

The same perspective can be seen in Jesus' reference in his Sermon on the Mount to the promise of the Psalms concerning the inheriting of the land, which was discussed earlier. What did Jesus mean when he spoke of the meek inheriting the earth (Matt. 5:5)? Although the Greek term found in the Beatitudes is the same as that used in the Septuagint for the 'land' (*gē*), the context of Jesus' Beatitudes requires that the perspective be stretched beyond mere possession of Palestine. Rather than the Jewish race inheriting the promised land, Jesus teaches that in the new covenant the 'meek', regardless of their ethnic background, will inherit the 'earth' – wherever in this world they might live.

Yet Christian and Jewish theologians in the present day continue to interpret the land-promise of the old covenant in terms of its typological dimensions rather than recognizing the greater dimensions of new-covenant fulfilments. In this regard, many would view the establishment of the modern State of Israel in the twentieth century as a fulfilment of the promise of the land as it was originally given to the patriarchs.[18] Some would go further and even see the use of force in displacing the current inhabitants of the land as a legitimate re-enactment of the conquest as it was ordered by God in the days of Joshua.[19] While some secular Jews view this process as merely a step necessary to secure their national existence, others interpret this policy in terms of a reclaiming of the land as promised to the patriarchs of old. In this very concrete way, the old-covenant typological concept of land-possession has been superimposed on the radically different circumstances of the new-covenant era.

In his letter to the predominantly Gentile church in Ephesus, Paul applies the promise of the inheritance of the land specifically to children of Christian believers who are obedient, rather than to people who are his Jewish kinsmen according to the flesh. The fifth commandment of the Decalogue had promised that children who honoured their father and their mother would 'live long in the land the LORD your God is giving you' (Exod. 20:12). Now Paul applies the same promise to children of Christian parents. If they submit willingly to the authority of their parents, they will enjoy long life on the 'earth' (Eph. 6:3). The context of Paul's writing to the church of Ephesus makes it clear that 'land' must be expanded to include the space-without-limits of the Gentile world. In this way the land has come to its new-covenant fulfilment within God's purposes. The limitation of the land-type of the old covenant has been broken so that it stretches, as does the Great Commission, to the uttermost parts of the earth (cf. Matt. 28:19; Acts 1:8).

And what of Jerusalem as a place of significance in the new covenant? This city obviously was a major focus of the ministry of Jesus. Yet most interestingly, it is not Jerusalem but Capernaum that is designated in the Gospels as 'his own town' (Matt. 9:1; 13:54). Why this prominence for Capernaum rather than Jerusalem? Because, as prophecy had anticipated, this town was located

[18] Davies's interest (1974: xv; 1982: xiii; 1991: xiii) has been prompted by current events in the land of the Bible. Yet he declines to discuss what happens when Judaism's understanding of its right to the land 'conflicts with the claims of the traditions and occupancy of its other peoples' (1991: xv).

[19] Palestinians might argue that their 'use of force' is also legitimate, but without this biblical appeal. For Israelis it is quite different, as Chapman notes: 'It is not surprising that cabinet ministers in Israel should quote from the Old Testament to support Israel's claim to the West Bank, or that the Israeli government should make the book of Joshua compulsory reading in all schools' (1983: 104).

'by the way of the sea' in the land of the Gentiles (Is. 9:1; Matt. 4:12–17). By choosing this locale for his ministry, Jesus makes a statement concerning the scope of his emerging kingdom. The 'way of the sea' was the narrow trade-route that linked three continents across the land-bridge that was Palestine. As a consequence of having this place for its beginning, the gospel of Jesus Christ could run at the fastest possible speed to the ends of the earth. This land, crafted by the one who shaped the continents, was designed from the beginning not as an end in itself but as a means to an end.

By the conclusion of the apostolic era, the focal point of the redemptive working of God in the world had shifted dramatically from Jerusalem to places like Antioch, Galatia and Ephesus. These centres became the hubs for the reaching out of the gospel 'to the ends of the earth' (read 'land'). So far as the Jerusalem of this new era was concerned, Paul was quite explicit. In his evaluation, the 'present Jerusalem' was 'in slavery with her children' because the Judaizers in Jerusalem had muffled the free gospel in favour of the bondage of legalism (Gal. 4:25). The Jews were inhabiting Jerusalem, but obviously it was no longer the 'city of God' as it had been under the typological administration of the old covenant.

The circumstance of Jerusalem today continues as it was in Paul's day. His reference to the 'present' Jerusalem and its bondage to a legalism that rejects the gracious gift of salvation coming through its own Messiah applies to the modern city of Jerusalem just as much as it did in the days of the apostles. It must not be presumed that those living in Jerusalem today without faith in Jesus as the Christ are the elect, the chosen of God unto salvation. Apart from a turning in repentance and faith, which is the same requirement for men and women all over the world, the inhabitants of the 'present Jerusalem' continue to be in bondage, and are 'without hope and without God in the world' (Eph. 2:13). To suggest anything else is to slight Jesus Christ and his sacrifice of life, while at the same time imperilling people's souls by encouraging false presumption.

But there is another Jerusalem, a Jerusalem that is above, from which the enthroned Son of God sends forth his Spirit. Apart from this Jerusalem, none of us would have a mother to bring us into the realm of God's redemptive working, for she is the mother of us all (Gal. 4:26). Only those who have been born from above by the outpouring of the Spirit from the throne of Christ situated in the heavenly Jerusalem can claim to be citizens in the kingdom of God.

This 'Jerusalem above' must not be viewed as an esoteric, spiritualized entity that has little contact with the realities of this world. On the contrary, only a thin veil keeps us in this world from perceiving its reality. That veil will be removed at the *apocalypsis*, the 'unveiling' that will occur when Christ returns. Then the curtain will be pulled back, and it will be made clear to all exactly what has been the state of things since the ascension of Jesus Christ. All this time he has been seated on his throne, exercising 'all authority in heaven and on earth' (Matt. 28:19). The locale for his reign is the place where Jerusalem has come to its fulfilment, and he sits enthroned as the legitimate heir to the throne of David (Acts 2:30–31). The exalted Christ rules from the heavenly Jerusalem (Heb. 12:22), manifesting his sovereignty over all nations until the end of the age.

Conclusion

In the process of redemptive history, a dramatic movement has been made from type to reality, from shadow to substance. The land which once was the specific locale of God's redemptive working served well within the old covenant as a picture of Paradise lost and promised. Now, however, in the era of new-covenant fulfilment, the land has expanded to encompass the cosmos.

It is this expanded land which is given graciously by God to the 'Israel of God' (Gal. 6:16). A full analysis of how this 'Israel of God' should be viewed within the era of the new covenant is considered elsewhere.[20] Yet it would be fully in keeping with the new-covenant perspective on the land to say that this new-covenant 'Israel of God' refers to those who have been 'born from above' by the Holy Spirit sent down from the 'Jerusalem that is above' (John 3:3 mg.; Gal. 4:26). It is they who are the true inheritors of the promises relating to the land; it is they who, in Jesus' phrase, will 'inherit the earth' (Matt. 5:5).

[20] Cf. among other treatments the present author's, Robertson 2000.

In this age of fulfilment, therefore, a retrogression to the limited forms of the old covenant must be neither expected nor promoted. Reality must not give way to shadow. By claiming the old-covenant form of the land-promise, the Jews of today may forfeit the greater new-covenant fulfilment of the land-promise. Rather than playing the role of Jacob as heir-apparent of the redemptive promises made to Abraham their father, they could be assuming the role of Esau by selling their birthright for a fleshly pot of porridge (Gen. 25:29–34; cf. Heb. 12:16). Evangelical Christians in particular should take care that they do not fail to apply the implications of Pauline theology to the current situation regarding the land. For Paul emphatically notes that 'if you let yourself be circumcised [an old covenant institution], Christ will be of no value to you at all' (Gal. 5:2). In a similar way, if the form of the old-covenant land-promise is presented as the blessed object to be achieved, then the real, substantial fulfilment of the new covenant could be missed. To claim the 'city with foundations, whose architect and builder is God' (Heb. 11:10), Abraham had to look beyond the shadowy form of the promise (which he never possessed) to the realities that could be perceived only by faith. How sad it would be if evangelical Christians who profess to love the Jewish people should become a primary tool in misdirecting their faith and expectation!

The land in its totality and in its final form belongs to the Lord (Lev. 25:23), but he is a gracious God who blesses his people with his gifts. Those who claim to be the heirs of this land must then be very careful to note from the documents of the new covenant what precisely is that 'final form' of the promised land, and to whom it is so graciously promised.

Bibliography

Alexander, T. D. (1995), *From Paradise to the Promised Land: An Introduction to the Main Themes of the Pentateuch*, Carlisle: Paternoster.

Block, D. I. (1998), *The Book of Ezekiel: Chapters 25 – 48*, Grand Rapids: Eerdmans.

Brueggemann, W. (1997), *Theology of the Old Testament: Testimony, Dispute, Advocacy*, Minneapolis: Fortress.

———— (1978), *The Land: Place as Gift, Promise and Challenge in Biblical Faith*, London: SPCK.

Chapman, C. (1983), *Whose Promised Land?*, Tring: Lion. Rev. edn.
Davies, W. D. (1974), *The Gospel and the Land: Early Christianity and Jewish Territorial Doctrine*, Berkeley: University of California Press.
——— (1991), *The Territorial Dimension of Judaism*, Minneapolis: Fortress.
Eichrodt, W. (1970), *Ezekiel: A Commentary*, London: SCM.
Feinberg, C. L. (1969), *The Prophecy of Ezekiel*, Chicago: Moody.
Holwerda, D. E. (1995), *Jesus and Israel: One Covenant or Two?*, Leicester: Apollos.
Keil, C. F., & F. Delitzsch (1976–7), *Biblical Commentary on the Old Testament: The Books of the Chronicles*, Grand Rapids: Eerdmans.
Rad, G. von (1943), 'The promised land and Yahweh's land in the Hexateuch', in *The Problem of the Hexateuch and Other Essays*, London: Oliver and Boyd, 1966: 79–93.
Robertson, O. P. (2000), *The Israel of God Yesterday, Today and Tomorrow*, Nutley, NJ: Presbyterian and Reformed.
Selman, M. J. (1994), *1 Chronicles*, Tyndale Old Testament Commentaries, Leicester: IVP.
Taylor, J. B. (1969), *Ezekiel*, Tyndale Old Testament Commentaries, Leicester: IVP.
Walker, P. W. L. (1996), *Jesus and the Holy City: New Testament Perspectives on Jerusalem*, Grand Rapids: Eerdmans.
Wright, C. J. H. (1993), 'Biblical reflections on land', *Evangelical Review of Theology* 17:153–167.
Zimmerli, W. (1983), *Ezekiel 2*, Philadelphia: Fortress.

4B
Dispensational approaches to the land

Stephen R. Sizer

Introduction

Dispensationalism is one of the most influential theological systems within the universal church today. Largely unrecognized and subliminal, it has increasingly shaped the presuppositions of fundamentalist, evangelical, Pentecostal and charismatic thinking concerning Israel and Palestine over the past one hundred and fifty years.

John Nelson Darby is regarded as the father of dispensationalism and its prodigy, Christian Zionism. But it was Cyrus I. Scofield and D. L. Moody who brought Darby's sectarian theology into mainstream evangelical circles. R. C. Sproul concedes that dispensationalism is now 'a theological system that in all probability is the majority report among current American evangelicals' (Gerstner 1991: ix). Most of the early popular American radio preachers such as Donald Grey Barnhouse, Charles E. Fuller and M. R. DeHaan were dispensationalists. Today, virtually all the 'televangelists' such as Jerry Falwell, Jim Bakker, Paul Crouch, Pat Robertson, Jimmy Swaggart and Billy Graham are also dispensationalists. Other leading dispensationalist writers include Charles Ryrie, Dwight Pentecost, John Walvoord, Eric Sauer, Charles Dyer, Tim LaHaye, Grant Jeffrey and Hal Lindsey. Notable political proponents include Jimmy Carter and Ronald Reagan. Probably the most significant Christian organizations to espouse dispensationalism have been the Moody Bible Institute, Dallas Theological Seminary and the International Christian Embassy, Jerusalem.

Dispensationalism defined

The basic text upon which dispensationalism is based is the Authorized Version of 2 Timothy 2:15, where the apostle Paul calls upon Timothy to show himself approved unto God, 'rightly dividing the word of truth'. Scofield took this verse as the title for his first book, which is a defence of this way of 'dividing' Scripture into discrete dispensations (1928: 1280). In its classical form, Charles Ryrie describes the essence of dispensationalism:

1. A dispensationalist keeps Israel and the church distinct.

2. This distinction between Israel and the church is born out of a system of hermeneutics that is usually called literal interpretation.

3. A third aspect ... concerns the underlying purpose of God in the world, namely the glory of God ... To the normative dispensationalist, the soteriological, or saving, program of God is not the only program but one of the means God is using in the total program of glorifying Himself (1965: 39–40).

The seven dispensations

Following Darby and Scofield, dispensationalists claim to find in Scripture evidence of seven distinct dispensations during which humanity has been tested in respect of specific revelation as to the will of God. In each dispensation, including the present sixth dispensation of the church, humanity has failed the test. These dispensations began with creation and will culminate in an exclusive Jewish kingdom on earth. Charles Ryrie (1995: 54) offers the clearest outline of the dispensations (see Table 1).

Table 1: The seven dispensations

Name	Scripture	Responsibilities	Judgment(s)
Innocency	Genesis 1:3 – 3:6	Keep garden	Curses
Conscience	Genesis 3:7 – 8:14	Do good	Flood
Civil government	Genesis 8:15 – 11:9	Fill earth	Forced scattering
Patriarchal rule	Genesis 11:10 – Exodus 18:27	Stay in promised land	Egyptian bondage
Mosaic law	Exodus 19:1 – John 14:30	Keep the law	Captivities
Grace	Acts 2:1 – Revelation 19:21	Believe in Christ	Death
Millennium	Revelation 20:1–15	Believe and obey	Death

These dispensations are seen by proponents as literally 'providing us with a chronological map to guide us' (Dyer 1991: 189) toward the seventh and final dispensation, which will be inaugurated by the imminent return of Jesus Christ and the climax to world history.

A distinction between Israel and the church

Dispensationalists believe that God has two separate but parallel means of working: one through the church, the other through Israel, the former being a parenthesis to the latter (Ryrie 1965: 48). Thus there is, and always will remain, a distinction 'between Israel, the Gentiles and the Church' (Ryrie 1995: 137).

Darby was not the first to insist on a radical distinction between Israel and the church. Marcion stressed the radical nature of Christianity *vis-à-vis* Judaism. In his theology there existed a total discontinuity between the Old and New Testaments, between Israel and the church, and even between the God of the Old Testament and the Father of Jesus (Gasque 1978: 620). It was, however, Darby who first insisted that 'The Jewish nation is never to enter the Church' (1856: 106). Scofield developed this idea further: 'Comparing then, what is said in Scripture concerning Israel and the Church, we find that in origin, calling, promise, worship, principles of conduct and future destiny, all is contrast' (1907: 23).

Lewis Sperry Chafer, the founder of Dallas Theological Seminary and a student of Scofield's, elaborated on this dichotomy between Israel and the church: 'The dispensationalist believes that throughout the ages God is pursuing two distinct purposes: one related to the earth with earthly people and earthly objectives involved, which is Judaism; while the other is related to heaven with heavenly people and heavenly objectives involved, which is Christianity' (Chafer 1936a: 107). For Chafer, 'Israel is an eternal nation, heir to an eternal land, with an eternal kingdom, on which David rules from an eternal throne' (1975: 315–323), that is, on earth, and distinct from the church, who will be in heaven.

A literalist hermeneutic

Dispensationalism is based on the hermeneutical principle that Scripture is always to be interpreted literally. Darby's approach might be summarized in one sentence in which he admitted, 'I prefer quoting many passages than enlarging upon them' (1962a: 363). Scofield, who popularized and synthesised Darby's theology, explains further: 'Not one instance exists of a "spiritual" or figurative fulfilment of prophecy ... Jerusalem is always Jerusalem, Israel is always Israel, Zion is always Zion ... Prophecies may never be spiritualised, but are always literal' (1907: 45–46).

Ryrie similarly asserts: 'To be sure, literal/historical/grammatical interpretation is not the sole possession or practice of dispensationalists, but the consistent use of it in all areas of biblical interpretation *is*' (1995: 40).

The logical deduction of a literalist dispensational hermeneutic, according to Dwight Pentecost, another former member of the Dallas faculty, is that 'Scripture is unintelligible until one can distinguish clearly between God's program for his earthly people Israel and that for the Church' (1958: 529). Donald Grey Barnhouse, another leading dispensationalist, insists: 'It was a tragic hour when the reformation churches wrote the Ten Commandments into their creeds and catechisms and sought to bring Gentile believers into bondage to Jewish law, which was never intended either for the Gentile nations or for the church' (Johnson 1963: 109, cited in DeMar & Leithart 1989: 24).

With breathtaking candour Chafer insists that dispensationalism 'has changed the Bible from being a mass of more or less conflicting writings into a classified and easily assimilated revelation of both the earthly and heavenly purposes of God, which reach on into eternity to come' (1936b: 410, 416, 446–447, cited in Fuller 1980: 24–25).

Ernest Sandeen critically observes that dispensationalism has 'a frozen biblical text in which every word is supported by the same weight of divine authority' (1967: 70, cited in Gerstner 1991: 100). Based on this interpretative principle, dispensationalists hold that the promises made to Abraham, and through him to the Jews, although postponed during this present church age, are nevertheless eternal and unconditional and therefore await future realization, since they have never yet been literally fulfilled. For example, it is an article of normative dispensational belief that the boundaries of the land promised to Abraham and his descendants from the Nile to the Euphrates will be literally instituted and that Jesus Christ will return to a literal and theocratic Jewish kingdom centred on a rebuilt temple in Jerusalem. In such a scheme the church on earth is relegated to the status of a parenthesis (Walvoord 1979: 25), a 'Plan B' (Mathison 1995: back cover), and 'a sort of footnote or side-track in contrast to God's main mission to save ethnic, national Israel' (Horton 1994: 1).

An apocalyptic eschatology

Crucial to the dispensationalist reading of biblical prophecy is the conviction that the period of tribulation is imminent, along with the secret rapture of the church and the rebuilding of the Jewish temple in place of, or alongside, the Dome of the Rock. This will signal the return of the Lord to restore the kingdom to Israel centred on Jerusalem. This pivotal event is also seen as the trigger for the start of the war of Armageddon, in which most of the world's population, together with large numbers of Jews, will suffer and die (Lindsey 1983: 20–30). As observers comment:

> Convinced that a nuclear Armageddon is an inevitable event within the divine scheme of things, many evangelical dispensationalists have committed themselves to a course for Israel that, by their own admission, will lead directly to a holocaust indescribably more savage and widespread than any vision of carnage that could have been generated in Adolf Hitler's criminal mind (DeMar & Leithart 1989: 26; see also Halsell 1986: 195).

Clearly, the consequences of such views, whether promulgated by academics from respectable theological institutions like Dallas Theological Seminary and the Moody Bible Institute or by Jewish fanatics such as Baruch Ben-Yosef and the Temple Mount Yeshiva (Pevtzov 1994: 6), can only be devastating, especially since dispensationalists have considerable political influence through which they seek the fulfilment of their apocalyptic vision of the future. This dispensational vision is comparatively young in terms of church history. It began in 1828 when Darby wrote his first tract against the prevailing optimism of the established church (Neatby 1901: 18).

John Nelson Darby: the father of dispensationalism

Darby is rightly regarded as the first to espouse dispensationalism as a discrete theological system. However, William Kelly and Edward Irving played no small part in the restoration of premillennial speculations out of which Darby's dispensationalism arose (Murray 1971: 191). Darby was not the first to use the term 'dispensation' to describe periods of biblical history, nor was his own scheme universally accepted even within Brethren circles. It was Darby, though, who first insisted that these dispensations were irreversible and progressive, speculating that the church would soon be replaced on earth by a revived national Israel.

Charles Ryrie attempts, unconvincingly, to show that Darby's ideas were latent in previous writers such as the mystic Pierre Poiret (1646–1719), the amillennial Calvinist John Edwards (1639–1716) and the hymn writer Isaac Watts (1674–1748). He does concede, however, that it was Darby who systematized and popularized the idea of dispensationalism (1995: 63, 65–71).

Darby was a charismatic figure and dominant personality, a persuasive speaker and zealous missionary for his dispensationalist beliefs. He personally founded Brethren churches in Germany, Switzerland, France and the United States, which in turn sent missionaries to Africa, the West Indies, Australia and New Zealand. By the time of his death in 1885, around 1,500 separatist Brethren churches had been founded worldwide. Don Wagner makes the point that 'During his lifetime, Darby wrote more hymns than the Wesleys, travelled further than the Apostle Paul, and was a Greek and Hebrew scholar. His writings filled forty volumes ... If Brightman was the father of Christian Zionism, then Darby was its greatest apostle and missionary' (1995: 89).

The clearest expression of Darby's thinking is to be found in *The Apostasy of the Successive Dispensations.* In this work it is noticeable, however, that Darby's views are vague and embryonic compared with later attempts by Scofield and Ryrie to systematize seven discrete dispensations. Ryrie's interpretation of Darby's dispensations is significantly at variance with Darby's own writings, but more consistent with, and probably reliant upon, Scofield. It is an understatement when Ryrie claims that Darby's scheme is 'not always easily discerned from his writings' (1995: 68). Ryrie appears to have read back into Darby's writings a scheme that suited his own purposes. From Darby's own works it is possible to reconstruct his dispensational chronology and compare it with Ryrie's interpretation, together with Scofield's 1909 version (see Table 2).[1]

Darby defended his dispensational interpretation on two grounds. First, he claimed that others had not studied the Scriptures correctly: 'The covenant is a word common in the language of a large class of Christian professors ... but in its development and detail, as to its unfolded principles, much obscurity appears to me to have arisen from a want of simple attention to Scripture' (1962c: 68). Secondly, Darby believed the Lord had revealed it to him personally: 'For my part, if I were bound to receive all that has been said by the Millenarians, I would reject the whole system, but their views and statements weigh with me not one feather. But this does

[1] Scofield's version was itself modified in a subsequent revision made by Schuyler English in the New Scofield Reference Bible in 1967.

Table 2: A comparison of Darby, Ryrie and Scofield

Darby's dispensations (1962b: 124–130)	**Ryrie's version of Darby** (1995: 68, 71)	**Scofield's dispensations** (1909: 5)
	1. Paradisaical state	1. Innocency (Gen. 1:28)
		2. Conscience (Gen. 3:23)
1. Noah (government)	2. Noah	3. Human government (Gen. 8:20)
	3. Abraham	4. Promise (Gen. 12:1)
2. Moses (law)	4. Israel under law	5. Law (Exod. 19:8)
3. Aaron (priesthood)	under priesthood	
4. Manasseh (kingly)	under kings	
5. Spirit (Gentile)	5. Gentiles	6. Grace (John 1:17)
	6. Spirit	
	7. Millennium	7. Kingdom (Eph. 1:10)

not hinder me from enquiring by the teaching of the same spirit ... what God has with infinite graciousness revealed to me concerning His dealing with the Church' (1962d: 6–7).

Even Roy Coad, in his otherwise sympathetic history of the Brethren movement, admits that 'for the traditional view of Revelation, another was substituted' (1976: 129). James Barr is less charitable, arguing that dispensationalism was 'individually invented by J. N. Darby [and] concocted in complete contradiction to all main Christian traditions' (1984: 6).

Darby was convinced that the visible church of his day was apostate. This assumption appears to have shaped his emerging belief that the church era was therefore merely a 'parenthesis' to the last days. Darby regarded the church as simply one more dispensation that had failed and was under God's judgment. Just as Israel had been cut off, so the church would be. Just as only a small remnant of Israel had been saved, so would only a small remnant of the church. And naturally, of course, the remnant taken from the ruins of the church were his own followers, the Brethren. 'The Church has sought to settle itself here, but it has no place on the earth ... [Though] making a most constructive parenthesis, it forms no part of the regular order of

God's earthly plans, but is merely an interruption of them to give a fuller character and meaning' to the Jews (1962e: 94).

Darby believed that the covenantal relationship between God and Abraham was binding for ever and that the promises pertaining to the nation of Israel, as yet unfulfilled, would find their consummation in the reign of Jesus Christ on earth during the millennium. Speaking of the imminent return of the Jews to Palestine, Darby predicted:

> The first thing, then, which the Lord will do will be to purify His land (the land which belongs to the Jews) of the Tyrians, the Philistines, the Sidonians; of Edom and Moab, and Ammon – of all the wicked, in short from the Nile to the Euphrates. It will be done by the power of Christ in favour of His people re-established by His goodness. The people are put into security in the land, and then will those of them who remain till that time among the nations be gathered together (1962f: 380).

Darby was as dismissive of the Jews as he was of Arabs. He not only taught that God would 'purify' the Arabs from between the Nile and the Euphrates and give all this land to the Jews, but he also believed that the majority of Jews would eventually identify with the Antichrist.

> The government of the fourth monarchy will be still in existence, but under the influence and direction of the Antichrist; and the Jews will unite themselves to him, in a state of rebellion, to make war with the Lamb ... Satan will then be displayed, who will unite the Jews with this apostate prince against heaven ... a remnant of the Jews is delivered and Antichrist destroyed (1962f: 379).

Clarence Bass summarizes the novel nature of Darby's emerging theological position:

> It is not that exegetes prior to his time did not see a covenant between God and Israel, or a future relation of Israel to the millennial reign, but they always viewed the church as a

> continuation of God's single program of redemption begun in Israel. It is dispensationalism's rigid insistence on a distinct cleavage between Israel and the church, and its belief in a later unconditional fulfilment of the Abrahamic covenant, that sets it off from the historic faith of the church (1960: 27).

Despite his prodigious efforts, Darby's dispensational views would probably have remained the exotic preserve of sectarian Brethren assemblies were it not for the energetic efforts of individuals such as William Blackstone and D. L. Moody. Above all, however, they were propagated by Scofield, who introduced them to a wider audience in America and the English-speaking world through his Scofield Reference Bible.

Cyrus I. Scofield: the author of the Scofield Reference Bible

The publication of the Scofield Reference Bible in 1909 by the Oxford University Press was something of a literary coup. For the first time, explicit dispensational notes were added to the pages of the biblical text. While such a systematic chronology was largely unknown prior to Darby and Scofield, the Scofield Reference Bible became the leading Bible used by American evangelicals and fundamentalists for the next sixty years. By 1945 more than two million copies had been published in the United States alone (Allis 1945: 267). Between 1967 and 1979 a further one million copies were sold (Fuller 1980: 1). In a move to make Scofield's work more accessible, in 1984 a new edition based on the New International Version was published, followed by a CD-ROM version.

Scofield's notes relied heavily on Darby's writings. Gerstner notes that the resemblance between Scofield and Darby 'is deep and systematic' (1991: 43). It is significant, however, that neither in the introduction nor in any of the accompanying notes does Scofield acknowledge his indebtedness to Darby.

In the Introduction to the Scofield Reference Bible, he claims that one of the 'remarkable results of the modern study of the Prophets' has been the 'recovering to the church of a clear and coherent harmony of the predictive portions'. Scofield defined his dispensations as periods of time 'during which man is tested in respect of obedience to some specific revelation of the will of God' (1909: 5).

> The Dispensations are distinguished, exhibiting the majestic, progressive order of the divine dealings of God with humanity, the 'increasing purpose' which runs through and links together the ages, from the beginning of the life of man to the end in eternity. Augustine said: 'Distinguish the ages, and the Scriptures harmonize' (1909: iii).

Whether Augustine understood 'ages' in terms of Scofield's dispensations is extremely unlikely. Nevertheless, Scofield believed that his scheme of seven was natural and self-evident in Scripture: 'There is a beautiful system in this gradualness of unfolding. The past is seen to fall into periods, marked off by distinct limits, and distinguishable period from period by something peculiar to each. Thus it comes to be understood that there is a doctrine of Ages or Dispensations in the Bible' (1914: 13).

Scofield's rigid adherence to these dispensations required him to make some novel assertions to ensure consistency. So, for example, in describing the transition between his fourth dispensation of promise to his fifth dispensation of law, Scofield claims:

> The descendants of Abraham had but to abide in their own land to inherit every blessing . . . The Dispensation of Promise ended when Israel rashly accepted the law (Ex. 19. 8). Grace had prepared a deliverer [Moses], provided a sacrifice for the guilty, and by divine power brought them out of bondage (Ex. 19. 4); but at Sinai they exchanged grace for law (1909: 20).

Similarly, in his introduction to the Gospels, Scofield imposes stark divisions before and after Calvary which lead him to the following assertions: 'The mission of Jesus was, primarily, to the Jews. The Sermon on the Mount is law, not grace. The doctrines of Grace are to be sought in the Epistles not in the Gospels' (1909: 989).

Strangely, Scofield ignored the one division that is self-evident – that between the old and new covenants. Mark 1:1 categorically declares itself to be 'The beginning of the Gospel of Jesus Christ', and Matthew 11:13 reads, 'for all the Prophets and the Law prophesied until John'. Yet Scofield places the life and ministry of Jesus within the dispensation of law, along with John the Baptist and the Old Testament prophets. He argues that the sixth dispensation of grace only 'begins with the death and resurrection of Christ' (1909: 1115). For Scofield, the Lord's Prayer, and in particular the petition 'Forgive us our debts, as we also have forgiven our debtors' (Matt. 6:12), is not applicable to the church, since it is what he terms 'legal ground' (1909: 1002). Scofield taught that salvation by works had been possible during the dispensation of the law, and that the apostasy of the church would signal the end of the dispensation of grace:

> As a dispensation, grace begins with the death and resurrection of Christ (Rom. 3. 24–26; 4. 24, 25). The point of testing is no longer legal obedience as the condition of salvation, but acceptance or rejection of Christ ... The predicted end of the testing of man under grace is the apostasy of the professing church (1909: 1115).

Scofield believed that the Gospels were essentially for the Jews and therefore not relevant for the church. In a footnote to Ephesians 3, for example, he claims, 'In [Paul's] writings *alone* we find the doctrine, position, walk, and destiny of the Church' (1909: 1252). Similarly, in perpetuating the distinction between Israel and the church, Scofield claimed that Israel is the earthly wife of God and the church is the heavenly bride of Christ.

> That Israel is the wife of Jehovah (see vs. 16–23), now disowned but yet to be restored, is the clear teaching of the passages. This relationship is not to be confounded with that of the Church to Christ (John 3. 29, refs.). In the mystery of the Divine tri-unity both are true. The N.T. speaks of the Church as a virgin espoused to one husband (2 Cor. 11. 1, 2); which could never be said of an adulterous wife, restored in grace. Israel is, then, to be the restored and forgiven wife of Jehovah, the Church the virgin wife of the Lamb (John 3. 29; Rev. 19.

> 6–8); Israel Jehovah's earthly wife (Hos. 2. 23); the Church the Lamb's heavenly bride (Rev. 19. 7) (1909: 922).

In many ways Scofield was representative of, but at the same time became a focus for, the growing prophetic and millennial fundamentalist movement in North America influenced by the Brethren. The views later popularized by Scofield were shaped by a series of Bible and prophetic conferences held across North America beginning in 1868, which followed the pattern established by Darby and Irving at Albury and Powerscourt from the 1830s. As Shelly (1978: 706) notes, 'Both the method of "Bible readings" and the topics of the conferences strongly suggest that the gatherings were a result of J. N. Darby's travels in the United States and the influence of the Plymouth Brethren.'

One of the resolutions adopted by the 1878 Niagara conference gives clear evidence of the influence of Darby's dispensationalism.

> We believe that the world will not be converted during the present dispensation, but is fast ripening for judgment, while there will be fearful apostasy in the professing Christian body; and hence that the Lord Jesus will come in person to introduce the millennial age, when Israel shall be restored to their own land, and the earth shall be full of the knowledge of the Lord; and that this personal and premillennial advent is the blessed hope set before us in the Gospel for which we should be constantly looking (Sandeen 1970: Appendix A).

William E. Cox (1974: 55–56), a former dispensationalist and subsequent critic, offered this appraisal of Scofield's abiding legacy.

> Scofield's footnotes and his systematized schemes of hermeneutics have been memorized by many as religiously as have verses of the Bible. It is not at all uncommon to hear devout men recite these footnotes prefaced by the words, 'The Bible says . . .' Many a pastor has lost all influence with members of his congregation and has been branded a liberal for no other reason than failure to concur with all the footnotes of Dr.

> Scofield. Even many ministers use the teachings of Scofield as tests of orthodoxy!

Craig Blaising (1992: 21), Professor of Systematic Theology at Dallas Theological Seminary, agrees: 'The Scofield Reference Bible became the Bible of fundamentalism, and the theology of the notes approached confessional status in many Bible schools, institutes and seminaries established in the early decades of this century.'

In 1890 Scofield began his Comprehensive Bible Correspondence Course, through which tens of thousands of students around the world were introduced to his dispensational teaching about a failing church and a future Israel. Scofield directed the course until 1914 when it was taken over by the Moody Bible Institute. In the 1890s, during Scofield's pastorate in Dallas, he was also Principal of the Southwestern School of the Bible. This was the forerunner to Dallas Theological Seminary, which was founded in 1924 by another of his students, Lewis Sperry Chafer, one of Scofield's most influential exponents.

> Chafer has, in the history of American Dispensationalism, a double distinction. First, he established and led Dispensationalism's most scholarly institution through the formative years of its existence. Second, he produced the first full and definitive systematic theology of Dispensationalism. This massive eight-volume work is a full articulation of the standard Scofieldian variety of dispensational thought, constantly related to the Biblical texts and data on which it claims to rest. Its influence appears to have been great on all dispensationalist teachers since its first publication, though it is fading today.
>
> All of Chafer's work and career was openly and obviously in the Scofieldian tradition. A few years before his death, Chafer, faithful to his mentor to the last, was to say of his greatest academic achievement, 'It goes on record that the Dallas Theological Seminary uses, recommends, and defends the Scofield Bible.' The major line of dispensational orthodoxy is clear and unbroken from Darby to Scofield to Chafer to Dallas (Gerstner 1991: 46).

It is perhaps therefore not surprising that the Moody Bible Institute in Chicago and Dallas Theological Seminary have since then continued to be the foremost apologists for Scofield's dispensational views, and for Christian Zionism in particular.

Hal Lindsey: the father of apocalyptic dispensational Zionism

Hal Lindsey, himself a former Dallas student, is undoubtedly the most influential contemporary dispensationalist. Lindsey has been described by *Time* as 'The Jeremiah for this Generation', and by the *New York Times* as 'the best-selling author of the decade' (Lindsey 1981: 179). The author of over twenty books, his latest publisher describes him as 'The Father of the Modern-Day Bible Prophecy Movement' (1995: back cover), and, 'the best-known prophecy teacher in the world' (1997: back cover). Lindsey's most famous book, *The Late Great Planet Earth*, has been described by the *New York Times* as the '#1 Non-fiction Bestseller of the Decade' (1970: back cover). It has gone through more than 108 printings, with sales of more than 18 million copies in English, and 18–20 million further copies in fifty-four foreign-language editions (Lindsey 1989: 195; Marsden 1991: 77; Lienesch 1993: 311).

Lindsey's popularity may be attributed to a combination of factors: his readable and journalistic style of writing; his imaginative if dogmatic insistence that contemporary geopolitical events are the fulfilment of biblical prophecy; and, above all, his categorical assertions that the end of the world is imminent. Like Darby and Scofield, Lindsey confidently asserts that his interpretation of the Bible uniquely shows what will happen in the future. 'Today, almost before I finish explaining a developing trend – it's already an accomplished fact' (1996: 3). In *The Final Battle* we read, 'This book describes in more detail and explicitness than any other just what will happen to humanity and to the Earth, not a thousand years from now, but in our lifetime – indeed in this very generation (1995: xiii).

Similarly, on the cover of *The Apocalypse Code*, Lindsey's publisher writes, 'In this riveting non-fiction book, the father of modern-day Bible prophecy cracks the "Apocalypse Code" and deciphers long-hidden messages about man's future and the fate of the earth' (1997).

In *Planet Earth: The Final Chapter*, we are promised:

> Hal will be your guide on a chilling tour of the world's future battlefields as the Great Tribulation, foretold more than two thousand years ago by Old and New Testament prophets, begins to unfold. You'll meet the world leaders who will bring man to the very edge of extinction and examine the causes of the current global situation – what it all means, what will shortly come to pass, and how it will all turn out (1998: back cover).

Like Darby, Lindsey also claims his interpretations were revealed to him personally by God.

> I believe that the Spirit of God gave me a special insight, not only into how John described what he actually experienced, but also into how this whole phenomenon encoded the prophecies so that they could be fully understood only when their fulfilment drew near ... I prayerfully sought for a confirmation for my apocalypse code theory (Lindsey 1997: 37; cf. Darby 1962d: 6–7, 108).

Lindsey may also be a popular writer because he tends to revise his predictions in the light of changing world events. Without carefully comparing each of his books, one would not necessarily realize that *The Final Battle* (1995) is a revision of *The Late Great Planet Earth* (1970); *The Apocalypse Code* (1997) is a revision of *There's a New World Coming* (1973b); and *Planet Earth 2000 A.D.* (in its two editions: 1994 and 1996) is a revision of *The 1980's Countdown to Armageddon* (1981). *Planet Earth: The Final Chapter* (1998) is the latest, but probably not the final, version in the 'Planet Earth' series.

A good example of Lindsey's prophetic revisionism concerns the future of the United States. In *Planet Earth 2000 A.D.* (1994) Lindsey specifically draws attention to a prophecy made in *The Late Great Planet Earth* (1970) as evidence of his prophetic accuracy. A comparison, however, shows that he has edited out his prediction of Communist subversion, which did not occur (see Table 3).

Table 3: Lindsey's changing predictions

The Late Great Planet Earth (1970: 184)	***Planet Earth 2000*** *A.D.* (1994: 15–16)
The United States will not hold its present position of leadership in the western world; financially, the future leader will be Western Europe. Internal political chaos caused by student rebellion and Communist subversion will begin to erode the economy of our nation. Lack of moral principle by citizens and leaders will so weaken law and order that a state of anarchy will finally result. The military capability of the United States, though it is at present the most powerful in the world, has already been neutralized because no one has the courage to use it decisively. When the economy collapses so will the military.	"The United States will not hold its present position of leadership in the western world," I wrote in *The Late Great Planet Earth.* "Lack of moral principle by citizens and leaders will so weaken law and order that a state of anarchy will finally result. The military capability of the United States, though it is at present the most powerful in the world, has already been neutralized because no one has the courage to use it decisively. When the economy collapses so will the military." Remember, folks, these words were written in 1969, not the 1990s!

Lindsey's particular kind of reading of history, coloured by an imaginative exegesis of selected biblical scriptures, is dogmatic, dualistic and highly speculative. The titles of Lindsey's books show an increasingly exaggerated and almost pathological emphasis on the apocalyptic, on death and suffering. These include *Satan is Alive and Well on Planet Earth* (1973); *The 1980's Countdown to Armageddon* (1981); *The Road to Holocaust* (1989); *Planet Earth 2000 A.D. Will Man Survive?* (1994); *The Final Battle* (1995) and *The Apocalypse Code* (1997). In each Lindsey insists that biblical prophecy is being fulfilled, uniquely, in this generation, and signals the imminent destruction of the world.

> We are the generation the prophets were talking about. We have witnessed biblical prophecies come true. The birth of Israel. The decline in American power and morality. The rise of Russian and Chinese might. The threat of war in the

> Middle East. The increase of earthquakes, volcanoes, famine and drought. The Bible foretells the signs that precede Armageddon ... We are the generation that will see the end times ... and the return of Jesus (1981: back cover).

Lindsey's last but one book, *The Final Battle* (1995) includes the statement on the cover: 'Never before, in one book, has there been such a complete and detailed look at the events leading up to "The Battle of Armageddon".'

Lindsey claims that the world is degenerating and that the forces of evil manifest in godless Communism and militant Islam are the real enemies of Israel. He describes in detail the events leading to the great battle at Megiddo between the massive Russian, Chinese and African armies that will attempt but fail to destroy Israel. He offers illustrated plans showing future military movements of armies and naval convoys leading up to the battle of Armageddon (1970: 155). These will merely hasten the return of Jesus Christ as King of the Jews, to rule over the nations from the rebuilt Jewish temple in Jerusalem (1983: 31–48).

> Obstacle or no obstacle, it is certain that the Temple will be rebuilt. Prophecy demands it ... With the Jewish nation reborn in the land of Palestine, ancient Jerusalem once again under total Jewish control for the first time in 2600 years, and talk of rebuilding the great Temple, the most important sign of Jesus Christ's soon coming is before us ... It is like the key piece of a jigsaw puzzle being found ... For all those who trust in Jesus Christ, it is a time of electrifying excitement (1970: 56–58).

Acknowledging that the Islamic world will not tolerate such a scenario, Lindsey graphically predicts the effect of a worldwide nuclear holocaust centred on Jerusalem, with the 200-mile valley from the Sea of Galilee to Eilat flowing with irradiated blood several feet deep (1995: 250–252): 'only a tiny fraction of the world's population will be left. Only a remnant will have survived. Many of the Jews would have been killed' (1970: 264).

In *The Final Battle*, Lindsey claims, 'The Jewish state will be brought to the brink of destruction' (1995: 184):

> The land of Israel and the surrounding area will certainly be targeted for nuclear attack. Iran and all the Muslim nations around Israel have already been targeted with Israeli nukes ... Zechariah gives an unusual, detailed account of how hundreds of thousands of soldiers in the Israel battle zone will die. Their flesh will be consumed from their bones, their eyes from their sockets, and their tongues from their mouths while they stand on their feet (Zechariah 14:12) ... But God's power is certainly stronger than any nuclear bomb ... We do know God will supernaturally strengthen and protect the believing Israelites so that they will survive the worst holocaust the world will ever see. Amen (1995: 255–257).

Lindsey's most controversial book is undoubtedly *The Road to Holocaust*. In it, like Darby (1962g: 154), he makes eschatology a test of orthodoxy. He accuses those who refuse to accept dispensationalism's distinction between the church and Israel of encouraging anti-Semitism, since they apparently deny any future role for the State of Israel within the purposes of God. This is, he claims, '... the same error that founded the legacy of contempt for the Jews and ultimately led to the Holocaust of Nazi Germany ...' (1989: back page).

> The purpose of this book is to warn about a rapidly expanding new movement in the Church that is subtly introducing the same errors that eventually and inevitably led to centuries of atrocities against the Jews and culminated in the Holocaust of the Third Reich ... They are setting up a philosophical system that will result in anti-Semitism (1989: 3).

Through his many books, his monthly Middle East political journal called *International Intelligence Briefing*, and his weekly television *Prophecy Watch* programmes, Lindsey has encouraged evangelicals and fundamentalists to support Israel's right-wing Zionist agenda. But there is great irony here: Lindsey claims to support Israel and to refute anti-Semitism, yet his 'Armageddon'-style theology (Wagner 1995: 25), may actually be a self-fulfilling prophecy, leading to the very holocaust which he abhors yet repeatedly predicts.

The International Christian Embassy, Jerusalem

From its foundation in 1980 the charter of the ICEJ has been to 'comfort' Israel. This has been defined as encouraging and facilitating the restoration of the Jews to Eretz Israel, although the geographical extent of greater Israel is not always made clear.

> The embassy believes that God wants us to stimulate, encourage, and inspire Christians amongst the many nations concerning their role and task in the restoration of Israel. The Bible says that the destiny of nations, Christians, and even that of the church is linked to the way in which these groups respond to this restoration (ICEJ 1991).

Those who founded the ICEJ were drawn from western evangelical, fundamentalist and charismatic circles. According to Don Wagner (1995: 100), virtually the entire ICEJ leadership are dispensationalists who, like Darby, Scofield and Lindsey, believe that the restoration of the Jews to Israel and the contemporary State of Israel are fulfilments of biblical prophecy. In 1985, Johann Luckoff, the Director of ICEJ, wrote, 'The return to Zion from exile a second time (Is. 11:11) is a living testimony to God's faithfulness and his enduring covenant with the Jewish people.'

With an international staff of fifty and representatives in over eighty countries, the ICEJ has gained significant status within Jewish political circles for its lobbying of foreign governments on behalf of Israel. Based on its dispensational convictions, the ICEJ sponsors an annual Feast of Tabernacles celebration attended by around 5,000 Christian Zionists from over seventy nations. Every Israeli Prime Minister since 1980 has attended and addressed this celebration. They proudly record the testimonials of many Jewish political and religious leaders. For example, Yitzhak Rabin said:

> Allow me to tell you how much I, and Israel, appreciate your [presence] here in Jerusalem, especially during these difficult days. Israel has experienced through her existence many difficulties. Therefore, whenever we see people that care, that are

> involved, and who show this by deeds, and by words – we appreciate this (ICEJ 1993: 7).

ICEJ claim that their Feast of Tabernacle celebration is the largest single annual tourist event in Israel.

In 1996, in rebutting criticism of their theological position, the ICEJ repudiated those who refused to acknowledge the central place of Israel within God's continuing purposes: 'While Gentile believers have been grafted into that household of faith which is of Abraham (the commonwealth of Israel), replacement theology within the Christian faith, which does not recognize the ongoing biblical purposes for Israel and the Jewish People, is doctrinal error.'

The ICEJ emphasizes that contemporary events are the fulfilment of Old Testament prophecy concerning Israel. They distinguish the church from Israel, speaking of 'the former and latter rains' (ICEJ 1993: 15). Whereas the New Testament emphasizes in Ephesians 2:14 that Jesus Christ has 'made the two one' so that, according to Galatians 3:28, in Christ there is now 'neither Jew nor Greek', the ICEJ insists on maintaining a distinction and superior status for those of Jewish ethnic descent who remain, even apart from faith in Jesus Christ, the chosen people, 'His Jewish sons and daughters' (ICEJ 1993: 9).

> In no uncertain terms God has made known His intention to regather the scattered Jewish people and to plant them in the land with His 'whole heart and soul' (Jeremiah 32:41). We believe that in the present massive wave of Soviet Jewish immigration to Israel (almost 400,000 since September 1989), the world is witnessing one of the most startling prophetic fulfilments of our time – one that should deeply touch the heart of every Bible-believing Christian and provoke him to action. Since its inception in 1980 the vision for the release of Soviet Jewry has been a vital aspect of the work of the ICEJ. Along with a growing number of Christians internationally, we have seen the Soviet Jewry issue as pivotal in God's unfolding plan for Israel and the nations ... It is an amazing fact that God, through His prophets, long ago ordained that He would use Gentiles to bring back His Jewish sons and daughters (1993: 9).

The ICEJ have taken their religio-political hermeneutic somewhat further than most dispensationalists and have effectively reinterpreted the Great Commission. In place of proclaiming the message of Jesus Christ, which, according to Romans 1:16 and 2:9–10, is 'to the Jew first', they have substituted a social gospel serving the expansionist political agenda of the modern State of Israel.

> In the same sense that the first apostles were commissioned by the Lord to be his witnesses from Jerusalem to the uttermost parts of the earth, we also feel compelled to proclaim the word of Israel's restoration, and the Christian's response to it, to every country and in every place where there are believers (1993: 22).

The ICEJ has repeatedly identified uncritically and unconditionally with the position of the right wing of the Likud party, using the Bible to defend Israel's military settlement and colonization of Syria's Golan Heights and the Occupied Territories despite international criticism. The ICEJ has also remained implacably opposed to the aspirations of the Palestinians for political autonomy and a shared Jerusalem, and to the right of return for refugees who have lost their property and land through war or confiscation.

Not surprisingly, the ICEJ is repudiated by the indigenous Christian Palestinian community, its theology regarded as nothing less than apostasy (Rantisi 1999), and as 'an anachronistic return to the Judaizing tendency the early church rejected at the first ecumenical council, recorded in Acts 15' (Wagner 1995: 104).

Diversity and contradiction within contemporary dispensationalism

A new generation of younger dispensationalists among the faculty of Dallas Theological Seminary have attempted to redefine their movement as 'progressive dispensationalism' (Ryrie 1995: 214; Blaising & Bock 1992 and 1993; Saucy 1993). Perhaps sensitive to criticisms of classical dispensationalism, they distance themselves from what they regard as the 'naïveté' of the founder's vision (Blaising & Bock 1992: 19), distinguishing the classical dispensationalism of Chafer and Ryrie (Ryrie 1953; 1965; 1995) from 'Scofieldism', as well as from 'the popular "apocalyptism" of Lindseyism' (Blaising & Bock 1992: 14–15, 21–23). They regard themselves as 'less land centered' and less 'future centered' (Bock 1992: 50).

Classical dispensationalism, however, remains strong within conservative circles. Ryrie is sceptical of these recent developments, and of their attempt at any revisionism. He describes the position of theologians such as Blaising and Bock as 'neo-dispensationalist' and as holding to what he terms a 'slippery' hermeneutic (Ryrie 1995: 171, 175, 178).

Ryrie also distinguishes what he terms 'normative' dispensationalism from 'ultradispensationalism'. This latter tendency is rooted in the teaching of Ethelbert W. Bullinger (1837–1913) and his successor Charles H. Welch, who, according to Ryrie, merely carried dispensationalism to its 'logical extremes'. Ultradispensationalists hold, for instance, that the church did not begin at Pentecost, but in Acts 28, when Israel was set aside; the Great Commission of Matthew and Mark is Jewish and therefore not for the church; the Gospels and Acts describe the dispensation of the law; only the Pauline prison epistles, that is Ephesians, Philippians and Colossians, relate to the church age; water baptism is not for the church age; and Israel, not the church, is the bride of Christ (Ryrie 1995: 199). Their teachings are perpetuated today by the Berean Bible Society, *Berean Expositor* and Berean Publishing Trust (Welch & Allen 1973).

Like Hal Lindsey, other contemporary dispensationalist writers compete to present the most accurate and timely interpretation of contemporary events as they unfold. We close by noting five key writers in this vein.

1. Billy Graham's father-in-law, Nelson Bell, former editor of the prestigious and authoritative mouthpiece of conservative Evangelicalism, *Christianity Today,* appeared to express the sentiments of many American evangelicals when, in an editorial in 1967, he wrote: 'That for the first time in more than 2,000 years Jerusalem is now completely in the hands of the Jews gives a student of the Bible a thrill and a renewed faith in the accuracy and validity of the Bible' (Wagner 1995: 4).

2. Charles Dyer, Professor of Bible Exposition at Dallas Theological Seminary, includes in *The Rise of Babylon* photographs allegedly showing Saddam Hussein's reconstruction of Babylon to the

same specifications and splendour as Nebuchadnezzar (1991: 128–129). Dyer warns that this is evidence that Hussein plans to repeat Nebuchadnezzar's conquest of Israel, the only Arab ever to have done so. 'The Middle East is the world's time bomb, and Babylon is the fuse that will ignite the events of the end times' (Dyer 1991: back cover).

3. John Walvoord, Professor Emeritus of Systematic Theology and Chancellor of Dallas Theological Seminary, as well as the author of the million-copy bestseller *Armageddon, Oil and the Middle East Crisis* (1990), writes in an earlier book, *Israel in Prophecy*: 'In the present world scene there are many indications pointing to the conclusion that the end of the age may soon be upon us ... In this generation. Never before in the history of the world has there been a confluence of major evidences of preparation for the end' (1962: 129).

4. In their provocatively titled book, *Ready to Rebuild*, which is about the 'Imminent Plan to Rebuild the Last Days Temple', Thomas Ice and Randall Price summarize the theological perspective of contemporary dispensationalism toward Israel and the future: 'After centuries of persecution and dispersion, Jews are back in their land and pursuing the rebuilding of the Temple with increasing fervor. This fascinating, fast-moving overview of contemporary events shows why the Temple is significant in Bible prophecy and how, more than ever, Israel is ready to rebuild' (1992: back cover).

5. Lastly, Mike Evans, founder and president of Lovers of Israel Inc., offers biblical justification for the continuation of American support for Israel. In his book *Israel: America's Key to Survival*, he writes:

> Only one nation, Israel, stands between Soviet-sponsored terrorist aggression and the complete decline of the United States as a democratic world power ... Surely demonic pressure will endeavour to encourage her to betray Israel. This must not happen. Israel is the key to America's survival. For God has said of the nations who will oppose Israel, 'Yea, those nations shall be utterly wasted ... I will bless them that bless thee, and curse them that curseth [*sic*] thee' (Isa. 60:12; Gen. 12:3). As we stand with Israel, I believe we shall see God perform a

> mighty work in our day. God is going to bless America and Israel as well. It is not too late. I believe this is the greatest hour to be alive, and the key is unity, standing tall, proclaiming with a voice of love our commitment to the House of Israel, and to the God of Israel (1980: 221).

Conclusions

Karen Armstrong is not alone in tracing within dispensationalism evidence of the legacy of the Crusades. They have, she claims, 'returned to a classical and extreme religious crusading' (1988: 377). Rosemary Radford Ruether also sees the danger of this kind of fundamentalism in its 'dualistic, Manichaean view of global politics – America and Israel together against an evil world' (1989: 176). Kenneth Cragg (1992: 237–238) comments satirically:

> It is so; God chose the Jews; the land is theirs by divine gift. These dicta cannot be questioned or resisted. They are final. Such verdicts come infallibly from Christian biblicists for whom Israel can do no wrong – thus fortified. But can such positivism, this unquestioning finality, be compatible with the integrity of the prophets themselves? It certainly cannot square with the open peoplehood under God which is the crux of New Testament faith. Nor can it well be reconciled with the ethical demands central to law and election alike . . . Chosenness cannot properly be either an ethnic exclusivism or a political facility.

The Middle East Council of Churches, which represents the indigenous and ancient oriental and eastern churches, has also been highly critical of the activities of dispensationalists.

> [They] force the Zionist model of theocratic and ethnocentric nationalism on the Middle East, [rejecting] the movement of Christian unity and inter-religious understanding which is promoted by the churches in the region. The Christian Zionist programme, with its elevation of modern political Zionism, provides the Christian with a world-view where the gospel is

> identified with the ideology of success and militarism. It places its emphasis on events leading up to the end of history rather than living Christ's love and justice today (MECC 1988: 13).

Finally, Clarence Bass makes this assessment of dispensationalism.

> No part of historic Christian doctrine supports this radical distinction between church and kingdom. To be sure they are not identical; but dispensationalism has added the idea that the kingdom was to be a restoration of Israel, not a consummation of the church ... (1960: 31).
>
> In the light of this principle, it is legitimate to ask whether dispensationalism is not orientated more from the Abrahamic Covenant than from the Cross. Is not its focus centred more on the Jewish kingdom than on the Body of Christ? Does it not interpret the New Testament in the light of Old Testament prophecies, instead of interpreting those prophecies in the light of the more complete revelation of the New Testament? (1960: 151).

Whether intentionally or otherwise, dispensationalism is being used today to give theological justification to what the United Nations regards as nothing less than a form of racism (Sharif 1983: 1, 120) and the denial of basic human rights: supporting the 'ethnic cleansing' of Palestinians from their historic lands; endorsing the building of Jewish settlements in the Occupied Territories; inciting religious fanaticism by supporting the rebuilding of a Jewish temple on Mount Moriah; dismissing moderate Jewish opinion willing to negotiate land for peace; and advocating an apocalyptic eschatology likely to become a self-fulfilling prophecy.

It is therefore not surprising that, among the indigenous Christians of the Holy Land especially, dispensationalism is regarded as a dangerous heresy, an unwelcome and alien intrusion, advocating an exclusive Jewish political agenda and undermining the genuine ministry of justice, peace and reconciliation in the Middle East.

Bibliography

Allis, O. T. (1945), *Prophecy and the Church*, Philadelphia: Presbyterian and Reformed.

Armstrong, K. (1988), *Holy War: The Crusades and their Impact on Today's World*, London: Macmillan.

Barr, J. (1984), *Escaping from Fundamentalism*, London: SCM.

Bass, C. (1960), *Backgrounds to Dispensationalism*, Grand Rapids: Eerdmans.

Blaising, C. A. (1992), 'Dispensationalism, the search for definition', in Blaising & Bock (eds.) 1992.

Blaising, C. A., & Bock, D. L. (eds.), (1992), *Dispensationalism, Israel and the Church: The Search for Definition*, Grand Rapids: Zondervan.

——— (1993), *Progressive Dispensationalism*, Wheaton: Victor.

Bock, D. L. (1992), 'For the love of Zion', *Christianity Today*, 9 March.

Chafer, L. S. (1936a), *Dispensationalism*, Dallas: Dallas Theological Seminary Press.

——— (1936b), 'Dispensationalism', *Bibliotheca Sacra* 93: 107.

——— (1975), *Systematic Theology*, Dallas: Dallas Theological Seminary Press.

Coad, R. (1976), *A History of the Brethren Movement*, Exeter: Paternoster.

Cox, W. E. (1974), *An Examination of Dispensationalism*, Philadelphia: Presbyterian and Reformed.

Cragg, K. (1992), *The Arab Christian: A History in the Middle East*, London, Mowbray.

Darby, J. N. (1828), 'Considerations on the nature and unity of the church of Christ', in W. B. Neatby (1901), *A History of the Plymouth Brethren*, London: Hodder and Stoughton.

——— (1856), *The Hopes of the Church of God*, London: G. Morrish.

——— (1962a), *The Collected Writings of John Nelson Darby*, ed. W. Kelly, Kingston-on-Thames: Stow Hill Bible and Trust Depot.

——— (1962b), 'The apostasy of the successive dispensations' in *The Collected Writings of John Nelson Darby*, Ecclesiastical 1.2.

——— (1962c), 'The covenants', in *The Collected Writings of John Nelson Darby*, Doctrine 1.3.

——— (1962d), 'Reflections upon the prophetic enquiry and the views advanced in it', in *The Collected Writings of John Nelson Darby*, Prophetic 1.2.

——— (1962e), 'The character of office in the present dispensation', in *The Collected Writings of John Nelson Darby*, Ecclesiastical 1.1.

——— (1962f), 'The hopes of the church of God', in *The Collected Writings of John Nelson Darby*, Prophetic 1.2.

——— (1962g), 'The rapture of the saints and the character of the Jewish remnant', in *The Collected Writings of John Nelson Darby*, Prophetic 4.2.

DeMar, G., & Leithart, P. J. (1989), *The Legacy of Hatred Continues: A Response to Hal Lindsey's The Road to Holocaust*, Tyler: Institute for Christian Economics.

Dyer, C. (1991), *The Rise of Babylon: Signs of the End Times*, Wheaton: Tyndale House.

Evans, M. (1980), *Israel: America's Key to Survival*, Plainfield: Logos.

Fuller, D. P. (1980), *Gospel and Law, Contrast or Continuum? The Hermeneutic of Dispensationalism and Covenant Theology*, Grand Rapids: Eerdmans.

Gasque, W. W. (1978), 'Marcion', in J. D. Douglas (ed.), *The New International Dictionary of the Christian Church*, Exeter: Paternoster. Rev. edn.

Gerstner, J. (1991), *Wrongly Dividing the Word of Truth*, Brentwood: Wolgemuth and Hyatt.

Goldberg, L. (1982), *Turbulence over the Middle East*, Neptune: Loizeaux Brothers.

Halsell, G. (1986), *Prophecy and Politics: Militant Evangelists on the Road to Holocaust*, Westport: Lawrence Hill.

Horton, M. (1994), 'The church and Israel', *Modern Reformation*, May/June.

Ice, T., & Price, J. R. (1992), *Ready to Rebuild: The Imminent Plan to Rebuild the Last Days Temple*, Eugene: Harvest House.

International Christian Embassy, Jerusalem (1991), *Prepare Ye the Way of the Lord*, Jerusalem: ICEJ.

——— (1993), *International Christian Embassy, Jerusalem*, Jerusalem: ICEJ.

——— (1996), *International Christian Zionist Congress Proclamation*, Jerusalem: ICEJ.

Ironside, H. A. (1908), *The Mysteries of God*, New York: Loizeaux Brothers.

Johnston, S. L. (1963), 'The paralysis of legalism', *Bibliotheca Sacra*, April/June.

Lienesch, M. (1993), *Redeeming America: Piety and Politics in the New Christian Right*, Chapel Hill: North Carolina Press.

Lindsey, H. (1970), *The Late Great Planet Earth*, New York: Bantam.

——— (1973a), *Satan is Alive and Well on Planet Earth*, London: Lakeland.

——— (1973b), *There's a New World Coming*, Santa Ana, CA: Vision House.

——— (1981), *The 1980's Countdown to Armageddon*, New York: Bantam.

——— (1983), *Israel and the Last Days*, Eugene: Harvest House.

——— (1989), *The Road to Holocaust*, New York: Bantam.

——— (1995), *The Final Battle*, Palos Verdes: Western Front.

——— (1996), *Planet Earth 2000 A.D.: Will Man Survive?* Palos Verdes, California: Western Front. 1st edn 1994.

——— (1997), *The Apocalypse Code*, Palos Verdes: Western Front.

——— (1998), *Planet Earth: The Final Chapter,* Palos Verdes: Western Front.

——— *International Intelligence Briefing* (monthly), Palos Verdes: Hal Lindsey Ministries.

Lukoff, J. (1985), *A Christian Response to Israel*, Jerusalem: ICEJ.

Marsden, G. (1991), *Understanding Fundamentalism and Evangelicalism*, Grand Rapids: Eerdmans.

Mathison, K. A. (1995), *Dispensationalism: Rightly Dividing the People of God?* Phillipsburg: Presbyterian and Reformed.

Middle East Council of Churches (1988), *What is Western Fundamentalist Christian Zionism*? Limassol: MECC. Rev. edn.

Murray, I. A. (1971), *The Puritan Hope: Revival and the Interpretation of Prophecy*, Edinburgh: Banner of Truth.

Neatby, W. B. (1901), *A History of the Plymouth Brethren*, London: Hodder and Stoughton.

Pentecost, D. (1958), *Things to Come*, Findlay: Dunham.

Pevtzov, L. (1994), 'Apocalypse now, Operation Conquest – the Temple Mount Yeshiva', *Jerusalem Post Magazine*, 18 February.

Rantisi, A. (1999), unpublished interview.

Ruether, R. R., & Ruether, H. J. (1989), *The Wrath of Jonah: The Crisis of Religious Nationalism in the Israeli–Palestinian Conflict*, San Francisco: Harper.

Ryrie, C. (1953), *The Basis of the Premillennial Faith*, Neptune: Loizeaux Brothers.

——— (1965), *Dispensationalism Today*, Chicago: Moody.

——— (1995), *Dispensationalism,* Chicago: Moody.

Sandeen, E. (1967), 'Toward a historical interpretation of the origins of fundamentalism', *Church History* 36: 70.

——— (1970), *The Roots of Fundamentalism: British & American Millenarianism 1800–1930*, Chicago: University of Chicago Press.

Saucy, R. L. (1993), *The Case for Progressive Dispensationalism*, Grand Rapids: Zondervan.

Scofield, C. I. (1907), *Scofield Bible Correspondence Course*, Chicago: Moody Bible Institute. 19th edn.

——— (1909), Scofield Reference Bible, Oxford: Oxford University Press.

——— (1914), *Addresses on Prophecy*, New York: Chas. C. Cook.

——— (1928), *Rightly Dividing the Word of Truth*, Philadelphia: Philadelphia School of the Bible.

Sharif, R. (1983), *Non-Jewish Zionism: Its Roots in Western History*, London: Zed Press.

Shelly, B. (1978), 'Niagara Conferences', in J. D. Douglas (ed.), *The New International Dictionary of the Christian Church*, Exeter: Paternoster Press. Rev. edn.

Wagner, D. (1992), 'Beyond Armageddon', *The Link: Americans for Middle East Understanding*, 25.4.

Wagner, D (1995), *Anxious for Armageddon*, Scotdale: Herald.

Walvoord, J. F. (1962), *Israel in Prophecy*, Grand Rapids: Zondervan.

——— (1979), *The Rapture Question*, Grand Rapids: Zondervan.

——— (1990), *Armageddon, Oil and the Middle East*, Grand Rapids: Zondervan.

Welch, C., & Allen, S. (1973), *Perfection or Perdition: An Exposition of the Epistle to the Hebrews*, London: Berean Publishing Trust.

4C

Ten questions for a theology of the land[1]

Colin Chapman

There cannot be many situations in the world today where the different ways in which a theme from the Bible is understood have such immediate practical consequences in the lives of every single person. To state the issue very simply: the many Jews and Christians who believe that the West Bank is part of the land once promised to the descendants of Abraham for all time are not likely to have much sympathy for Palestinian claims to the same piece of land and theiq longings, resulting from centuries of occupation, for a Palestinian state. While biblical scholars and theologians sit around reading papers to each other, politicians, builders and water engineers are busy creating facts on the ground. And they do so because they are convinced that, because of what the Bible says, the whole land and this part of it in particular, *belong* in some profound sense to the Jews rather than to anyone else. Politics and theology are interwoven in this part of the world.

[1] This is a revised version of a paper published in *Mishkan* 26.1 (1997): 4–15.

The fundamental *political* question at the heart of the debate in recent years has been this: what are we to think of a situation in which two peoples lay claim to the same piece of land for different reasons? Two competing nationalisms related to the same area have emerged and clashed during the last 120 years – with disastrous consequences for both sides. But at this particular point in time the question about ownership of the land needs to be focused even more sharply. Do we believe that the Israeli government should resist Palestinian aspirations for statehood, and maintain direct or indirect control over the Occupied Territories on the West Bank at all costs? Or do we believe that, in the interests of human rights, Palestinian claims to peoplehood and nationhood need to be heard by Israel and the rest of the world, and allowed to find expression in land and statehood?

If this is the *political* question, the fundamental *theological* questions for Christians at the heart of this debate are these: does the existence of a Jewish state in the land today have profound theological significance in the economy of God? Is this understanding of the land consistent with the gospel proclaimed by, and summed up in, the person of Jesus Christ? Are there good biblical and theological reasons for giving whole-hearted support to the Zionist vision? When the questions are framed in this way, it becomes clear that there is a fundamental divide between those Jews and Christians who believe that the Jews have some kind of divine right to the land for all time, and those people (whether Jews, Christians, Muslims or people of no faith) who believe that the Jews do *not* have any such right.

It will be obvious by now that I come to the subject of the land with a set of questions that are very different from those of someone whose main interest is 'pure' biblical theology or the particular area of eschatology. As a result of living in Egypt and Lebanon for many years and later teaching in western contexts, the burning questions in my mind have to do with human rights, with Judaism and Islam, with the survival of Christianity in the Middle East, and with the mission of the churches in and around the Holy Land. So, for example, my engagement with Muslims has forced me to recognize the enormous stumbling-block created in their minds all over the world by the apparently blind and unthinking Christian support of Zionism and the policies of Israel. I am not, however, seeking to formulate a 'Palestinian theology of the land', but rather a Christian theology which can be commended to Jews and Arabs, to Muslims, Jews and Christians.

In this essay I want to do two things: first, to state some of the principles which have guided me in my thinking on these issues over the years since I began writing *Whose Promised Land?* in Beirut in the early 1980s;[2] secondly, to respond to some of the criticisms which have been levelled against the approach that I have adopted. I do this by elaborating a series of ten propositions and questions. Each of these can stand on its own, but each also forms a vital link in the chain of the argument.

1. The Abrahamic covenant: a 'package deal'?

The four strands of the Abrahamic covenant constitute a kind of 'package deal' and therefore need to be taken closely together.

A people requires a land, and there is something special about the relationship between peoplehood and land in the case of the Jews, since the promises given to Abraham concerning the land were intimately bound up with the promises concerning the nation, the covenant relationship and blessing for all peoples of the world (Gen. 12:1–3; 17:1–8).

Any Christian interpretation of the divine right to the land promised in Genesis, therefore, cannot be separated from our interpretation of other strands in the covenant promise. As Christians we have no difficulty in believing that the promises concerning the nation, the relationship between God and his people and the blessing for all peoples of the earth find their deepest fulfilment in the coming of Christ, who blesses people of all nations by drawing them into a covenant relationship with God as members of a holy nation (e.g. 1 Pet. 2:9–10). But if these three strands of the one covenant find their fulfilment in Christ and his church, how can we put the promise concerning the land into a different category? Can it be right to say that, while these three promises can legitimately be given a spiritual interpretation by Christians, the promise about the land requires a literal interpretation?

[2] A revised version of *Whose Promised Land?* (Tring: Lion, 1983) appeared in 1992.

Christian Zionists say to me: 'But why can we not have it both ways? Why can we not have an interpretation which is both literal and spiritual? Even if it is right to give a spiritual interpretation to the promise about the land, as the writer of Hebrews does, surely this need not preclude a literal interpretation? Can the promise not relate *both* to the inheritance of all Christian believers, and *also* to the divine covenant which gives to the Jews a divine right of ownership for all time?'

Part of my answer would be that the insistence on a literal fulfilment could be a double-edged weapon. God promised that the Aaronic priesthood would continue 'for ever' (1 Chr. 23:13). Has he fulfilled that promise literally? The Old Testament also promises that a descendant of David will sit on his throne 'for ever' (2 Sam. 7:12–16). Has that promise been fulfilled literally? No, but both have been fulfilled (really, if not literally) in Jesus.

The more fundamental problem, however, lies in the misleading and unhelpful distinction made between a 'literal' and a 'spiritual' interpretation. The New Testament encourages us to see the coming of the kingdom of God in Christ as the real and substantial fulfilment of every aspect of the Abrahamic covenant. It is therefore impossible to distinguish between literal and spiritual fulfilment of Old Testament promises and prophecies.

2. The modern return to the land: does it match the biblical pattern?

There are too many substantial differences between the return to the land after the exile in Babylon and the return in the last 120 years to accept that they are following the same pattern and can both be interpreted by the same biblical categories.

The prophets are full of predictions of the return to the land, and Ezra and Nehemiah describe several stages of the return after the exile. The modern return of the Jewish people to the land in the nineteenth and twentieth centuries has frequently been compared with the return of Jews to the land after the Babylonian captivity. Yet there are significant differences. These modern Jews were not returning to their ancestral homes in the same way as the exiles were (Ezra 2:70). The returning exiles also expected to have 'aliens' (or non-Israelites) living alongside them with full rights of inheritance (Ezek. 47:21–23). Above all, events since 1880, when taken as a whole, have more in common with the conquest under Joshua than with the peaceful return after the exile. This makes it hard for me as a Christian to see the recent return as a repetition of the return in the sixth century BC and therefore as a further stage in the fulfilment of the same prophecies.

A further problem I have in identifying the recent return with the sixth-century BC return revolves around the question of repentance. Moses speaks of God banishing his people from the land because of disobedience, but restoring them to the land after repentance: 'when you and your children return to the LORD your God ... then the LORD your God will restore your fortunes and have compassion on you and gather you again from the nations where he scattered you ... He will bring you to the land' (Deut. 30:1–5).

In books relating to the exile and the return, Daniel and Nehemiah are given as examples of people who express genuine repentance and confess the sins of the people (e.g. Dan. 9:1–19; Neh. 1:4–11). Thus when God brings the remnant back to the land, he does so in accordance with the conditions quoted above from Deuteronomy. The people then confess their sins corporately at a later stage after the return (e.g. Ezra 10:1–4; Neh. 9:1–37). Yet nevertheless, even before the return, a significant number of individuals have expressed repentance on behalf of the people.

My Jewish Christian friends in Israel, who live constantly in the atmosphere of Ezekiel 33 – 39, say to me, 'The Jews have returned in unbelief, but repentance and belief will follow their return.' Something like this can perhaps be seen in Ezekiel. Even there, however, the cleansing and the resettling seem to go together: 'On the day I cleanse you from all your sins, I will resettle your towns, and the ruins will be rebuilt' (Ezek. 36:33). But in Deuteronomy, repentance is clearly the condition of return.

If the temple was destroyed in AD 70 and Jews exiled from the land, as Jesus taught, as a judgment for their failure to recognize him as Messiah (Luke 19:41–44), the repentance required in the terms of Deuteronomy 30 would, from a Christian perspective, mean recognition of Jesus as Messiah. This would be the condition of return.

For all these reasons, there seem to be major difficulties in putting the return in recent centuries in the same category as the return in the sixth century BC. There are far too many significant differences.

3. Jesus' 'kingdom of God': the true fulfilment of Old Testament hope?

Jesus spoke of the kingdom of God as the fulfilment of what was promised in the Old Testament (e.g. Mark 1:15). If there is any single, over-arching concept in the teaching of Jesus, it is surely the coming of the kingdom of God. The kingly rule of God which began to come in the person of Jesus was the fulfilment of all the promises in the Old Testament covenants and all the prophecies about God's action to bless Israel and the nations. If this is true, however, what would be a genuinely Christian interpretation today of verses such as these from Psalm 102?

> But you, O LORD, sit enthroned for ever . . .
> You will arise and have compassion on Zion,
> for it is time to show favour to her;
> the appointed time has come.
> For her stones are dear to your servants;
> Her very dust moves them to pity.
> The nations will fear the name of the LORD,
> all the kings of the earth will revere your glory.
> For the LORD will rebuild Zion
> and appear in his glory
>
> (Ps. 102:12–17).

Jesus' teaching that 'the time has come' was announcing the arrival of the time spoken of by the prophets and the psalmist. Using the language of Psalm 102, therefore, the coming of the kingdom meant that the appointed time had come for God to 'arise and have compassion on Zion', 'to show favour to her', to 'rebuild Zion and appear in his glory'. In other words, if Jesus related God's compassion for Zion in a special way with the coming of the kingdom, it may be illegitimate for Christians today to relate his compassion for Zion with the Zionist vision.

I have often been accused of subscribing to so-called 'replacement theology'.[3] I do not, however, believe that the church has 'taken the place of Israel'. While New Testament writers give the church titles reserved for Israel in the Old Testament, they do not describe the church as 'the new Israel'. Instead, Gentiles are grafted *into* Israel (Rom. 11:17–24), which is thereby transformed to become the 'one new humanity' (Eph. 2:15). Unlike some of my Arab and western Christian friends, I still believe there is something special about the Jewish people. 'They are loved on account of the patriarchs' (Rom. 11:28). But I also believe that the fulfilment of all that was promised to Abraham and his descendants is found in the kingdom of God which came in Jesus.

As a result, when Christians agree with Jews in seeing their return to the land as the fulfilment of prophecy, I suspect that it may in many cases make it harder, not easier, for Jews to see Jesus as Messiah. If I pray for Jewish people as Paul did in Romans 10:1, I will long for them to be able to make the connection between the hopes of the Old Testament (summed up in the words of Zechariah, 'The LORD will be king over the whole earth': Zech. 14:9) and the claim of Jesus that through his coming 'the kingdom of God is near' (Mark 1:15).

4. The land in Jesus' teaching: a silence with reason?

Teaching about the land is conspicuous by its absence in the teaching of Jesus. In his magisterial work *The Gospel and the Land*, W. D. Davies finds just four verses in the Gospels where there is an indirect reference to the land, and only one explicit reference. This is in the Beatitudes (Matt. 5:5), where Jesus is quoting from Psalm 37:11: 'Blessed are the meek, for they shall inherit [not "the world" or "the earth", but] the land'. The meek, the humble, the poor in spirit, says Jesus, will inherit the promised land, and enter the kingdom of God. Davies (1974: 68) quotes a rabbi who said in effect, 'If you are saying grace before a meal and forget to thank God for the land, it does not count as a proper grace.' He goes on to argue that since the land was such a

[3] As, for example, in the review of *Whose Promised Land?* in *Mishkan* 1 (1984): 58–62.

fundamental part of Judaism at the time of Christ, his relative silence must have been deliberate.

It would be good to see some of my Christian Zionist friends engaging with Davies's argument, which is so well summed up in these eloquent words:

> In the last resort this study drives us to one point: the person of a Jew, Jesus of Nazareth, who proclaimed the acceptable year of the Lord only to die accursed on a cross and so to pollute the land, and by that act and its consequences to shatter the geographic dimension of the religion of his fathers. Like everything else, the land also in the New Testament drives us to ponder the mystery of Jesus, the Christ, who by his cross and resurrection broke not only the bonds of death for early Christians but also the bonds of the land (Davies 1974: 375).

It is also worth pointing out here a significant contrast between Jesus and the prophets who preceded him. When Jesus predicted the destruction of Jerusalem as a judgment on the Jewish people (Luke 19:41–44), this was fully in keeping with several of the Old Testament prophets. But, unlike them, he did not predict a return to the land (Mark 13:1–36; Matt. 24:1–51; Luke 21:5–36). Instead, he predicted the coming of the kingdom of God in terms drawn from Daniel's vision of the Son of Man who comes to the Ancient of Days to receive his kingly authority (Matt. 24:30–31; Luke 21:25–28; cf. Dan. 7:13–14). It cannot be an accident that Jesus had so little to say specifically about the land.

5. A turning-point for the disciples – and for us?

Luke 24:13–49 and Acts 1:1–8 mark a turning-point in the thinking of the disciples concerning the land, the Messiah and the kingdom of God. Until this point they would have been thinking in the same terms as other Jews of the first century. They had looked forward to God's decisive intervention in history which would restore political sovereignty to the Jews, enabling them to live in peace and obey the law in the promised land.

This is the idea reflected in the words of the disciples on the road to Emmaus: 'We had hoped that he was the one who was going to redeem Israel' (Luke 24:21). It must also have been the idea in the minds of the disciples when, during the period between the resurrection and the ascension, they asked, 'Lord, is this the time when you are to establish once again the sovereignty of Israel?' (Acts 1:6, NEB). It was John Calvin (in his commentary on Acts) who commented pointedly that 'there are as many mistakes in this question as there are words'.

The Christian Zionist interpretation of Jesus' reply (Acts 1:7–8) is that he accepted fully the idea that the Jews would one day regain their independence as a sovereign state in the land, but that he was simply correcting their ideas about the timing of it all. I suggest that the other possible interpretation is far more convincing, because it is much more consistent with the rest of the New Testament. Jesus was not only challenging their ideas about the timing, but trying to correct the very idea itself. When he went on to speak about the coming of the Spirit and about their witness 'in Jerusalem, Judea, Samaria and to the ends of the earth', he was trying to give them a new understanding of the kingdom of God that was not limited either to the land or to the chosen people. Israel's kingdom would be established as people of every race came under the rule of Israel's Messiah/King.

6. The apostles and the land: did they get it right?

The apostles seem to have ceased to believe that the establishment of a Jewish state had any significance for the kingdom of God. Unlike other Jewish teachers, the apostles had nothing to say about the theological significance of the land in the kingdom of God, and they used Old Testament language concerning the land in new ways. There is no suggestion that the apostles believed that the Jewish people still had a divine right to the land, or that Jewish possession of the land would be an important part of God's plan for the world. The penny had dropped; they had at last got the point!

I am sometimes accused here of building an argument on silence. My response is that this is not really an argument from silence, since there are several examples of New Testament writers who use vocabulary related to the land but give it new meaning. Paul speaks of 'the word of his grace, which can ... give you an inheritance among all those who are sanctified' (Acts 20:32). Peter speaks about 'an inheritance' which, unlike the land, 'can never perish, spoil or fade' (1 Pet. 1:4). Hebrews 4:1–13 interprets the theme of the land for Jewish Christians. And the climax of the letter comes in 12:22: 'But you have come to Mount Zion, to the heavenly Jerusalem.' The main argument of Hebrews is well summed up by C. J. H. Wright as follows:

> Hebrews' affirmations of what 'we have' are surprisingly comprehensive. We have the land, described as the 'rest' into which we have entered through Christ, in a way which even Joshua did not achieve for Israel (3:12 – 4:11); we have a High Priest (4:14; 8:1; 10:21) and an Altar (13:10); we have a hope, which in the context refers to the reality of the covenant made with Abraham (6:13–20). We enter into the Holy Place, so we have the reality of the tabernacle and temple (10:19). We have come to Mt. Zion (12:22) and we are receiving a kingdom, in line with Haggai 2:6 (12:28). Indeed according to Hebrews (13:14), the only thing which we do not have is an earthly, territorial city! (in Walker 1994: 18).

7. The hopes of Israel: unaffected by Jesus' coming?

To see the Jewish state today as the fulfilment of Old Testament prophecies, or even as a sign of God's faithfulness, misunderstands the nature of the kingdom that came in Jesus, and ignores the teaching of Jesus concerning the judgment explained in the eschatological discourses. Although the New Testament writers were not addressing the kind of political questions we face today, we cannot ignore their theology of the kingdom when we have to address political questions they did not have to face.

My fundamental disagreement with Christian Zionists is that they do not seem to me to take seriously enough the question: what difference did the coming of the kingdom of God in the person of Jesus make to traditional Jewish hopes and expectations about the land and the people? If they address the teaching of Jesus and the apostles on these subjects at all, they seem to interpret the Old

Testament today as if the coming of Jesus made little or no difference to these particular aspects of the hopes of first-century Judaism. They seem to read the Old Testament with the spectacles worn by the first disciples *before* the resurrection and their encounters with the risen Christ. It is as if the coming of the kingdom in Jesus simply meant a postponement of Jewish hopes for restoration, rather than the fulfilment of these hopes in the Messiah and the messianic community.

8. Paul's vision for Israel – or the world?

While Paul seems to look forward to a more glorious future for the Jewish people (Rom. 9 – 11), there is no suggestion that the future salvation of 'Israel' is related in any way to the land.

In Romans Paul clearly looks forward to a more glorious future for the Jewish people. But when he says, 'and so all Israel will be saved' (11:26), he can hardly mean that at some time in the future *all* Jews then alive will be saved, since this would contradict his earlier statement that 'not all who are descended from Israel are Israel' (9:6). And there is no suggestion that the future salvation of 'Israel' is related in any way to the land. Paul's silence about the land does not suggest that he still held on to his traditional Jewish theology of the land, but rather that he had modified it very considerably.

This is the conclusion of Kenneth Bailey, who has taught for many years in Lebanon and the Middle East. He points out that in his reference to the promises given to Abraham in Genesis 12 and 17, Paul speaks of the promise that Abraham and his descendants 'should inherit' not the land, but 'the world' (*kosmos*). After showing how these promises were interpreted in the intertestamental period, Bailey (1994: 63) concludes: 'For Paul, the "children of Abraham" are those Jews and Gentiles who through faith in Christ have been made righteous. The "land" becomes the "world" (*kosmos*), which is the inheritance of the righteous.'

Is Paul twisting Scripture? Is he deliberately playing with the text when he substitutes 'world' or 'universe' (*kosmos*) for 'land'? Bailey believes that Paul is simply giving us a distinctively Christian interpretation of promises about the land. Once again Davies

(1974: 179) sums up the thinking of Paul so well: 'In the Christological logic of Paul, the land, like the Law, particular and provisional, had become irrelevant.'

9. The 'redemption of Israel': achieved recently or long ago?

If Luke related 'the redemption of Jerusalem' and the 'consolation of Israel' to the life and ministry of Jesus (Luke 2:25, 38; 21:28; 24:21), it is hard to see how Christians today can use the same terminology to interpret the significance of Zionism.

Books written by Christian Zionists are full of expressions such as 'the restoration of Israel', 'the redemption of Jerusalem', 'the restoration of the Jews', 'the rebirth, regeneration or renewal of the nation'. These expressions are all based on Old Testament prophecy which looks forward to the restoration of the nation after the exile. It is perfectly understandable that Jews should have kept hopes like these alive as they longed for a new return after their centuries-long diaspora. But I have great difficulty understanding how Christian Zionists can use the same terminology without any qualification whatever. They do not seem to recognize that Luke at least believed that 'the redemption of Jerusalem' and 'the consolation of Israel' had already been accomplished in Christ.

The response of some Christian Zionists is to say that we are limiting God. If we agree that an Old Testament promise or prophecy has been fulfilled in a spiritual way, why can it not also be fulfilled in a literal way?

But this is a step backwards which we cannot take. If Jesus really was, and is, the 'new temple', as he claimed to be, and if we have seen the Shekinah glory of God resting not on a restored temple but on the Word made flesh (John 1:14; 2:20–22), how can Christians ever even contemplate the rebuilding of a temple in Jerusalem? Or again, if the Old Testament vision of water welling up from Jerusalem's temple and flowing down to the Dead Sea (see Ezek. 47:1–12; Joel 3:18–20; Zech. 14:8–9) is related by Jesus to the giving of the Holy Spirit (John 7:37–39), how can we apply these same passages to Israeli irrigation schemes on the West Bank?! (I was astonished to hear this particular interpretation expounded some years ago by an evangelical Arab pastor in Amman, Jordan.) Or finally, how can we apply the expression the 'redemption of Israel' to the events of the last hundred years, when that expression has been used for nearly two thousand years to describe the incarnation and the atonement?

10. Old Testament prophecy – mere prediction or ethical challenge?

We may recognize that a people requires a land, and that Jews will want to use Old Testament language to express their hopes. But the more Jews (and Christians) appeal to Scripture to undergird and justify Zionism, the more they must ask for Zionism to be judged by all of the ethical and eschatological teaching of the Old Testament.

That Jews (both religious and secular) should use the Old Testament as the basis of their Zionism is perfectly understandable. What I do not understand is how Christians can use the Old Testament in the same way, affirming that it gives the Jews the title deeds to the land for all time. But if, for the sake of argument, I were to agree with this use of the Old Testament, I would want to press home the implications of this approach by arguing as follows: 'If you use part of the Old Testament this way, are you not putting yourself under the judgment of the whole? If you look to Genesis to claim the promise of the land, what about Exodus and the commandments not to steal, kill or covet? If you believe in the predictive element of prophecy, what about the prophetic concern for justice? Is not the present Israeli government's policy of Judaizing East Jerusalem a modern parallel to Ahab stealing Naboth's vineyard? Where are the Elijahs among the Christian Zionists who are prepared to speak a prophetic word to the Ahabs in Israel today? If you believe in the vision of a restored Zion, can you show us where is the blessing of the nations in all of this? Is it to be seen in the exporting of Israeli technology to Africa? And, tell me, what has the suppression of the *intifada* done to the soul of Israel and of Judaism? Is this the fulfilment of all those wonderful visions, so full of biblical terminology, which were put forward by generations of Zionists?'

In short, we have a right to say to Zionists, both Jewish and Christian: 'The stronger you press your claim to the land on the basis of Scripture, the more you must expect and even invite the whole world to judge what the Jews have done in the land by the moral and spiritual standards found in those same Scriptures. You have no grounds for accusing us of double standards, complaining that we judge the State of Israel by higher standards than we use to judge the Arabs!'

I end with a question, a challenge and an appeal.

A question: what progress has there been, if any, in the dialogue between Christians who are Zionists and Christians who are not Zionists in recent years? I do not share many of the assumptions of Christian Zionism, because I believe they are based on flawed theology and flawed exegesis of Scripture, and because they seem to me to lead in practice to disastrous political and human consequences. While there have been a number of occasions in recent years when the two sides have spoken to each other, I have an uncomfortable feeling that we are still speaking at cross-purposes and not really engaging with each other at any deep level.

A challenge: can Christian Zionists support their case with recent scholarship? The case against Christian Zionists has been supported by new scholarship, as, for example, in the writings of N. T. Wright (1996) and Peter Walker (1994, 1996). Can work of this quality be matched by Christian Zionists, or are they simply, dare I say, repeating the same old arguments that have been put forward in the past?

An appeal: is it not possible to address some of the real, live issues out there in the world today? I am sad that the agenda for most Christians has for so long revolved largely around questions about the fulfilment of prophecy and divine rights to own the land. I fear that we shall need to go on discussing these questions for many years to come, since assumptions about the way the Old Testament should be interpreted are so deeply ingrained in the minds of Christians all over the world. But if we are not careful, we may find that we are addressing old questions and old agendas at a time when everything is changing as a result of what is happening on the ground. The goalposts are moving!

What I am asking for is that, instead of simply asking, 'How, if at all, can the establishment of the Jewish state and its policies towards the Palestinian Arabs be justified?', we begin to address a new set of questions, such as these:

- What are we to understand about nationhood and peoplehood?
- What makes a person a Jew, and how do Jews today, both in Israel and the West, understand their identity?
- What do our Scriptures say about human rights, and about the status of minorities?
- How are we to understand Islam and Islamic responses to Israel?
- How can we develop a critique of Islamic fundamentalism that is both sympathetic and rigorous?
- Can we give our minds to the question of Jerusalem and try to work out a political formula for a city of peace – a formula that enables two peoples and three faiths to live side by side with mutual respect and recognition?
- Is there a prophetic word to the Palestinians that can help them in their task of nation-building? Is there a word about styles of leadership, about integrity, and about the kind of pluralism that safeguards the rights of minorities?
- How in the midst of all that is happening in the Middle East can we help Jews to see Jesus of Nazareth as Daniel's Son of Man and Isaiah's suffering Servant? How can we help Muslims to see what is distinctive in the way Jesus responded to blindness, perversity, injustice and violence, and by so doing inaugurated the kingly rule of God on earth?
- Is there any hope for the survival of Christianity in the Middle East beyond the next twenty years or so? What does Christian mission mean in that context today?
- How helpful has been the contribution of western Christians throughout this unfolding drama?

In Jeremiah 37:17 King Zedekiah asks, 'Is there any word from the LORD?' We should be asking the same question today, but recognizing that we are seeking a word *for a new and changing situation.*

Bibliography

Bailey, K. E. (1994), 'St Paul's understanding of the territorial promise of God to Abraham: Romans 4:13 in its historical/theological context', *Near East School of Theology Review.* 15.1: 59–69.

Davies, W. D. (1974), *The Gospel and the Land: Early Christianity and Jewish Territorial Doctrine*, Berkeley: University of California Press.

Walker, P. W. L. (ed.) (1994), *Jerusalem Past and Present in the Purposes of God*, Carlisle: Paternoster. Rev. edn.
——— (1996), *Jesus and the Holy City: New Testament Perspectives on Jerusalem*, Grand Rapids: Eerdmans.
Wright, C. J. H. (1994), 'A Christian approach to Old Testament prophecy concerning Israel', in Walker 1994: 1–19.
Wright, N. T. (1996), *Jesus and the Victory of God*, London: SPCK.

5. *VIEWS FROM THE LAND TODAY*

5A

People, land and Torah: a Jewish Christian perspective[1]

Baruch Maoz

In this paper we explore three vital biblical themes – people, land and Torah – and the relationship between them. The history of the people of Israel may legitimately be described as that of a constant journey, but it is not a journey void of a goal. Israel is portrayed in the Bible as constantly journeying either towards the land or away from it, but always in some kind of relation to it. What is so important about the land? How can we best describe the relationship the people of Israel have towards it? How does the Torah affect the people of Israel living in the land today?

The land in Israel's history and experience

God's first act in relation to Israel was to call the people's founding father away from his previous dwelling 'to a land which I will show you' (Gen. 12:1). In other words, biblical history – which, to a very

[1] This is a revised version of a paper first published in *Mishkan* 5 (1986): 59–72.

large extent, is synonymous with the history of the people of Israel – is 'landed history', firmly grounded in a specific location. Much of what took place in the land could have taken place nowhere else, and took place there precisely because of the people of Israel.

The very beginning of human history teaches us to expect as much. Adam was not only created, given a ruler's mandate, gifted with a marriage relationship and enthroned over all the earth. No, the peak of God's blessing to him was a specific location, geographically defined by rivers and a garden. It was there that Adam and Eve communed with God and acted out their calling to subdue the earth, to replenish and rule over it. When (following their sin) they were cast out, their exile from the garden was equal to their being exiled from God.

Similar guidelines apply to Israel. They did not earn their land any more than Adam earned the Garden of Eden (Gen. 12:1; Jer. 31:20–40, 32:30–44). Once placed in the land, however, through the mercies of God, the people's enjoyment of the land was contingent upon their faithful obedience to the God who had graciously placed them there (Deut. 27 – 29). If ever they sinned, they lost the right to enjoy the land and were consequently exiled. Exile from the land was, and is, equal to being exiled from God (Ps. 42; 2 Kgs. 13:23; 17:18–20; 24:20; Jer. 32:31). It is a kind of disembodied national existence which tears at the very roots of a normal existence, threatening to extinguish it if it is not remedied by a return.

Moreover, Israel as a people cannot truly fulfil its duties to God apart from the land. Please note this is not 'land' in general, nor even any land in particular, but only one certain and specific land. This is the land repeatedly designated in the Bible by way of its borders (Gen. 15:18; Exod. 23:31; Deut. 11:24; Josh. 1:4), its topography (Deut. 1:7; Judg. 1:9, 15; 1 Sam. 14:4–5), its climate (Deut. 11:10–11; Judg. 6:40; Is. 18:4, 55:10; Jer. 18:17; Hag. 2:17) and its history. Israel's worship of God is contingent upon a certain order of seasons (Lev. 23:9–10, 39–40; 26:4; Josh. 1:15; Job 5:26; Ps. 1:3), upon certain animals, fruit or grain which are available only locally (Lev. 11), and on modes of dress (Is. 22:21; 2 Sam. 13:18; 2 Kgs. 1:8; Deut. 25:9) and buildings (Ezek. 41:8; Zech. 9:15; Lev. 14:37; Ps. 118:22; Josh. 2:6) which are suitable for some areas but not for others. Most particularly, it is a 'place the LORD your God will choose as a dwelling for his Name' (Deut. 12:11; 1 Kgs. 11:36; Neh. 1:9). Consequently, Israel could not serve its God as well in Tibet, western Europe or North America as it could in that specific plot of land wedged between the Anti-Lebanon and the River of Egypt, between the Great Sea and the Arabian Desert.

The amount of biblical material on this subject is astounding to a measure equalled only by the paucity of theological enquiry into the subject. Land is a central theme of biblical faith. Small wonder, then, that the land has been given so many loving names by the people who were called to dwell in it. Here are only a few examples: 'my own homeland' (Gen. 30:25), 'the land of your fathers' (Gen. 31:3), 'native land' (Gen. 31:13), 'home' (Lev. 18:9), 'beloved' (Is. 62:4), 'the Beautiful Land' (Dan. 11:16) – even simply 'this land' (Num. 14:3), since for Israel there is none other.

The land as divine presence and blessing

The land of Israel is not merely a piece of turf. It is God's blessing (Gen. 1:22; 26:3; Num. 24:1, 5–7) and it is God's presence (Gen. 15:18; Exod. 23:31; Deut. 11:24; Josh. 1:4). It is evidence of an ongoing relationship between God and the people of Israel (Deut. 7:12–13; 2 Kgs. 21:14; Jer. 23:39; Lam. 5:16–22). The land is the covenant made concrete (Gen. 17:7–8; Exod. 6:8; Neh. 9:8; Jer. 31:31, 38–40; 32:37–41).

The land, as far as Israel is concerned, is God's 'holy habitation' (Exod. 15:3; Ps. 28:2). This is particularly indicated by the temple, serving as what W. D. Davies has aptly (though somewhat quaintly) described as 'the quintessence of the land' (see 1 Kgs. 8:17–19, 33). This is so fundamental that for Israel to be carried away into exile from its own land is equal to its being 'removed' from God's presence (2 Kgs. 17:18–19). The Lord reigns from Zion (Ps. 2:6), which is the scene of his presence and saving power (Ps. 14:7; 46:4–5; 63:2). Nothing is so heart-rending to the psalmist as to be away 'at the heights of Hermon', instead of being able to appear before God (Ps. 42). Elsewhere he cries out on behalf of all his people, 'How can we sing the songs of the LORD while in a foreign land?' (Ps. 137).

The land is not only where God dwells; it is where he is constantly active in blessing. God's eyes are constantly upon the land (Deut. 11:12; 1 Kgs. 9:3), governing its seasons by bringing or withholding its rains (Deut. 29:22; Jer. 14:1–8), protecting it from enemies (2 Kgs. 7:6–7; 19:5–8, 35–37; Is. 7:3–7, 16–17), directing the growth of its produce (Lev. 26:4; 1 Kgs. 17:14; Ps. 68:10; Amos 4:7; Zech. 10:1; Lev. 25:19; Deut. 16:10, 15; Mal. 3:9–10), and either preserving it from or exposing it to locusts, frost and mildew (Deut. 28:22, 38; 1 Kgs. 8:37; Ps. 78:46–47; Joel 1:4; Amos 4:9). Do enemies invade the land, rob its inhabitants of its fruit and burn the rest? God has done this (Judg. 3:7–8, 12–14; 4:1–2; Is. 7:18–25; Jer. 17:3–4). Has the invading enemy been defeated? This, too, is God's handiwork (Judg. 3:9, 15; 4:3; Is. 46:1–4). Is a plague stalking the land, or wild beasts? These are the Lord's doings (2 Sam. 24:15; Ps. 106:29; Lev. 26:22; Deut. 32:24; Ezek. 34:28). Everything that ever happens in the land is God's work: giants are defeated (Deut. 3:3; Josh. 17:18; 2 Sam. 21:15–22), well-fortified cities collapse (Josh. 6), rivers overflow and cause chariots to drown in the ensuing mud (Judg. 4:12–13; 5:4–5, 12–13); even the sun and the moon stand still when God so orders it (Josh. 10:12–14). The land is nothing less than God's amazing presence.

The intimate connection between the people and the land

It is an interesting phenomenon of the English language that, with regard to all people but the people of Israel, we may easily distinguish between a land and its people by linguistic means. We say 'Greece' and 'Greeks', 'China' and 'Chinese', 'Nigeria' and 'Nigerians'; but 'Israel' denotes both people and land. It therefore should come as no surprise to us to discover that the Bible lays a similar identification at the foundations of our thinking on the subject.

The land is no passive observer, a mere sphere in which Israel as a people operate. It is spoken of as altogether at one with the people – so much so that it becomes liable for the people's actions (Lev. 26:14; Deut. 6:12). It is also a privilege granted to the land (Lev. 25:4–5). Israel's sin brings punishment to the land (Lev. 26:33; Deut. 24:4, 28–29), for God will be 'angry with the land' because of the people's sin. Conversely, when the people are true to God, he will bless them and the land (Deut. 30:9). Israel's destiny is that of the land (Pss. 122:1–2, 6; 147:2).

So the prophets speak of land and people as one: blessing upon the people is blessing to the land (Is. 7:22; Jer. 44:22; Mal. 3:10–11). The people's sinning is equal to the land's committing sin (Lev. 19:29; Deut 24:4). Mourning (Hos. 4:3; Zech. 12:12), sorrow (Is. 3:26), pain (Mic. 1:9) and joy (Joel 2:21; Amos 9:13) are often shared by the land and people alike. As a result, it is sometimes impossible to determine if the terms employed refer to the people or to the land. In fact, they often speak of both. When God addresses Jerusalem, speaking tenderly to her, or when he refers to a glorified new Jerusalem (Is. 41), can we confidently say whether the reference is to people in terms of land or to the land as somehow identified with the people? When God pours out his Spirit upon the people, the very land radiates with his glory (Ezek. 43:2) and joyfully celebrates his goodness to the people (Hos. 2:18–23).

The land was the sphere in which the people experienced blessing; it was a means for their enjoyment of God. It was to be constantly celebrated by annual observance of the feasts related to its seasons, and its fruits were continually offered to God in sacrifice. It must be disposed of (Lev. 25:23–24) and tilled (Lev. 25:2–5), and its fruits must be enjoyed (Lev. 25:6–7), in accordance with God's commands. Its 'edges' are to be left for the needy (Lev. 23:22), for the people are forbidden to exhaust its resources for private gain. The climax of blessing in the land is the divine promise: 'I will be your God' (Lev. 25:17, 55). The land is thus the epitome of God's promises, and an important part of the whole without which the remainder is incomplete. Nowhere in the Scriptures are the people of Israel considered to be blessed outside of the land. Nowhere is blessing promised to the people apart from blessing to the land (Deut. 28:65–68; Pss. 69:35–36; 85:10, 12). Small wonder, then, that the people of Israel have come to love the land so vehemently:

If I forget you, O Jerusalem,
  may my right hand forget its skill!
May my tongue cleave to the roof of my mouth
  if I do not remember you,

if I do not consider Jerusalem
  my highest joy!...
O daughter of Babylon, you devastated one,
  how blessed will be the one who repays ...
who seizes and dashes your little ones against the rock!'
(Ps. 137:5–9, my translation of vv. 8–9)

Possession of the land

A biblical term used to express one aspect of the divinely intended relationship between the people and the land is the term 'possess' (Gen. 22:17; 23:4; Acts 7:5; Heb. 11:8–9). The people of Israel were not only meant to dwell in the land, as did Abraham, but to 'possess' it (1 Kgs. 21:15; 2 Kgs. 17:24; Is. 14:21). As early as at Jacob's bedside we come across the concept of political independence in relation to the land. However seminal the form in which the concept here appears, Jacob nevertheless assures Judah of a 'sceptre' (Gen. 49:8–10). This is the symbol of government and kingly power. Possession denotes control of the land: its resources (Lev. 26:16; Deut. 28:4–5; Judg. 6:3–6), highways (Lev. 26:22; Judg. 5:6), agricultural produce (Lev. 26:20; Deut. 28:11–12), and the freedoms of its inhabitants (Deut. 28:48–52; Judg. 3:14; Jer. 30:8). Loss of such control was always conceived of as divine punishment (Lev. 26) due to the people's unfaithfulness to the covenant (Deut. 28 – 29; 5:31–32; 11:8, 22–25).

Consequently, the returnees in the days of Ezra and Nehemiah realized that renewal of a physical presence in the land was but one step toward the ultimate goal. They must labour for the renewal of national, economic, political, social and religious life in the land to which they had returned (Ezra 9:10; Neh. *passim*; Hag. 2:4–5, 20–23). Such aspirations are faithful representations of earlier prophetic utterances, of which Ezekiel's following statement is but one example: 'They will know that I am the LORD, when I break the bars of their yoke and rescue them from the hands of them who enslaved them. They will no longer be plundered by the nations' (Ezek. 34:27b–28).

Of course, the right to enjoy such a national blessing is conditional, as we have already indicated. Possession and physical presence are not, so far as the divine purposes are concerned, ends in themselves; they serve greater purposes. For this reason, the people are to exercise great care as to how they conduct their political independence and what they do to secure it. All such deeds must be acts of faith (Is. 7:9; 2 Kgs. 19) and expressions of covenant loyalty (Lev. 25:18–19, 26:3–6, 9–10; Josh. 1:7; 2 Kgs. 17). The people must not mingle with the other nations so as to lose their distinct moral and religious identity (Deut. 6:12–19; Josh. 23:9–16; Jer. 7; Ezek. 8).

The land and salvation

We have said that the people's right to enjoy the land is contingent upon their covenant loyalty. But no-one ever earns the right to God's goodness, any more than human sinfulness can ever undo the faithfulness of God. While God declares that he will punish the people of Israel's unfaithfulness with terrible stringency, 'Yet ... I will not reject them or abhor them so as to destroy them completely, breaking my covenant with them. I am the LORD their God' (Lev. 26:44). Those who are not consumed by the just deserts of their sin will discover that their salvation issues out of God's unchangingly merciful nature. Even when we do not believe, he continues to be faithful because he cannot deny himself. God's self-consistency is our salvation and only hope.

The people will be restored to the land if they repent (Deut. 30:1–10); otherwise they will be brought back to the land, and will there repent (Jer. 50:20; Ezek. 36:4–21, 30:27–29). Even then the people and land are inseparable. The land sins (Deut. 24:4), is defiled by the people's sin (Lev. 18:25; Num. 35:34; Jer. 2:7; 16:18) and is later redeemed and blessed (Is. 62:4). Psalms, Ezra, Nehemiah and earlier books such as Leviticus, Deuteronomy and Judges all speak of the land and the people as one. Nation, city, land and political entity all have a shared destiny, so that one cannot be redeemed without the others. At times they may be distinguishable, but they are never separable except as spirits may be separated from bodies – an excruciating abnormality which constantly cries out for remedy.

Consequently, Israel can be redeemed nowhere else but in the land of Israel. 'There in Zion, the city of our appointed feasts ...

the Majestic One, the LORD shall be for us' (Is. 33:20–24, my translation). Indeed, salvation itself is conceived of in terms of a joyful return to the land (Is. 35:10; Amos 9:15; Zech. 10:9–10), and comfort is addressed indistinguishably to people, city and land (Is. 40:1, 9–10; 50:3–16; Jer. 4:14; 8:5; 22:29). Jerusalem is the people that has sinned (Jer. 6:6) and that stands in need of forgiveness (Jer. 5:1). Spiritual restoration and a return to the land are linked (Jer. 23:7–8; 24:6–7; 30:1–9; Ezek. 34:13–27; 36:16–38; 37:21–27; Mic. 4:1) so that the people are never considered blessed, forgiven or redeemed except in the land promised to their fathers: 'You will know that I am the LORD, when I bring you into the land of Israel' (Ezek. 20:42).

> 'On that day they will say to Jerusalem,
>   "Do not fear, O Zion;
>   do not let your hands hang limp.
> The LORD your God is with you,
>   he is mighty to save.
> He will take great delight in you,
>   he will quiet you with his love,
>   he will rejoice over you with singing." '
>
> (Zeph. 3:16–17)

The New Testament and the land

The New Testament neither contradicts nor corrects what we have deduced from the Old Testament data. On the contrary, Old Testament expectations are heightened in the New Testament by the sheer fact that their fulfilment is described as having begun. After all, the New Testament claims to be a fulfilment of Old Testament promise, the reliable description of a climax of hope being realized and clarified by the coming of Messiah. Jesus is not a cancellation of Old Testament hope but its unequivocal affirmation (Luke 24:38–44; John 11:24; 20:24–27; Acts 24:15; Rom. 8:18–24; Phil. 3:21; Rev. 21 – 22).

This is not to say that Old Testament expectations are now fully realized, or that whatever has not yet been fulfilled is now replaced with a different hope. Israel is yet to experience salvation (Rom.

9–11) – an assurance which necessarily connotes essential continuity with Old Testament promise. Nor is there any New Testament modification of what we have learned from the Old Testament regarding Israel, except by way of clarification. Consequently, we must necessarily conclude our reading of the New Testament with the same conceptions as we did the Old Testament. There is a real continuity between Old and New Testaments, as well as a kind of discontinuity.

It is true that redemption from sin is not to be conceived of in terms that are primarily material. On this point the New Testament is as clear as the Old, though much more emphatic. But salvation is not to be thought of as exclusively spiritual and moral, as if Israel's living in the land had no spiritual and moral implications! The gospel message is replete with appreciation for the material realm. The New Testament makes it quite clear that the material is the arena in which ultimate salvation is to take place (Rom. 8:18–25), thus reconfirming Old Testament expectation. Even our bodies are to be redeemed (Rom. 8:23; 1 Cor. 15).

Of course, salvation is not exclusively or primarily a matter of material realities (Heb. 4:8); nor are the Old Testament promises exhausted by exclusively material accomplishments as opposed to heavenly ones (Heb. 11:16). The contradictions found between 'heavenly' and 'earthly' lie not in terms of geography but in terms of the priority of things: Godward or otherwise, holy or sinful. The new heaven and new earth are said to 'descend'. There are spiritual bodies and natural ones (1 Cor. 15:36–44), and the New Testament doctrine of resurrection implies a spiritual kind of material existence rather than a non-material state of being (Exod. 3:6, 8; Num. 32:11; Deut. 30:20; Neh. 9:7–8).

To summarize our argument up to this point:

- Israel as a people and the land of Israel are inseparable in so far as the divine purposes are concerned. God promised the land to the people in his covenant with Abraham. In the unfolding of this promise, God has made the land a focal point for all his promised blessings: the people are blessed, walk in God's ways and enjoy his presence only in the land.
- This land is not just any land, but one specific land repeatedly

designated in Scripture by its borders, cities, climate, topography, former inhabitants and such like.

- The gospel is the fulfilment of Old Testament promise and, consequently, not a replacement. God's gifts and his calling are not revoked. However wide the gifts and graces of the gospel may now be, however their dispersion, the New Testament may in no rightful sense be construed as replacing the covenant made with Abraham.
- Hence, Israel as a people (and therefore Israel as a people in its divinely promised land) remains a focal point of New Testament expectation. God has not forsaken his people; he has consigned them over to unbelief that he might have mercy upon all (Rom. 11:32).

The Mosaic Torah and the Abrahamic covenant

Such conclusions immediately present us with a problem. It is obvious from many of the texts quoted that Israel's relation to the land is not only the product of the Abrahamic covenant, but also of the Mosaic (Lev. 26; Deut. 28 – 29). Are we then to conclude that Israel's divinely purposed, continued existence also implies an equally divinely intended duty toward the covenant made at Sinai?

This is an issue which sharply divides many Jewish Christians and which has never been satisfactorily resolved by our Gentile brethren. Antinomianism, legalism, Judaizing and liberalism have plagued the church from the moment of its inception, and are hardly liable to be decisively resolved in the course of this paper! Nevertheless, it is high time that there should be formulated a biblical doctrine of the law, thoroughly and carefully conceived. Meanwhile the following brief remarks may suffice.

Contrary to what the rabbis would have us understand, the basic covenant which lies at the root of Israel's national existence is not the covenant instituted at Sinai. It is the covenant which God made with Abraham. Other biblical covenants flow from and are subservient to the purposes of this basic, fundamental covenant. The covenant with Abraham is the covenant which lies at the foundation of Israel's national being. It was because God remembered this covenant that he led Israel out of Egypt (Exod. 6:5–8). Israel's deliverance from Egypt had the accomplishment of the Abrahamic promise as its goal (Exod. 6:6–8, cf. 3:6–8). The Mosaic covenant, on the other hand, is secondary to that made with Abraham (Exod. 3:7–8, 6:5–8; Deut. 6:10–11; 7:1, 7–10). Israel's continued enjoyment of the land was indeed contingent upon their keeping of the Mosaic covenant but only because that Mosaic covenant fulfilled the divine purposes of the Abrahamic covenant for one particular era within salvation history – namely from the departure from Egypt (Exod. 20:2) until the appearance of the Seed (Gal. 3:19; cf. Jer. 31:31–32; Heb. 8:8–12, 9:1–15, 10:15–18).

So the people's relation to the land has a twofold contingency. As its primary ground it is contingent upon the Abrahamic covenant (Lev. 26:14; Deut. 29:21–24; 2 Kgs. 18:11–12; Jer. 34:12ff.). As a secondary ground it is contingent upon the people's faithful adherence to the Mosaic covenant (Jer. 11:3–5), but this subserves the purposes of the former covenant (Lev. 26:27–28, 40–46; Is. 54:10, 59:21; Mic. 7:18–20; Rom. 11:28–29; Gal. 3:17–18).

The Abrahamic covenant continues in the face of transgressions against the Mosaic covenant even while the people are being punished because of their sin (Hos. 5:14–16, 11:1–9; Rom. 11:1–2, 26). Jesus then fulfils the Abrahamic covenant. He is the deliverer, destined to 'turn godlessness away from Jacob' (Rom. 11:26) in accordance with the (Abrahamic) covenant (Matt. 1:21; Luke 1:54–55, 68–73).

Consequently, Israel is not displaced by the church. Rather, the church enters into the enjoyment of Israel's blessings as a strange branch 'grafted in ... contrary to nature', but never in place of the natural branches, who will be grafted in again (Rom. 11:23–24). This is not to say that Israel's redemption bears no relation to the Torah (however we may choose to define that term) or to Torah in general. Israel's redemption is the fulfilling of Torah – a renewing of covenant, or a 'new covenant' (Is. 42:6, 49:4; 55:1–3, 61:1–8; Jer. 31:31–39).

Here too, as in other areas, the Torah is fulfilled by Christ, who was given as 'a covenant for the people' (Is. 42:6; 49:8; Luke 22:20). Israel is still bound – in Christ and by Christ – to God in covenant, but the covenant in view is no longer that which God made with our fathers when he took them by the hand to lead them out of Egypt. The promised Seed has come (Gal. 3:1–19). We now have another priesthood, empowered by an endless life and after an order different from that of Aaron. A change in the priesthood of necessity implies a change in the law (Heb. 7:12). We are no longer subject to the 'schoolmaster', nor are we free to live as if we were still subject, 'for the slave woman's son will never share in the inheritance with the free woman's son' (Gal. 4:1–30).

The implications of the above may be summarized in three short statements:

- Jews in Christ are no longer bound by the Mosaic covenant.
- Israel is still bound to God in covenant, that is to say, in the Abrahamic covenant.
- Jesus brings to Israel a new covenant. He does not do so by cancelling the Mosaic covenant but by fulfilling it. Hence, no lasting comfort is available to Israel outside of Christ and no greater comfort is possible than the comfort of the gospel. We must preach Christ! We must call Israel to repentance! Our people's destiny depends on this to a terrifying extent.

Conclusion

What, then, does this mean for the complex relationship which exists between people, land and Torah? The observant reader may have noticed that many of the references above (such as Is. 42:6; 49:4, 55:1–3; 61:1–8; Jer. 31:31–39) make reference to the land as well as to the covenant. Further such examples could be cited. It is as true of God's earthly promises as it is of the heavenly, that 'God's gifts and callings are irrevocable' (Rom. 11:29). God's purposes for Israel include the land.

These references also make mention of Israel's obedience. Israel's right to enjoy God's goodness is contingent upon Israel's obedience. That, in a nutshell, is the message of the prophets. Herein lies the crucial importance of Israel being meaningfully confronted with the gospel, for obedience to God is impossible without submission to Christ. The Mosaic Torah has its fulfilment in him, and the new Torah is established in his blood. To reject Christ is to disobey God in the most radical manner. In other words, Israel's right to continued enjoyment of the land is to a great extent contingent upon its relation to Jesus. May God give us the courage to call Israel to Christ.

> How beautiful upon the mountains
> are the feet of him who brings good tidings,
> who publishes peace, who brings good tidings of well-being,
> who publishes salvation,
> who says to Zion, 'Your God reigns!'
> Listen! Your watchmen raise their voices.
> Together they sing for joy, for eye to eye they gaze at
> the return of the LORD to Zion.
> Break forth joyously! Sing together,
> you wasted ruins of Jerusalem!
> For the LORD has comforted his people;
> he has redeemed Jerusalem
> The LORD has bared his holy arm
> before the eyes of all the nations,
> and all the ends of the earth shall see
> the salvation of our God.'
>
> (Is. 52:7–10, my translation)

5B

Zionism and the land: a Palestinian Christian perspective[1]

Naim Ateek

Jewish and Christian Zionism

In its inception, the modern struggle over Palestine was not a religiously motivated conflict but a political one. It arose as a result of Jewish experience in Europe. Jewish leaders in Europe concluded that anti-Semitism was a malaise that would not go away. The only remedy was for Jews to find a home far away from European Christians. Such was the assessment of the Zionist secular Jewish leaders of the time. In other words, it was not based on any biblical claim to the land of Palestine. In fact, the early Zionists were ready to establish their state in other countries – Uganda, Argentina, Cyprus and others – if only they could escape anti-Semitism and alleviate the misery of their fellow European Jews.

[1] This is an expanded version of a paper originally delivered at the first consultation on 'The Theology of the Land' held in Droushia, Cyprus, in July 1996 and published in *Mishkan* 27 (1997).

The Zionist movement was nurtured by the spirit of its day – nationalism, imperialism and colonialism. Quite understandably Jewish people, as other national minorities in Europe, entertained ideas of independence and liberation. Yet such ideas remained anathema for the *religious* Jewish communities within Europe. Indeed, each of the three main Jewish denominations, Orthodox, Conservative and Reform, rejected Zionism and considered it an aberration. For, religiously speaking, they insisted that the return to the land could be heralded only by the Messiah.

So it took a long time for Zionism to be accepted by a majority of religious Jews. This gradual conversion to Zionism took place as a result of several events: the Holocaust, the establishment of the State of Israel in 1948 and the success of the 1967 war. These three events, more than anything else, contributed to the success of Zionism and its victory over any strong religious opposition from within the Jewish community.[2]

At the same time, long before the establishment of the Zionist movement, there was a strand of western 'Christian Zionism' that was beginning to show its face within some Christian circles. As far back as the 1840s, Lord Shaftesbury linked the idea of Jewish restoration to the land of Palestine with Queen Victoria's political agenda. He was influential in promoting the establishment of the Jerusalem Bishopric in 1841 as a joint venture between the Church of England and the Lutheran Church of Prussia. It was also Lord Shaftesbury who first coined the phrase 'a country without a nation for a nation without a country'. This was later transposed by the Zionists to 'a land of no people for a people with no land' (Hodder 1887: 14).

In a similar way John Nelson Darby (1800–82), an Irish minister of the Church of England, was promulgating his views of dispensationalism as early as 1829.[3] He believed that the concept of Israel is the key factor in Bible prophecy, and that God had two plans and two groups of people with whom to work. Israel was God's kingdom on earth and the church was God's heavenly kingdom. It was important, therefore, for the State of Israel to be

[2] Nevertheless there remain religious Jewish groups that have remained anti-Zionist: for example, the American Council of Judaism, and *Neturei Karta*, an ultra-Orthodox group.

[3] For an explanation of the dispensational system, see e.g. Beegle 1978: 164–182.

established on earth in order for these prophecies to be fulfilled in a literal way.

Darby's views spread to the United States and Canada. He made seven extended trips, spending a total of six years preaching and teaching in North America. One of those who was influenced by Darby's teachings was William Blackstone, who was probably the first person to launch a major lobby effort in the United States on behalf of the Jewish State. In 1891, six years before the establishment of the Zionist movement, Blackstone lobbied President Harrison to support the creation of a state for Jews in Palestine. Blackstone heard that Herzl was beginning to waver in his commitment to Palestine as the potential site of the Jewish State. So he sent him a copy of the Bible with all the verses that mention the return of Jews to the land marked in red. He wanted to reinforce his conviction that Jews must return only to Palestine according to biblical prophecy (see Wagner 1995).

One of the important spokesmen for Christian Zionism at the beginning of the nineteenth century was an Anglican clergyman named Louis Way. Three key elements were important within his thought: a careful monitoring of contemporary events that indicated the imminence of Jesus' return; the restoration of the Jews to Palestine as a fulfilment of biblical prophecy; and an insistence that this restored Jewish State must be exclusively Jewish, making no provision for the Arabs.

The growing sympathy for Zionism in Britain was no doubt due in part to the love and attachment that many people had to the biblical stories of the Old Testament and the history of ancient Israel. For example, both Lord Arthur Balfour and David Lloyd George, two of the prominent British political figures who played a significant role in the legitimization of Zionism early in the twentieth century, were influenced by a literal interpretation of the Bible.

Balfour is best known for his Balfour Declaration, issued in 1917, which committed the British Government to establishing in Palestine a 'national home for the Jewish people' (Crombie 1991: 155–158). In those days the Jewish population in Palestine was fewer than 80,000, while the Palestinian Muslim and Christian population exceeded 600,000. Yet it was Balfour's biblical predisposition that led him to support a Jewish home in Palestine long before he met the early Zionist leaders, Theodor Herzl and Chaim Weitzmann. Balfour believed that God's plan must be fulfilled.

So the Christian Zionists gave a significant impetus to the early Jewish Zionists. Long before there were any Jewish religious Zionists, there were western Christian Zionists who were using the Bible to promote their distinctive approach to the Bible and the land.

The conversion of religious Jews to Zionism was ultimately due to the success of the 1967 war. Israel's victory carried with it the most convincing argument. Israel was able with great military ease to conquer the surrounding Arab countries and occupy vast areas of their territories. Most significantly, in addition to the Gaza Strip, Israel now came to occupy both the area of the West Bank (i.e. 'Judea and Samaria', their ancient homeland), and above all East Jerusalem, which included the area of the Temple Mount and the Western Wall.

For many religious Jews, this was the final proof of God's faithfulness to the Jewish people. God had given them a great victory over their enemies. Consequently, most of the religious sceptics were won over to supporting Zionism. This then led to the transformation and metamorphosis of Zionism itself – a gradual mellowing of the secular Zionism of Herzl and the other early Zionists, and the emergence of a vibrant religious Zionism inspired by the Jewish biblical tradition.

So from the early 1970s, the primary argument for Jewish claim to the land was not the traditional argument of anti-Semitism or even the tragedy of the Holocaust, but the religious argument – namely that God had given the land to the Jewish people and it was therefore theirs by divine right. The biblical argument had become paramount. This is where Christian Zionism and Jewish Zionism met in full speed, connecting with and nourishing each other. Both were based on a literal reading of the biblical text, even though ultimately they had quite different hopes and agendas.

Religious Jews needed the active support of western Christian Zionists to confirm Israel's claim over the land of Palestine. They needed them to lobby for them, especially in the United States, to safeguard and promote Israeli sovereignty over the whole land without giving in to Palestinian claims or international pressure. They also desperately wanted to prevent the establishment of a

Palestinian State on the West Bank and the Gaza Strip. For some Jewish religious groups, this whole process was part of 'the redemption of Israel' – redeeming the land and hastening the first coming of their Messiah.

Meanwhile, Christian Zionists supported Israel because of their own interpretation of the Bible regarding the end of history and the second coming of Christ. According to this view of the Bible, the signs of the end-times are very clear: Israel stands at the centre of history, so believers must keep their eyes on what happens to it and to the Jewish people. Ever since 1948 there has been a rising crescendo of jubilation. Christian Zionists have sensed that the Old Testament prophecies are being fulfilled: the return of Jews to the land of Palestine, the establishment of the State of Israel, and the capture of East Jerusalem in 1967. Some of them now await the rebuilding of the temple and the reintroduction of the animal sacrifices (see e.g. Ice & Price 1992).

These and other events are all signs within this scheme of the approaching end-times and the second coming of Christ. It is an elaborate system of events where a major battle, Armageddon, will take place in the valley of Jezreel. Two-thirds of the Jewish people will be destroyed and the last third will confess their faith in Jesus the true Messiah. The second coming of Christ will usher in the millennial reign of Christ (Lindsey 1981).

Undoubtedly, Jews detest this Christian Zionist agenda. They tolerate it, however, due to the political and financial support they receive from it. One recalls, for example, the close bond of friendship between the late Prime Minister of Israel, Menachem Begin, and the American televangelist Jerry Falwell. Almost certainly Begin was well aware of Falwell's beliefs and must have personally viewed them with distaste – the belief that there will be another major holocaust of Jews at the end of history. Yet he befriended Jerry Falwell and expressed his appreciation to him for his faithful support of Israel by giving him a small private jet. In fact Falwell was one of the first people whom Begin telephoned to inform him of Israel's destruction of Iraq's nuclear reactor in 1981 (Halsell 1986).

Another example of the collaboration between Christian and Jewish religious Zionists can be cited in the work that has been going on to breed a red heifer that will be suitable for the services associated with any rebuilt temple in Jerusalem. In the time of Jesus no Jew was supposed to enter into the inner courts of the temple without being ritually pure. Impurity could come in a number of ways, but especially through contact with a corpse.[4] According to Numbers 19, the ritual for becoming purified was a complex, seven-day process. The person had to be sprinkled with water that contained the ashes of a red heifer administered by a pure Jewish priest. This method of purification may well have been practised as late as the sixth century AD, with some Jews retaining a supply of these ashes and thereby keeping themselves ritually clean in the hope that the temple would soon be rebuilt (Shahak 1997: 106–109). Since that time, however, all Jews have in this respect been considered ritually unclean and impure. As a result, no Jew is to enter the site where the temple stood without being purified first. Yet if unclean Jews cannot even step on the site of the temple, neither can they begin to rebuild it in their state of impurity. It is a Catch-22 situation.

Be that as it may, Christian and Jewish Zionists have been collaborating on breeding a red heifer in order to prepare for the possibility of rebuilding the temple and the reinstitution of the sacrificial system. These two contradictory brands of Zionism have both been working very hard to breed a red heifer according to the biblical specification – each, of course, meanwhile pursuing its own eschatological hope while the breeding is going on. The breeding was started on a ranch in the United States by some Christian Zionists and later transferred to a kibbutz in Israel. The heifer must be entirely red. If two of its hairs are not red, it is disqualified (Shahak 1997: 106–109).

From these examples it is clear how much the Bible and its interpretation have influenced and continue to influence Middle East politics. A number of years ago, when Archbishop Desmond Tutu visited Jerusalem during the Christmas season, I went with him to visit some Israeli government officials. As we were leaving the office of one of the government ministries, a man followed us shouting, 'Genesis 12:3!' What does the verse say? 'I will bless those who bless

[4] According to the Talmud, impurity of a Jew is caused through contact only with a Jewish corpse or any tiny part of the corpse's body. A non-Jewish corpse does not have the same effect.

you, and the one who curses you I will curse; and in you all the families of the earth shall be blessed.' As recorded, these were the words of God to Abraham when God called Abraham to go to Canaan. Desmond Tutu was being warned of the curse that might befall those who support Palestinian rights and abandon Israel. The man shouting at us was using the Bible as an authoritative weapon, assuming on the basis of Genesis 12:3 that unless we bless Israel we must be cursed by God.

One could continue to cite numerous examples of how the Bible is being used and abused by people. Yet obviously the issue of the land stands at the heart of this argument. This is the bottom line of the conflict. The whole peace process is dependent on this question of land. To whom does the land belong? Does it belong to the Jewish people or to the Palestinians? How can their claims be reconciled? Is peace possible between them? For people of faith, the answer to these questions and many others depends on one's theology of land, which is itself dependent on one's interpretation of the Bible.

Clearly, then, this is one of the most crucial issues in biblical interpretation. So it is of utmost significance to ask: what is the basic message of the Bible, and what does it say about the land? How does a Christian read it in a distinctive way that is true to its own central theme – the reality of Jesus Christ?

Now that Zionism, as outlined above, has shifted from being a secular phenomenon to having a distinctly religious base, the development of a Christian theology of land has become an urgent necessity. For many people, the religious arguments for Zionism, which use religious language and are based on the biblical promises regarding the land, have become the most convincing. So Christians must respond with their own, alternative theology of land. On this may depend the future of peace in the region – not least because Jewish religious parties are currently a strong component within the Israeli government.

The centrality of Christ

The heart of the Bible is Jesus Christ. From a Christian perspective Jesus stands at the centre of history. History is the story of

God's love for the world in Jesus Christ to bring justice, healing, peace, salvation and liberation to all. Apart from Christ, this world is an enigma. Christians can understand the meaning of history only when they view it through what God has purposed for it in Christ.

The Old Testament is very much a part of that background. Christians may differ in their understanding of revelation and inspiration, yet they believe that the Holy Spirit was active in guiding the writers as they recorded the story of salvation which God eventually accomplished in Jesus Christ. So the Old Testament has a vital and unique role. Yet there is also a crescendo in the biblical books that reaches its climax in the coming of Christ.

From this perspective, therefore, the biblical material cannot be viewed in a straightforwardly horizontal way. The Old Testament cannot stand on its own, nor can it be understood apart from the New Testament. It cannot be fully comprehended apart from its completion and fulfilment in Christ. In fact, without the New Testament, many parts of the Old Testament might be considered, in today's language, either Zionist or racist. Without Christ, the Old Testament is not only incomplete. It can also be, in some of its parts, a potentially dangerous document. For example, the commands to Joshua concerning the Canaanites might lead some fanatical people to pursue a policy of ethnic cleansing.[5] So we highly value the Old Testament because of Christ, but on its own we see it as insufficient for salvation.

Christ, then, is the heart of the Bible. He is its hermeneutic, the criterion for its interpretation and understanding. As Christians we cannot begin our study of the Bible from Genesis. We must begin with what God has done in Christ and then move into the Old Testament in order to understand the background of the faith. As we do so, we find that the outcome was not precisely what one might have expected from a plain reading of the Old Testament. What God did for the world in Christ far exceeded the best that the prophets predicted and anticipated. The best illustration of this is the resurrection of Christ. It is possible to discover certain hints of the resurrection here and there in the Old Testament (as the

[5] This alarming consequence is noted and criticized by e.g. Prior 1997.

early church did), but the event itself far exceeded anything that they had imagined. It was God's great surprise.

In other words, in order to understand any issue in the Bible, we must understand it in the light of its fulfilment in Christ. For example, if we want to study the topic of chosenness or election, our point of departure must be the teaching of Christ and the New Testament. What the New Testament teaches about election becomes authoritative, because in Christ we have received the full picture. So we adopt and embrace the New Testament's teaching because it is the completed and fulfilled version.

From this foundational understanding of the centrality of Christ, let us now reflect on the issue of the land.

A theology of the land

The Synoptic Gospels make clear that Christ was interested in the issue of the kingdom of God rather than the land. In the Old Testament the word or words designating the 'land' appear more than 1,600 times, but in the New Testament fewer than fifty times. At the same time, the expressions 'the kingdom of God' or 'the kingdom of heaven' are frequently on the lips of Jesus and are recorded more than a hundred times in the Synoptics alone.

So the concept of the kingdom in the New Testament is the counterpart to the concept of the land in the Old Testament, but with one major difference: the consistent stress on the inclusive nature of God's kingdom. The kingdom of God does not differentiate between gender, race or ethnicity. It is for all the world and for all peoples. Jesus then practised what he preached in his attitude to Jews, Romans, and Greeks, to Canaanites and Phoenicians, to men and to women. The New Testament has abundant illustrations of this (e.g. Matt. 8:5–13; 15:21–28; Mark 7:24–30; Mark 10:2–12; Luke 17:11–19; John 4:4–42).

By contrast, Jesus did not appear to be interested in the issue of the land. In fact, he tried to stretch his disciples' understanding away from their narrow understanding of God and the land. He wanted to shatter any narrow nationalism which they exhibited (Matt. 15:21–28; Luke 9:51–56; 24:13–27; Acts 1:6–8). The whole spirit of the ministry of Christ in the Gospels puts us on a different ground from that of the Old Testament. Ethnocentricity is opposed, ethnic arrogance is challenged, and any superior feeling is discouraged and shattered (Mark 12:1–12; Luke 20:9–19; Matt. 20:1–16).

After the resurrection, for example, the two Emmaus disciples expressed their hope that Jesus might have been the one 'to redeem Israel'. Jesus responded by helping them to understand the Scriptures: 'Then beginning with Moses and all the prophets, he interpreted to them the things about himself in all the scriptures' (Luke 24:13–33). Jesus himself, it turns out, is the key and the focus – not Israel. In him the redemption of Israel, as well as of others, has been accomplished.

In the Gospel of John, *all* those who believe in Jesus Christ have become children of God, 'who were born, not of blood or of the will of the flesh or of the will of man, but of God' (John 1:13). God's supreme revelation is no longer the law that Moses gave to the children of Israel, but rather God's grace given through Christ to all the world (John 1:17–18). In John's most famous verse (3:16) we read that 'God so loved the *world*' – not only the children of Israel or Eretz Israel. Theologically, neither Jerusalem nor Gerizim is any longer important; for 'God is spirit and those who worship him must worship in spirit and truth' (John 4:24).

So at every point and turn, the focus now is not on one land (the land of Israel) or one people (the Jewish people), but rather on what God is doing for the whole world and for all the people of the world in Christ. The land of Palestine is only the launching-pad for God's activity in and for the world.

That is why the land of Palestine was not seen as theologically important in the early church. The focus was on Christ and the importance of preaching the gospel to the world. It was only after the fourth century that the land began to be perceived as holy and Christian pilgrimages to the land ensued (see e.g. Walker 1990).

Indeed, for the early church, the destruction of the temple was an indication of the disappearance of the old order, the old covenant and the dawning of the new. For the early Christians it revealed a divine response to the failure of Israel to welcome her Messiah. Most importantly, Christ himself has replaced the temple; and believers in Christ have become themselves the temple of the Holy

Spirit of God (2 Cor. 6:16; 1 Cor. 6:19; 3:16). Faith in Christ has thus shattered any geographical restrictions; and the message of Christ can no longer be limited to one locale.

The same basic theology is present in almost every one of the New Testament writings. God's purposes for the world have been revealed in Christ, and they are inclusive of all people. Any narrow understanding of God or the land is shunned. One of the most telling examples is Stephen's sermon in Acts 7. Stephen pointed out that the temple did not represent the original plan of God. For God's original purpose was seen instead in the instructions he gave for the tabernacle, which travelled with his people through the wilderness. This tabernacle was not bound to any one geographic location, and so was able to symbolize the universal presence of God (Acts 7:44). Solomon was permitted later to build the temple, but at its dedication God made it quite clear that he would not be in any way limited to it (7:48–50).

So God had never limited himself to one land; no one land as such was holy. True holiness resides not in the land nor in the temple, but rather in Christ. At the same time, there is a profound sense in which the incarnation has sacramentalized the whole world. The material world, far from being desacralized, has been sanctified in its entirety.

The New Testament thus reinterprets the promises of the land in the light of Christ. A good example of this is in Romans 4:13, where Paul says something quite revolutionary: 'For the promise that [Abraham] would inherit the *world* did not come to Abraham or to his descendants through the law but through the righteousness of faith' (my emphasis). Yet nowhere in the Old Testament was Abraham given such a promise relating to the whole world! Instead, Paul has taken the promise made to Abraham concerning the land and has reinterpreted it in the light of the coming of Christ. Christ is the true seed of Abraham (Gal. 3:16) and in his coming he has brought salvation and redemption for the whole world. So in the light of their universal fulfilment in Christ, the narrow Old Testament promises regarding the land have acquired a new meaning. They are now seen to be transitory and provisional in their intention. They are time-bound, and because of their completion in Christ, have become theologically obsolete.

The New Testament, however, not only reinterprets the Old Testament. It also 'de-Zionizes' it. One can illustrate this by comparing, for example, what Jesus said in John 1:51 with its counterpart in Genesis 28:12–13. In the latter passage, we read:

> And [Jacob] dreamed that there was a ladder set up on the earth, the top of it reaching to heaven; and the angels of God were ascending and descending on it. And the LORD stood beside him and said, 'I am the LORD, the God of Abraham your father and the God of Isaac; the land on which you lie I will give to you and to your offspring.'

In John, Jesus says to Nathanael, 'you will see heaven opened and the angels of God ascending and descending upon the Son of Man'. Jacob's ladder was set on the earth. The land was seen as important and the promise to inherit the land was reiterated to Jacob. In John, however, the land is no longer of any importance. It is replaced by Jesus the Messiah. The angels in John are ascending and descending not on the land but on the Son of Man. This represents, I suggest, a definite de-Zionizing of the biblical faith. It is no more Israel or the land that is the all-important centre, but rather Jesus the Christ.

In the Old Testament there are also frequent references to the exclusive role of Israel within God's purposes and to the land being theirs in an exclusive way. The New Testament shatters this exclusivity at every turn. One of the classic examples is found in Jesus' sermon in Nazareth (Luke 4:16–30). Jesus reads from Isaiah 61 but stops before the verses which describe the 'vengeance of our God' against other nations (vv. 2b, 5–6). This no longer has any place in the kingdom of God. The fact that Jesus then refers to the widow of Sidon and to Naaman the Syrian makes quite plain what he now sees as God's true concern: a love for all lands and for all people.

It is only in the light of this theology, centred around Christ, that we can then evaluate the Old Testament concept of land. The overall trajectory moves from a generally exclusive theology within the Pentateuch to one that is more inclusive after the exile. Yet even within the Pentateuch there are verses that reflect a more inclusive view. For example, we read in Leviticus 25:23: 'The land shall not be sold in perpetuity, for the land is mine; with me you are but aliens and tenants.' This then is very similar to the universal vision of the psalmist: 'The earth is the LORD's and all that is in it, the world, and those who live in it' (Ps. 24:1).

After the exile there is a gradual shift towards a more inclusive understanding of God and the land. The experience of exile must have stretched the people's understanding of God. One of the most exciting books in the Old Testament that reflects this inclusive theology is the book of Jonah. The story seems to have been written by a Jewish theologian who was rebelling against the traditional view of God and the land. Repeatedly the point is made in the book that God cares for people other than Jews (even for the most hated enemy, the Assyrians) and for a land other than the land of Israel.

In this movement towards inclusivity, Ezekiel 47:21–23 reflects a new realism. Here it is accepted that the land belongs not only to the Israelites returning from exile but also to the people who had since come to live in the land. In some parts of the Torah we read that the current occupants of the land must be totally exterminated (Num. 21:1–3, 31–35; 33:51–52; Deut. 7:1–2, 22–24). Now in Ezekiel the Israelites are commanded to live with these occupants, thought admittedly they are described from the Jewish perspective as 'aliens in their midst'. Evidently, the experience of exile had forced them to embrace a more universal perspective on God and his purposes. Even though there remains within the writings of these post-exilic prophets some exclusive approaches to the land, the shift to a more inclusive theology had started. This is then picked up again in the New Testament and finds its truest and clearest expression in Christ himself with his inclusive concept of the kingdom of God.

Conclusion

The Bible, when read from a Christian perspective and with the resolve to honour Christ as the key to the Scriptures, endorses this inclusive approach to the land. What, then, is the implication of all this for our modern debates about the land and its future?

Simply put, it is this. The land of Palestine/Israel is part of God's world. It belongs to God in the same way as does the rest of the world. God is its creator and owner – just as God is the maker and owner of the whole world. Today, God has placed on this land both Palestinians and Jews. They must then share it under God and become good stewards of it. It does not belong to either of them exclusively. They must share it equitably and live as good neighbours with one another. Both nations must 'do justice, love mercy, and walk humbly with God' (Mic. 6:8). Once those biblical demands of justice have been satisfied, a good measure of peace will be achieved. The result will then be a new and deeper security enjoyed by all throughout the land. 'For the effect of justice will be peace, and the result of righteousness, security and trust forever' (Is. 32:17).

Bibliography

Beegle, D. M. (1978), *Prophecy and Prediction*, Ann Arbor: Pryor Pettengill.

Crombie, K. (1991), *For the Love of Zion*, London: Hodder and Stoughton.

Halsell, G. (1986), *Prophecy and Politics: Militant Evangelists on the Road to Holocaust*, Westport: Lawrence Hill.

Hodder, E. (1887), *The Life and Work of the Seventh Earl of Shaftesbury, K.G.*, London: Cassell.

Ice, T., & Price, J. R. (1992), *Ready to Rebuild: The Imminent Plan to Rebuild the Last Days Temple*, Eugene: Harvest House.

Lindsey, H. (1981), *The 1980's Countdown to Armageddon*, New York: Bantam.

Prior, M. (1997), *The Bible and Colonialism: A Moral Critique*, Sheffield: Sheffield Academic Press.

Shahak, I. (1997), 'Jerusalem and the Jews', in V. Melander (ed.), *Culture, Confrontation and Local Mobilization: Essays in Honour of Sigbert Axelson*: Uppsala: Swedish Institute of Missionary Research: 106–109.

Walker, P. W. L. (1990), *Holy City, Holy Places?* Oxford: Clarendon.

Wagner, D. E. (1995), *Anxious for Armageddon*, Scotdale: Herald.

6. THE LAND AND CHRISTIAN RESPONSIBILITY

6A
Stewardship of the land: a Christian mandate

Carl E. Armerding

Introduction

Questions of the stewardship of the land can incorporate a wide variety of topics, from ancient to contemporary. It is important to attempt some working definitions, not least because 'land' can be understood in two quite different senses: one relating to the 'earth' as a whole, the other to the particular 'land of Israel'.

The land or earth?

These two senses – one universal in scope, one more particular – are both inherent in the common Hebrew noun *'ereṣ*, which translates into English as both 'land' and 'earth' (as well as 'ground'). In the Genesis account of creation (Gen 1:10, 24; 2:4) *'ereṣ* means 'earth'. Elsewhere in Genesis, however, and frequently in the historical books, *'ereṣ* refers to some particular geographical entity, especially, but not exclusively, the 'land of Israel'. In the poetic books of Job and Psalms, where the word is frequent (e.g. Ps. 2:2, 8, 10), *'ereṣ* often takes on its more universal sense. Other instances leave the ambiguity intact: for example, the several references in Psalm 37 (vv. 11, 22, 29, 34) concerning who will 'inherit the land'. When we come to the New Testament the Greek *gē* reflects the same semantic range as the Hebrew *'ereṣ*, though there appears to be a shift in emphasis from the particular to the universal meaning. English readers must therefore decide for themselves in both Testaments whether 'land' refers to a particular geopolitical entity, or to the 'earth' in the creational sense.

In this chapter, rather than be forced into a choice among legitimate alternatives, we shall revel in the breadth of the term 'land', incorporating into our remarks *both* the geopolitical sense of the Pentateuch and the Former Prophets, *and* the creational and universal sense of the more poetic sections of the Old Testament. This will enable us to broaden the discussion, and ensure that the contemporary church has not missed any part of its divine imperative.

Stewardship

This inevitably affects the corresponding meaning of 'stewardship'. 'Steward' originally applied to an individual appointed to care for another's property, as reflected in Jesus' parable of the steward (Luke 16:1–12). The Greek word-group (noun *oikonomia*) signifies the responsible management of an asset by a steward appointed by the owner for that purpose. In this present debate, however, because of the two meanings of the word 'land', the term can be applied in two ways.

1. In a theological sense, 'stewardship' has gained currency to describe humanity's original responsibility for the earth in the creation covenant, with prominence given to two key verbs in Genesis 2:15, 'till' (*'ābad*) and 'guard/keep' (*šāmar*). These verbs are frequently contrasted with 'have dominion' (*rādāh*) and 'subdue' (*kābaš*), found in Genesis 1:26–28. The latter terms, with both military and economic overtones, are frequently understood to envisage a hostile relationship with the earth, in contrast to the more

stewardly verbs in Genesis 2. Such verses, which introduce the notion of the stewardship of the land in the Bible, may then serve in contemporary debate as a basis for an ecological strategy for the Christian church in relation to the world.

2. However, when applied to the 'land' of Israel rather than to the created 'earth', 'stewardship' can equally refer to Israel's responsibility to maintain its land according to the divine covenant requirements. As Leviticus 25:23 reminds us, all the land belonged to Yahweh, and the covenant (as outlined in Exodus to Deuteronomy) supplies numerous examples of how Israel was to care for God's property. The children of Abraham in the land, no less than Adam in the original creation, are responsible to care for Yahweh's vineyard. As seen in previous chapters, 'stewardship' in this second sense also raises large contemporary issues: should stewardship of this particular land be given to the Israelis, to the Palestinians, or to both? Although for many people the question of who owns the land of Israel is far more theologically relevant than the more universal questions of creation theology, my own interest is primarily in the latter.

Christian responses

Surprisingly, however, the importance of both these issues has frequently been missed by the church. In the environmental debate Rachel Carson was able to argue in *Silent Spring* (1962) that Christian lack of concern was responsible for the sorry state of the relationship between humanity and nature, and that this was the direct result of a Bible-based worldview that supposedly suppressed the natural order.

Meanwhile, the land of Israel too has known seasons of neglect within Christian thought. In the last two millennia only three periods have been distinguished by intense active interest in the land of Israel.

The first such period was that of Byzantium, distinguished from the later eras by the absence of an Islamic antagonist. The Byzantine rulers in Constantinople and Palestine were Christian successors to the Romans. In addition to significant building activity in cities such as Jerusalem, they created from the semi-arid conditions of

Palestine a remarkable agricultural system that would serve as a model for Zionist settlers over a thousand years later. Palestine was part of an emerging 'Christendom', with Jerusalem a world centre on a par with Constantinople in the scheme of imperial geography. As such, the Byzantine rulers came closer to a real stewardship of the land than any of their Christian successors.

A second period is marked by the Crusader movement of the eleventh century to the thirteenth. Fuelled by millennial speculation, and the restlessness of under-employed nobility and clergy in Europe, the crusading impulse swept through a continent slowly emerging from medieval feudalism. Tied to the preaching of Christian idealist prophets such as Bernard of Clairvaux, the real motivation for many, at least among the leaders, was a mixture of earthly adventurism and the hope of heavenly reward. If there was any sense of 'stewardship' in the kingdom of Jerusalem, or its successor enclaves in Acre, Rhodes or Malta, it was too bound up with the imperialist tendency to be obvious. Unlike the Byzantines, the Crusaders rarely concerned themselves with the broader needs of the land, as most were forced to content themselves with exercising nominal control over the countryside through strategically placed castles.

A final period of Christian interest in the Holy Land can be traced to modern millennial movements, especially premillennial dispensationalism (see above, ch. 4B). This hermeneutical scheme sees Israel and the church as two separate divine entities. Darby's so-called 'earthly people of God', the Jews, had been given the land of Israel as an eternal inheritance. Since many of these expectations for the land were inspired by Old Testament prophecies such as Amos 9, involving supernatural fruitfulness and blessing, the movement was more than receptive to the idealism surrounding the return of European Jews to Palestine at the end of the nineteenth century. When stories of the desert beginning to bloom started to circulate, as European technology and investment transformed an under-utilized agricultural system, it seemed that ancient prophecies were being fulfilled before the world's eyes. Darby's prophetic scheme explained all this in Christian terms and lent credibility to both movements.

While successive British administrations from the mid-nineteenth century onward were undoubtedly motivated by political and economic considerations, the memoirs of prominent figures such as the Seventh Earl of Shaftesbury (Anthony Ashley Cooper) show that convictions about the role of Israel's return in biblical prophecy formed a powerful incentive for eastern expansion of the British Empire. The securing of a League of Nations mandate for the new entity of Palestine in the treaties that ended the first World War was understood by those who had 'ears to hear' as the unfolding of the divine plan for the land.

From this wave of prophetic enthusiasm, the practical implications for the Christian church were not as clear as they were for European Jews. For the latter, the Zionist movement under the visionary Theodor Herzl provided a stimulus to concrete action. However, as millenarian enthusiasm grew, Zionistic Christians assiduously watched the Middle East to discover signs that prophecies were being fulfilled. A few of these Christians settled in the land themselves, either as missionaries or simply because they wished to be near the place where they believed Christ would return – on the Mount of Olives. But, for most Christians, even Christian Zionists of that era, these concerns resulted in limited direct contact with the land or its people. A cornerstone of the millenarian movement was the powerfully emotive conviction that Christ's return was 'imminent'. This cut a broad swathe among Christians and churches for whom the earlier postmillennial doctrine had seen Christian mission activity as a precondition for the coming of the Lord. In contrast to the earlier postmillennialism, which had frequently spawned Christian social activism, this new premillennialism all too often encouraged a spectator mentality. So the land of Israel, as the Zionist population grew, was seen as the arena where the prophetic clock was ticking, but there was little that Christians needed to do about it – except watch the clock and 'be ready'!

From this overview it can be seen how Christian interest in the 'land', with the possible exception of the Byzantine era, should probably be seen not in terms of stewardship at all. A better description might be 'curiosity' – or something worse.

What, then, does stewardship of the land mean for the Christian church, seeking to be faithful to the calling of its Lord at the start of the new millennium? The goal must be to understand rightly the teaching of the Scriptures, and especially what Jesus and his apostles had to say about these things. This, for faithful followers of 'the Way', is basic to discipleship.

But Christian history shows this is not easy. In the ecological debate, for example, one need only think of the way Constance Cumbey (1983) responded so critically to the year-long symposium at Calvin College which brought together Christian scholars concerned with environmental issues (cf. Wilkinson 1980). They issued a clarion call for Christian involvement in environmental issues, basing their appeal on the concept of Christian stewardship as found in the creation narratives of Genesis. For Cumbey, however, the catastrophic suffering of the environment is simply one more proof that the Lord's coming is near. Christians who join environmentalists are making common cause with New Age thought and with a 'worldly agenda', rather than standing with those waiting for the parousia!

Clearly there is not yet a consensus as to what Christian stewardship of the land might involve – whether in the ecological realm or in connection with Israel. Partly this is because Christians, like any other group, represent a wide variety of political and economic viewpoints. Messianic believers in Israel, for example, clearly span the political spectrum from right to left (see Skjøtt 1997). The real barriers, however, are genuinely theological. What are the places, then, where Christian theology needs further work?

The theological gap

Mainstream Protestant theology: no concept of land

Several of the chapters in this book allude to the widespread view that the new covenant, in contrast to the covenant with Abraham, is essentially spiritual, and therefore is not concerned with something as material as land. Inherent in this belief can lie the idea that for something to be spiritual, it must be non-material. But for many this means it is less than real, because reality consists of what can be touched – substantial matter that occupies space. Yet advocates of this spiritual interpretation would argue that if Jesus, who once had a physical body, is now known through the incorporeal Holy Spirit, then the new covenant is best understood as no longer limited by the physical or material. The people of God is itself a spiritual concept, so it naturally follows that the idea of place is now equally spiritual.

Complicating the process is the theological priority given to the doctrine of redemption, and the widespread conviction, even among biblical theologians, that creation is a doctrine subordinate to redemption within Scripture (see, for example, the Old Testament theologies of W. Kaiser and E. Martens). Redemption is seen in the new covenant as having to do primarily with people, not space. By contrast, land (or earth) is spatial and material, and functions merely as the arena for the redemptive drama. Anything more might even be seen as investing the creation with an undue importance, or returning to pantheism. Old Testament models, in which a land was given sacred status, are seen as temporary, like other aspects of the old covenant relegated by the writer of Hebrews to the realm of shadow (Heb. 8:5; 10:1).

This holds true for those on both the amillennial and the dispensational premillenarian ends of the spectrum. In each case, it is argued, Jesus proclaimed a 'kingdom ... not of this world' (John 18:36), which, when taken with the absence of any New Testament emphasis on territory in relation to the church, convinces both sides that the spiritual home of new-covenant believers is something less (or more) than an earthly territory. Even the term 'kingdom of God', with its overtones of a specific realm, is now better understood as '*kingship* of God', emphasizing the relationship of sovereign to subjects rather than the idea of a specific territory.

In Europe, spatial concepts such as Christendom or the Holy Roman Empire have long since lost any meaning. Each in its time conjured up a vision of 'holy space', or a visible and corporeal kingdom, in contrast to the current idea of a universal, invisible and spiritual communion known as the church. The church, which quite rightly knows no geographical limits, and is understood to be equally at home in *every* place, has often understood itself to be fully at home in *no* place.

All of this has left the Protestant Christian church with little basis for a theology of land. Where any sense of holy territory is retained, it is usually reserved for some form of nationalistic 'manifest destiny', in the American sense, or lingering ideas of 'building Jerusalem in England's green and pleasant land'. These concepts are still at home in Russian circles, where Moscow (or Kiev) is seen as the third holy city after Jerusalem and Constantinople, and where a holy national church still inhabits holy national geography.

In the Protestant West, therefore, the image of a Christian kingdom has always tended to be more spiritual than institutional. Unlike Russians, Americans have never trusted their government to bring in a literal kingdom, and would certainly not hand that task over to bishops, or even a Christian emperor! Biblical kingdom images may have exerted a powerful influence on both British and American society (see e.g. Tuchmann 1988), but the focus has been on holy people rather than holy place. Protestants easily envisage themselves as a 'holy nation' or a 'royal priesthood' (cf. Exod. 19:6; 1 Pet. 2:9); but to extend this to a particular land is a much greater leap, though some of the imagery we have mentioned points in that direction.

Moving from the national to the more local, the concept of sacred space is still alien to Protestantism. Beginning with Luther's rejection of the Sacred Steps in Rome, and Henry VIII's dissolution of the monasteries in England, Protestantism has turned its attention from locations to ideas – the Word and words. Although the sacred monastery or healing shrine survives in Roman Catholic and Orthodox circles, for Protestants the 'high places' have been destroyed. Even battle sites across Europe, which once carried an aura of sacredness, have largely become tourist attractions rather than places of pilgrimage. The typical western Protestant worshipping community is certainly more at home in a simple English chapel than in a baroque cathedral.

The conclusion is inescapable: these are bad days for those who suggest that the new covenant properly includes not only the idea of a holy nation, but also that of a holy land or sacred space. The one *Terra Sancta* that remains (i.e. the land of Israel) is for most Protestant Christians little more than a once-in-a-lifetime sentimental pilgrimage destiny. For many a western tourist it is easier to embrace the concept of a continuing Jewish Holy Land than a holy land with which a full-blooded Christian identity has any ongoing living relationship.

Protestants therefore have little theology of land – and sometimes little theology of creation in general. Such ideas, it is felt instinctively, belong to the old covenant, which has either become anachronistic in Christ (as in centrist Protestant theology) or belongs to another people (as in dispensationalism). The land or the earth has lost its significance in traditional Protestant Christian theology, except at the extremes. The new covenant is seen as spiritual, and land is simply too physical, too real, to fit.

Dispensational premillenialism: a special view of the land

By contrast to mainstream Protestantism, one stream of popular theology looks at the question quite differently. Dispensational premillennialism retains an interest in land, but the land in question has little directly to do with the new covenant. Fundamental to dispensational thought is an ongoing role for the 'people Israel', but unlike the church, whose homeland under dispensationalism is heavenly, old-covenant Israel still finds its destiny tied to the territory given by covenant to Father Abraham. For the church, this might be little more than a theological curiosity, were it not for the fact that Israel's return to the land is understood to presage 'the last days' – with the establishment of the State of Israel in 1948 marking the close of 'the times of the Gentiles' (Luke 21:24) and the renewed ticking of God's prophetic clock. As a result, although the doctrine of the imminent return of Christ would seem to render unnecessary any signs, dispensational teachers sometimes exhibit an almost obsessive interest in events in the Middle East. The presence of God's covenant people in God's covenant land is proclaimed as proof that the Lord's return is near (in 'this generation': Matt. 24:34).

What has this produced for a Christian theology of the land, and especially its stewardship? Certainly dispensational prophetic thinkers take an active interest in the land of Israel, but can this be called stewardship? Because they have been tied to a doctrine of the church as a heavenly people with a heavenly destiny, dispensationalists have found it almost impossible to concentrate the mind on stewardship of any earthly territory. Their interest in the land of Israel has been simply as the subject of prophecy. They have looked to the future new creation, not to the present, often seeing this earth as ultimately destined for the fire (cf. 2 Pet. 3:1–13). This old earth, including even the land of Israel, has only temporary significance.

Thus, despite dispensationalism's highly developed sense of the importance of the land in an old-covenant context, it shares with other Protestant theologies a spiritualized new covenant and, in the final analysis, lacks a viable theology of land/earth.

Thus in both mainstream and dispensational branches of Protestantism, there has been this tendency to spiritualize the new covenant, and in particular its view of the land. This has made it difficult to speak effectively on the broader issues of creation theology. And on the narrower issue concerning the land of Israel, Protestant Christians have fallen into radically opposite camps. Protestants have either had nothing to say on important land-related issues, or have spoken with sharply different voices. In the so-called evangelical wing of Protestantism, in particular, this paralysis reflects a disunity that at times baffles outsiders, including conservationists of all stripes, together with both Jews and Arabs. It is hoped that this present volume may begin to play a part in addressing this issue, in much the same way as Wilkinson's *Earthkeeping* (1980) has proved seminal on the issues of creation.

A way forward?

There are, however, some areas where evangelicals may be moving toward a greater consensus. Partly this may be because of a new political climate in Israel, which begins to make it possible for Christian theologians, on both sides of the Protestant debate about Israel, to re-examine some outmoded theological formulations and seek fresh consensus.[1] Certainly, on the environmental questions, the rediscovery in the years since the Second World War of a more holistic theology and more comprehensive gospel has resulted in many groups, both fringe and mainline, taking up the environmental issue from a Christian perspective.[2] There are also some her-

[1] Cf. Chapman, above, p. 185.

[2] Cf. Henry 1947; in the UK, for example, the Jubilee Centre (Cambridge) and the A Rocha Trust.

meneutical givens, on which evangelical scholars would now find general agreement.

First, there is a wide agreement that the centre of Jesus' teaching was the kingdom of God. If so, it would seem to follow that a non-spatial and non-material kingdom could hardly do justice to the very earthed categories of Old Testament theology that spawned the idea. Both creation and land may need to be re-evaluated in the light of this.

Secondly, many would now argue that the New Testament still retains some significance for ethnic Israel. To be sure, the New Testament may primarily look for fulfilments of Old Testament promises in Christ, and 'Israel' may now be something more than merely the physical seed of Abraham (Rom. 9 – 11; Gal. 3 – 4).[3] Nevertheless, a future role for ethnic Israel cannot be ruled out – not least because of Romans 11. This is a view which clearly needs more debate, but which also presents a challenge to both sides of the Protestant discussion concerning Israel and the land.

Thirdly, it is increasingly recognized that the return from exile under Zerubbabel was only a partial fulfilment of the prophetic promises. The prophecies are either hopelessly idealistic or awaiting a fulfilment more glorious than anything seen by the returnees. For those who take the latter course, the critical question then becomes whether the kingdom ministry of Jesus (and the apostles' interpretations of it) is the complete fulfilment, or whether some further fulfilment is to be expected.

Finally, many are struck by the remarkable preservation of the Jewish people and their re-establishment of national Israel in the land after two thousand years of exile. Since 1948, Christian theologians have found it much more difficult to ignore modern Israel. Christians may still wrestle with what Israel means, but few will say it means nothing. And in contrast to the pre-Israel world, where the Jewish people found their identity in the dispersed community, it is now widely agreed that the spiritual heart of Judaism is somehow, mysteriously, tied up with their land.

[3] See e.g. Murray 1959–65, a commentary in the Reformed tradition, which acknowledges that those who spiritualize Israel must consider Paul's argument in Rom. 9 – 11 more carefully.

In the light of all this, the way forward in this debate would seem to require us to assert the following theological convictions.

1. Creation is primary

Biblical theology must begin and end with creation rather than redemption.[4] When this is done, the whole earth and all humanity are seen clearly as the original and the ultimate focus of Scripture. Israel and the church do not supersede this, and both have a mission larger than themselves: to bring the whole creation under God's kingly rule. Neither institution can be identified with the kingdom; instead they both serve as witnesses to the kingdom.

This then softens the critique of replacement theology which, because it sees the church as the new Israel, is understood to diminish the literal significance of God's promises to Abraham. If the promises to Abraham were given so that all nations and all creation might 'be blessed' (Gen. 12:3), then Abraham's covenant both prepares for and shares in the subsequent mission of the church. Neither body is the final kingdom, or the final tree of Romans 11, but both become part of one people and one purpose: to bring all creation under the lordship of Jesus Christ. Just as the law was to 'lead us to Christ' (Gal. 3:24), so Israel's mission is ultimately fulfilled in Christ and the restoration (or blessing) of all creation.

2. Earth and land are important in both Old and New Testaments

If God's original creation, the fully populated 'heavens and earth', are not only the beginning of his work but the goal as well, again certain emphases follow. The triangle scheme developed by a number of teachers, and illustrated in various of C. J. H. Wright's articles, pictures the original covenant as bringing together (a) God, (b) humanity, and (c) the earth. If all subsequent covenants involve some combination of the same players, then there is no covenant without a place for the earth, or the land. This is obvious in a

[4] This is well argued in Old Testament studies by both C. J. H. Wright 1983 and Dumbrell 1984.

number of the covenant forms of the Old Testament (Noahic, Abrahamic, Davidic), in each of which the concept of holy space is clearly present. Even the new covenant of Jeremiah 31, quoted and applied to the church in Hebrews 8 and 10, can hardly be separated in Jeremiah's Zion oracle from its fulfilment within the holy space of Jerusalem and Judah.

So the covenant inaugurated by Christ, bringing others into the blessings of Abraham, will equally include a focus on land in some sense. Nowhere in the Bible are people found apart from place. Even the writer of Hebrews, when refocusing the covenant to centre in Jesus, holds out the promise of a place of rest. Believers come ultimately to 'the heavenly Jerusalem, the city of the living God' (Heb. 12:22) – an image consistent with the writer's continual emphasis that in Christ the new space is *more* real, not *less* real, than the old.

Within this framework, the concept of holy place, which, like the concept of holy people, is focused on a particular family for a specific time and mission, can never be abandoned (see e.g. Pritz 1997). Neither Jesus nor Paul abandons the role of place in the new covenant; instead, they teach that holy space can never again be *limited* to Jerusalem and its temple. The earlier limitation was, from the time of Abraham, part of God's particular grace to one nation, and that for purposes of mission. In the new covenant, far from abandoning the idea of place, Paul argues that '*in the very place* where it was said to them, "You are not my people", they will be called "sons of the living God"' (Rom. 9:26, my emphasis). This new people, which includes both Jews and Gentiles, is inevitably located, like its older counterpart, in a specific place; for neither Paul nor any other apostle could have envisaged a people without a home.

But now that home is 'all creation'. The new home, for this new people, could never be captured by the limitations of a small territory on the eastern fringe of the Mediterranean Sea – nor should it be, in the days of the new covenant. Paul asserts that in the new economy it is not solely the land of Israel that belongs to the Lord, but the earth and its fullness (1 Cor. 10:26). Thus holy place has not diminished, but expanded. The new covenant, no less than the old, unfolds in the arena of God's created world. So, even if the focus of holy space in the New Testament has shifted from the particular to the universal, the legitimacy of particular holy space within the old-covenant order can also be maintained in the expanded worldview of the new.

Israel and Jerusalem are not therefore automatically *less* holy in the new days of the new covenant. Even in the old covenant, when God displayed his glory in Solomon's temple, this did not limit his holiness to a 'temple made with hands' (1 Kgs. 8:22–30). Now that the whole earth has taken the place of Solomon's temple and its localized picture of the cosmic glory of God, the symbol has given way to the reality. All creation, as from the beginning, is the arena for the glory of God, a truth recognized even at the dedication of Solomon's great building (1 Kgs. 8). Yet, in another sense, these scenes of the earthly presence of God's glory continue to carry a special meaning for both Jewish people and followers of Messiah Jesus. For it was at these places, just as through these chosen people (the Jews), that God worked his gracious mission to humanity. Even as the people of Israel are still 'beloved' in God's sight (as part of the expanded family tree of Romans 9 – 11), so too the land where Israel met God remains holy.

If, then, the whole earth is now 'holy to the Lord', a holiness that Christians and Jews alike can affirm as fundamental to God's work in the world, can we not celebrate *both* the universality of holiness in all God's creation *and* the specificity of those special places where God has met his people in the great redemptive acts? If God's purpose in redemption is remembered not as an end in itself, but as the means by which God would restore all creation, then both the sites of redemptive history (the particular land) and the goal of that history (the whole creation) are holy. This may be why Paul can say that 'The earth is the Lord's' (1 Cor. 10:26), rather than focusing on the land of Israel, which is merely the place in which the redemption of all creation was secured.

This refocusing does not eliminate the holiness of the land, but sets it in perspective. As creatures of space and time we need never shy away from the fact that God came to us specifically, within history, in covenants, in relationships, in great acts of mercy and grace, and in places which are concretely part of our geography. These 'battlefield moments' and these 'historic sites' provide the setting for our redemption. Yet it must be remembered that their holiness is, like the re-enactment of redemption in the Lord's Supper, derived from their value as witnesses to the cosmic work of bringing 'all things' into submission. In the contemporary world, we still need our holy places, just as we need our holy moments.

3. As the people of Israel are loved by God, so too their land is holy

Because 'God's gifts and his call are irrevocable', the Jewish people remain 'loved' (Rom. 11:28–29). Paul affirms their sacred role within redemptive history. Even though God no longer has an exclusive covenant with Israel, the Jewish people remain beloved because of the patriarchs. In other words, God continues to honour the fact that, historically, these were the people of the covenant, through whom he has now blessed the entire world.

Yet, if the people remain beloved or holy for the sake of their history, should not the land be equally honoured? Do not Christians, like Jews, have a stake in the stewardship of that small piece of real estate, where Abraham wandered 'looking forward to the city with foundations' (Heb. 11:10), and where the Lord of glory was crucified and rose victorious from the grave? Should followers of the risen Lord, who belong to a universal kingdom, not honour the places where the early apostles waited for the promise of the Father, and from which they took the good news to the ends of the earth (Acts 1:4–8)?

None of this should turn us away from the concern for justice and righteousness in the land of Israel, as in the earth more generally. If Jesus came to restore the earth, in order that he might 'rule in righteousness' and have dominion 'from the River to the ends of the earth' (Ps. 72:8), it follows that part of our stewardship is to witness to God's kingly rule of justice throughout the earth. The ecological aspect of this justice, no less than the social aspect, must remain a priority for Jesus' people. And the call for the same must be heard in Israel, as throughout the world.

But, just as we must never exempt modern Israel from God's concern for both peace and justice, neither can we turn a blind eye when God's ancient people and land are the target of special enmity. If they remain 'loved' and their land remains the arena of God's great works of salvation, we as the contemporary church must share responsibility for what goes on in that ancient land. The land, which in old times needed her Sabbaths to fulfil her purpose (2 Chr. 36:21), groans with all creation waiting for the day of redemption (Rom. 8:22–23). The land of Israel, together with all creation, is looking for that day, and we who follow the crucified Lord must agonize with it.

Conclusion

So the God who in the beginning created the heavens and the earth and pronounced each part of them good, has a continuing commitment to his creation. His covenant of creation blessed the whole earth, and blessed the whole race of Adam who was called to live in harmony (*šālôm*) both with God and with the land or earth (*'ereṣ*). The earth, as the arena of God's activity, and the home set apart for humanity, was sanctified as holy, an act given substance and specificity when God established the Sabbath (Gen. 2:1–3). Space, no less than people and animals, was given a day to celebrate and rest: a truth clearly set forth in the covenant statutes of Israel (e.g. Lev. 25).

When God narrowed his focus by choosing the family of Abraham, and the land of promise, he never abandoned his commitment to holiness in the land or the earth. Through the witness of Abraham and his children walking in the way of the Lord and doing righteousness and justice (Gen. 18:19), the promised blessing would be fulfilled, and all the nations of the earth [would] be blessed (v. 18). The law, as the standard which defined 'the way of Yahweh' for Abraham's children, contained extensive and explicit instructions about the land, and about how it was to be set apart in holiness. As the holy seed walked in the way of Yahweh, they were called to live out holiness in the land which, no less than the people, shared in Yahweh's covenant love. Now that the promises to Abraham have been fulfilled through his offspring Jesus (Gal. 3 – 4), the New Testament writers quite rightly turn their attention away from the children of Abraham and their specific rules of stewardship in their God-ordained territory to the universal people of God within all creation.

The focus returns, in Christ and his seed, as it was in the beginning with Adam and his seed, to the whole earth, and its fullness. Our stewardship of the land, while it carries a worldwide responsibility, finds a model in Yahweh's loving instructions for the care of the land in the old dispensation. We can be *more* creative, and *more* universal, in our stewardship of the earth, but we can never be less. The fact that some day our King will return to rule over this earth in righteousness, whatever the new heavens and new earth might mean, can only increase our longing for the principles of divine stewardship to be seen in our own earth, in our own day. To do less is to blaspheme the Creator, to despise his good gifts, and to reject the call of our God in both covenants.

Bibliography

Carson, R. (1962), *Silent Spring*, Cambridge, MA: Houghton Mifflin.

Cumbey, C. (1983), *Hidden Dangers of the Rainbow: the New Age Movement and Our Coming Age of Barbarism*, Shreveport: Huntington House.

Dumbrell, W. J. (1984), *Covenant and Creation: A Theology of the Old Testament Covenants*, Exeter: Paternoster.

Henry, C. F. H. (1947), *The Uneasy Conscience of Modern Fundamentalism*, Grand Rapids: Eerdmans.

Murray, J. (1959–65), *Epistle to the Romans*, New International Commentary on the New Testament, Grand Rapids: Eerdmans.

Pritz, R. (1997), 'Jerusalem, the Holy City', *Mishkan* 26: 39–43.

Skjøtt, B. F. (1997), 'Messianic believers and the land of Israel – a survey', *Mishkan* 26: 72–81.

Tuchman, B. W. (1988), *Bible and Sword*, New York: Ballantine.

Wilkinson, L. (ed.) (1980), *Earthkeeping: Christian Stewardship of Natural Resources*, Grand Rapids: Eerdmans.

Wright, C. J. H. (1983), *Living as the People of God: The Relevance of Old Testament Ethics*, Leicester: IVP.

6B

The land and the book: a personal response

Gordon J. Thomas

This chapter is very different from all that precede it, because it is not written by an expert or by someone with a particular axe to grind. In my own mind, at least, I represent the punter in the church, whom this book is meant to help. So, when asked to offer some concluding reflections, I accepted with the proviso that I was not setting myself up as any form of pundit on the theology of the land of Israel – more like a one-man focus group.

My need to be informed and challenged

A few weeks before the Tyndale Fellowship Biblical Theology Study Group was due to consider this topic, I was asked whether I thought that Israel as both land and people had a significant part to play in the future purposes of God. Partly from reluctance to give hostages to fortune, and partly out of sheer agnosticism, I dodged the question. I replied that I hoped to be in a more informed position to answer the question after attending the forthcoming conference in Cambridge. Now that I have attended it, participated in the discussion and read the supplementary chapters in this volume, am I in any better position to answer the question? Come to that, now that you have read all the preceding chapters, are you any clearer?

Like many Christians, I have at times been intensely interested in this controversial subject, but also, like many Christians, I have felt the lack of time and information with which to think things through. In my childhood in a Christian home I must have absorbed some of the 'largely unrecognized and subliminal' dispensationalist influences that Stephen Sizer refers to. Somehow, without being able to pinpoint exactly how, I just took it on board that the return of the Jews to Palestine in 1948 was a fulfilment of prophecy and that world history was all going to bubble up to a cataclysmic end in the Middle East, probably in my lifetime. As a layperson in my early twenties I read Hal Lindsey's *The Late Great Planet Earth* and *There's A New World Coming*, saw the film *Thief in the Night* and attended a number of Bible studies on the last things. There I became fascinated by various and sundry stances taken on the great tribulation, the rapture and the millennium, not to mention timetables involving clever calculations concerning Daniel's seventy weeks of years. All kinds of weird and wonderful theories crossed my horizon. John F. Kennedy was the beast of Revelation 13, who had received a mortal wound but would recover and win the hearts of millions. Henry Kissinger was the second beast, who acted as PR man for Kennedy's Antichrist. The number 666 referred to a barcode which would be laser-tattooed on to everyone's right hand and forehead and used instead of a credit card. The nations of the European Common Market (as it was then) represented a revived Roman Empire, which would be the power-base of Antichrist. Then of course there was the mother of all battles at Armageddon and the bodily return of Jesus Christ on to the Mount of Olives. Human history would apparently reach its consummation in the land of Israel. The strange thing about those days was that I would never have called myself a dispensationalist, and would not have recognized the label if pinned on anyone else. As far as I was concerned, I was a fairly middle-of-the-road evangelical Christian, who took the

Bible seriously, and who was not much different from most other Christians I knew.

Since those days, I have had the enormous privilege of formal biblical and theological study, which has provided new tools for interpreting Scripture, and also of a range of other experiences, which have prompted fresh questions to ponder. For example, in the mid-1980s my family and I enjoyed the hospitality of a Christian Arab family in Nazareth, and I began to realize that there was another perspective on the land which I had never really considered. Somehow I had failed to absorb the fact that there was a tradition of Orthodox Christianity among the Arabs going back two thousand years. Apart from hearing from their lips what life was like, caught between Jewish and Islamic fundamentalisms, I found myself for the first time asking serious questions about their place in the divine economy under the new covenant inaugurated by Jesus.

In the years that have followed I have sometimes been perturbed by belligerent demands that I declare where I stand on the Israel issue. Do I subscribe to a replacement theology? What do I make of the teachings of various Messianic Jews? Will I repudiate a 'land for peace' deal in the Middle East? For the people who frame the questions, the issues at stake are clear cut. There is a right and a wrong answer. There are the good guys and the bad guys over there in the Middle East and back here in the western church.

Some specific responses to the contributors

Since so much hinges on the meaning of the promises to Abraham in Genesis, Paul Williamson and Desmond Alexander perform a valuable service for us all by their careful unpacking of these promises. Alexander helpfully points out that the promise of land is intimately bound to a number of other theological ideas, such as rest, sacred space, identity, faith and obedience, and blessing or cursing. Williamson notes that the territorial promise was fulfilled, but only incompletely, in the days of Joshua and of Solomon.[1] He also draws

[1] Cf. David Clines' classic words (1978: 29): 'The theme of the Pentateuch is the partial fulfilment – which implies also the partial non-fulfilment – of the promise to or blessing of the patriarchs.'

attention to the variability of the scope of the boundaries in different texts, which ought to give us pause before we make dogmatic claims about God's inflexible purposes and unrepentable promises. In case we miss the point, Alexander likewise points out the shift from Ephraim to Judah as the expected channel of blessing. These essays make a similar overall point that 'the climax of God's programmatic agenda is not the establishment of a nation, but rather the blessing of the nations'.

Deryck Sheriffs' chapter, with its five snapshots of the land at scattered times in history, is very stimulating both exegetically and hermeneutically. Like Alexander, he ties land into a nexus of interrelated issues. This approach also enables him to retrace a narrative pathway through the Old Testament, which reveals anything but a straight-line, forward movement. Tantalizingly he utters the odd throwaway line which is pregnant with theological significance, but does not stop to develop what he means. Thus, for example, notions of biblical inerrancy and divine inexorability of purpose, held by many on the dispensationalist side of this controversy, do not sit well with the fallibility of the prophets and iconoclasm of God identified by Sheriffs.

Peter Walker bravely covers the whole New Testament interpretation of the subject, and, in my judgment, carries it off extremely well. I found myself unable to do more than nod my head in agreement over the way he handled so much of his material, whether it be Jesus fulfilling the hopes of the restoration of Israel or Paul's widening the Abrahamic promise of inheritance from the land to the world (Rom. 4:13).

Palmer Robertson's hermeneutic is based on the view that the relationship of old covenant to new covenant is that of 'prophetic shadow to substantial fulfilment', as expounded in Hebrews. I found myself agreeing with his view that the old covenant was conditional. I was intrigued by his exposition of Isaiah as radically altering the Israel land-ideology *vis-à-vis* Egypt and Assyria. But I was rather dubious about his interpretation of resurrection in Ezekiel 37. He rightly expresses concern that 'by claiming the old covenant form of the land-promise, the Jews of today may forfeit the greater new-covenant fulfilment of the land-promise'. I wonder whether invoking the old covenant is even an option, since Hebrews

8:13 declares it 'obsolete'. I certainly go along with his reminder that the land is not 'an end in itself but . . . a means to an end'.

Of all the papers here, the one which ruffled me the most was that by Stephen Sizer. He presents a systematic exposure of dispensationalism, elements of which, as I confessed earlier, permeated my more youthful outlook. Having the theological moorings of this approach made explicit was very shocking. To be frank, I was appalled at many things written by the arch-proponents. For instance, 'The Jewish nation is never to enter the Church' (J. N. Darby). 'It was a tragic hour when the reformation churches wrote the Ten Commandments into their creeds and catechisms and sought to bring Gentile believers into bondage to Jewish law, which was never intended either for the Gentile mission or for the church' (D. G. Barnhouse). 'The Dispensation of Promise ended when Israel rashly accepted the law . . . at Sinai they exchanged grace for law' (C. I. Scofield). 'In his [Paul's] writings *alone* we find the doctrine, position, walk and destiny of the Church' (C. I. Scofield). And there is Scofield's teaching that the Gospels were essentially for the Jews and not for the church, and his repudiation of the Lord's Prayer and especially its petition for forgiveness, since it is 'legal ground'.

Sizer's final two paragraphs also make for uncomfortable reading, as they spell out the repercussions of dispensationalism on the political realities of the Middle East.

Colin Chapman's first three paragraphs make it crystal clear that this is no esoteric hair-splitting debate over the niceties of theology. He makes his case with the aid of ten points, all of which struck me as valid, and several of which were very telling. One was point 7, about the difference that the coming of Jesus makes to traditional hopes and expectations. Another was point 10, which asks whether prophecy is mainly prediction or mainly ethical challenge. But the most cogent of Chapman's arguments, for my money, is located in Ephesians 2:15. The creation of one new humanity in place of Jew and Gentile is not an isolated proof text. It coheres with Paul's explanation in Ephesians 1:10 that God's ultimate purpose is to unite the whole cosmos under the headship of Christ. Chapman's closing questions are designed to move the debate beyond territorial claims, and I look forward to the responses of others to them, as well as to grappling with them myself.

Baruch Maoz provides a wealth of material to illuminate the Old Testament picture of a symbiotic relationship between the people of Israel and the land. He also helpfully links possession of the land with obedience and Torah. However, I question some of his theological assertions. For instance, he equates exile from the land with exile from God, without noting the New Testament witness that Christians are aliens in this world while citizens of another. He speaks of Israel being unable to fulfil its duties to God apart from the land, without exploring the theological function of the wilderness in the Bible (cf. Deut. 8; Hos. 2; Is. 40; Mark 1:12). I also have some questions about his straight-line view of history and lack of global perspective.

Naim Ateek's social and political sketch about recent events in Israel was very informative, especially regarding the impact of the 1967 war. It is a pity not to have a Zionist perspective on the same events. From the point of view of biblical theology and hermeneutics, Ateek raises a much larger question with his insistence on a Christological reading of the Old Testament. What it achieves is fine; what it omits is the problem. There is a danger of failing to read the Old Testament in its own canonical context and of illegitimate Christian reading back. I am happier with Deryck Sheriffs' dual-reading strategy, which reads an Old Testament text twice in different ways. Yet I can only say a resounding 'amen' to Ateek's concluding paragraph.

Last but by no means least, we have the ruminations of the elder statesman of the study group, Carl Armerding. I appreciate his irenic tone, as he strives to balance the need to demand peace with justice in the land of Israel with the need to defend God's chosen people from the enmity which has so often been their lot. In setting his whole discussion against the broader backdrop of a creation theology, Armerding points up various other directions in which our exploration of this subject could go: putting stewardship of land above ownership, heeding the warnings of ecology, revisiting the concept of 'sacred space'.

A more general response

On these matters, as on so much else, instead of good and bad guys, there are equally intelligent and sincere Christians holding opposing views. How can this be, if they hold in common a high view of the authority of the Bible and a personal allegiance to Jesus Christ as Saviour and Lord?

Some of the differences may stem from different life experiences – where one has lived, the people among whom one has ministered, and so on. But the core differences are the stuff of which biblical theology is made. Every single chapter in this volume is informed by implicit or explicit principles of biblical interpretation, by a view on how texts are to be read, how the two Testaments relate to each other, how an eternal God relates to time-bound history. The key problem is that there appears to be insufficient real consensus among evangelicals, let alone in the wider Christian church, as to what constitutes a valid hermeneutic.

In the medieval Roman Catholic tradition the matter was taken from one's hands. According to the Tridentine Profession of Faith (1564), a true child of the faith had to affirm the following: 'I acknowledge the sacred Scripture according to that sense which Holy Mother Church has held and holds, to whom it belongs to decide upon the true sense and interpretation of the Holy Scriptures, nor will I ever receive and interpret the Scripture except according to the unanimous consent of the fathers.'

By contrast, once the Reformers had put the Bible into the language and hand of the ploughboy, a Pandora's box of interpretation was opened. The multiplicity of Protestant denominations owes as much to diverse methods of scriptural interpretation as to church politics and personality clashes. The notion that Scripture interprets itself replaced the dogma that the church controlled interpretation – but unfortunately the Bible seems to interpret itself differently to different people! Invoking the aid of the Holy Spirit makes little improvement either, since the Spirit apparently says various things to various people. All this helps to account for the differences of theological opinion to this day.

If the authority of church, Bible and Holy Spirit, taken separately, has proved insufficient to establish an interpretative methodology, are we any further forward in our search for a hermeneutic that will yield a legitimate contemporary application of the biblical text? Some of the elements in my own approach towards an evangelical hermeneutic can be summarized in the following imperatives:

- Seek to integrate the authority of church, Bible and Holy Spirit, considering input from all three sources.
- Engage in exegesis that takes account of the plurality of contexts surrounding a biblical text.
- Ask at least the following two questions: (1) What further light does the rest of the *canon* shed on this subject? (2) What difference does the life and teaching of *Jesus Christ* make to our understanding?

My experience in teaching the Bible to students of many ages, races and denominational backgrounds is that the closer the consensus we reach on interpretative method, the less polarized are the conclusions we draw.

Some provisional personal conclusions

- Yahweh's ownership of the whole earth relativizes any human territorial claims, recasting them in terms of humankind's stewardship responsibilities, even over Israel.
- The function of Israel in the land was to be a prototype of a redeemed society and thereby a conduit for his redemption of the whole earth.
- Israel largely failed to carry out the missionary vocation given it in Exodus 19:6.
- The vocation originally entrusted to Israel in the land is now passed on to Jesus in his church. He is the seed of Abraham through whom the nations are blessed.
- In drawing an inerrant straight line between promise and fulfilment, the dispensationalist viewpoint underpinning Christian Zionism is seriously flawed.
- By calling the 'church age' a mere parenthesis in God's ongoing plans for the Jewish people, dispensationalism marginalizes the birth, life, death and resurrection of our Lord Jesus Christ in salvation history, resulting in a very deficient theology.
- The challenge to today's church is the same as to yesterday's Israel: to be a 'kingdom of priests' and a 'holy nation'. Immorality in the church and injustice in the world profane God's holy name among the nations just as surely as did Israel's sin before the exile.

- As God's co-labourers, we have a responsibility not to wait fatalistically for Armageddon but to pray and work for God's will to be done 'on earth as it is in heaven'.
- The ongoing task of biblical theology is to continue to grapple with the bends and forks in the road of the biblical narrative and to interpret them coherently.[2]
- The fact that God's Word reveals so many twists and turns in his dealings with humanity must inform our understanding of who God is and how he deems to work.

I doubt whether this book (or any other) will change the minds of Christians totally convinced of their interpretation, but it has helped me to realize and to articulate better where I stand. I share Palmer Robertson's misgivings: 'How sad it would be if evangelical Christians who profess to love the Jewish people should become a primary tool in misdirecting their faith and expectation!' My prayer is that this book will do for others what it has done for me: give a better understanding of the land of promise in the Bible and for today.

Bibliography

Clines, D. J. A. (1978), *The Theme of the Pentateuch*, Sheffield: JSOT Press.

Habel, N. C. (1995), *The Land Is Mine: Six Biblical Land Ideologies*, Minneapolis: Fortress.

[2] Habel (1995) describes six different land ideologies in the Old Testament, but does not attempt a theological value-judgment on them and on how they relate to one another.